THE TWILIGHT OF BYZANTIUM

THE TWILIGHT OF BYZANTIUM

ASPECTS OF CULTURAL AND RELIGIOUS HISTORY
IN THE LATE BYZANTINE EMPIRE

Papers from the Colloquium
Held at Princeton University
8–9 May 1989

Edited by

SLOBODAN ĆURČIĆ

and

DOULA MOURIKI

DEPARTMENT OF ART AND ARCHAEOLOGY
PROGRAM IN HELLENIC STUDIES
PRINCETON UNIVERSITY

Copyright © 1991 by the Trustees of Princeton University
Published by the Department of Art and Archaeology,
Princeton University, Princeton, New Jersey 08544-1018

Library of Congress Cataloging-in-Publication Data

The Twilight of Byzantium : aspects of cultural and
religious history in the late Byzantine empire : papers from
the colloquium held at Princeton University 8–9 May
1989 / edited by Slobodan Ćurčić and Doula Mouriki.
    p.   cm.   Includes index.
1. Arts, Byzantine—Congresses.   2. Byzantine Empire—
Civilization—Congresses.   I. Ćurčić, Slobodan.
    II. Mouriki, Doula.
    NX449.T85 1991
    700′   .9495—dc20   91-2772
    ISBN 0-691-04091-5 (alk. paper)

This book is printed on acid-free paper,
and meets the guidelines for permanence and
durability of the Committee on Production Guidelines
for Book Longevity of the Council on Library Resources.
Printed in the United States of America
by Princeton University Press
Princeton, New Jersey 08540

10 9 8 7 6 5 4 3 2 1

Contents

Foreword

THIS VOLUME was made possible by the concentrated effort, commitment, and teamwork of many individuals. We must first of all thank the authors whose papers, read at the colloquium on May 8 and 9, 1989, have been transposed into the articles which constitute this volume. The success of the Princeton colloquium and the enthusiasm generated by the participants contributed in a major way to the idea of publishing the proceedings of the colloquium in book form. Our thanks also go to Elizabeth Powers, Fine Arts Editor of Princeton University Press, who enthusiastically welcomed the idea of the Press producing the book. The resulting volume is one in a series of occasional publications produced by the Department of Art and Archaeology. Its production would have been unthinkable without the superb work of Dr. Christopher Moss, the Department's Editor of Publications. He has borne responsibility for the design, copy-editing, and typesetting, and has been instrumental in many other aspects of the production of this book.

The materialization of this volume would not have been possible without the financial support of the Department of Art and Archaeology through its Publications Fund, and the Program in Hellenic Studies under the auspices of the Stanley J. Seeger Fund. To Prof. Yoshiaki Shimizu, Chairman of the Department of Art and Archaeology, and to Dr. Dimitri Gondicas, Director of the Program in Hellenic Studies, go our profound thanks. The support received from these two individuals reflects a much broader support base at Princeton which has nurtured this project from its inception. Last, but certainly not least, we wish to thank the graduate students who were enrolled in our joint seminars during the spring semester of 1989. Their challenging presence gave rise to the idea of holding the colloquium and, ultimately, may be said to have planted the seed which has grown into this volume.

SLOBODAN ĆURČIĆ
Princeton

DOULA MOURIKI
Athens

Notes on Contributors

SLOBODAN ĆURČIĆ, Professor of Art and Archaeology at Princeton University, is the author of *Gračanica. King Milutin's Church and Its Place in Late Byzantine Architecture* (University Park and London, 1979), *Art and Architecture in the Balkans: An Annotated Bibliography* (Boston, 1984), *Gračanica: Istorija i arhitektura* (Belgrade and Priština, 1988), and numerous other publications on art and architecture in the Byzantine world. With A. St. Clair, he was co-editor of *Byzantium at Princeton* (Princeton, 1986). He has recently written on the architecture of St. Mary's of the Admiral (in E. Kitzinger, *The Mosaics of St. Mary's of the Admiral in Palermo*, DOS 27, forthcoming), and is currently preparing a book on architecture in the Balkans, 300–1500, as well as working on a corpus of late medieval churches in Serbia.

SMILJKA GABELIĆ is a permanent member of the Institute of Art History, University of Belgrade. She is the author of numerous articles on various aspects of Byzantine art, focusing largely on iconographic issues. Her book on the Cycle of the Archangels in Byzantine art is in press.

THALIA GOUMA-PETERSON is Professor of Art History and Museum Director at the College of Wooster in Wooster, Ohio. Her research and writing have been concentrated in two distinct fields: Byzantine painting and contemporary art. Her scholarship has appeared in the *Art Bulletin*, *Dumbarton Oaks Papers*, *Gesta*, *Storia del Arte*, and elsewhere. She has also organized and curated a number of exhibitions and has written on such artists as Miriam Schapiro, Joyce Kosloff, and Athena Tacha. Her most recent article deals with originality and innovation in Byzantine religious painting.

ANGELA CONSTANTINIDES HERO, Adjunct Professor of Byzantine History at Queens College of the City University of New York, served as philological editor of the forthcoming Dumbarton Oaks translation of *Byzantine Monastic Typika*, and has contributed to the *Oxford Dictionary of Byzantium*. Her other publications include *The Letters of Gregory Akindynos* (Washington, D.C., 1983); *A Woman's Quest for Spiritual Guidance: The Correspondence of Princess Irene Eulogia Choumnaina Palaiologina* (Brookline, MA, 1986), and *The Correspondence of Theoleptos Metropolitan of Philadelphia* (in press).

DOULA MOURIKI is Professor of History of Art at the School of Architecture of the National Technical University of Athens. She is the author of several books and numerous articles on Byzantine painting, including wall painting, mosaics, icons, and illustrated manuscripts. Among her books are *The Frescoes of St. Nicholas at Platsa in the Mani* (Athens, 1975); *The Mosaics and Frescoes of St. Mary Pammakaristos (Fethiye Camii) at Istanbul* (Washington, D.C., 1978); in collaboration with Hans Belting and Cyril Mango; and *The Mosaics of Nea Moni at Chios* (Athens, 1985). She has recently published important studies on icons in Cyprus and Sinai, and is currently preparing a monograph on the wall paintings of the Pantanassa at Mistra.

ROBERT OUSTERHOUT is Associate Professor of Architectural History in the School of Architecture at the University of Illinois at Urbana-Champaign, where he has taught since 1983. He is the author of *The Architecture of the Kariye Camii in Istanbul*, Dumbarton Oaks Studies, 25 (Washington, D.C., 1987); and *The Blessings of Pilgrimage*, Illinois Byzantine Studies, 1 (Urbana-Chicago, 1990); as well as numerous articles on Byzantine and medieval architecture.

MARCUS RAUTMAN is Assistant Professor of Art History and Archaeology at the University of Missouri, Columbia. He has recently discussed some of the buildings and people of late Byzantine Thessaloniki in articles in *Byzantion, Jahrbuch der österreichischen Byzantinistik*, and *Revue des études byzantines*. A field archaeologist, he is currently excavating in Cyprus and Turkey.

STEPHEN REINERT, Associate Professor in Byzantine and Early Turkic History at Rutgers University, holds both a Ph.D. in Byzantine History and an M.A. in Turkic languages and literature. His research focuses on the political and cultural evolution of late Byzantine and early Ottoman society, and the contacts between the two. His translation *The Beggar at the Door: The Dīvān of Gadā'ī, A Fifteenth-Century Chaqatay Poet* will be published by Caratzas, and he is completing a book entitled *The Emperor and the Sultan. Manuel II Palaiologos' Encounter with Yıldırım Bāyazīd and the Early Ottoman World.*

ALICE-MARY TALBOT, Executive Editor of the *Oxford Dictionary of Byzantium* is a historian specializing in the Palaeologan period. Her particular interests are in monasticism ("The Byzantine Family and the Monastery," forthcoming in *DOP*), hagiography, and the status of women ("A Comparison of the Monastic Experience of Byzantine Men and Women," *Greek Orthodox Theological Review* 30.1 [1985]; "Byzantine Women as the Donors and Recipients of Charity," forthcoming). She has also edited and translated the letters of Athanasios I (*The Correspondence of Athansius I, Patriarch of Constantinople*, [Washington, D.C., 1975]) and the text of Theoktistos the Stoudite on the posthumous miracles of Athanasios I (*Faith Healing in Byzantium: The Posthumous Miracles of the Patriarch Athanasios I of Constantinople by Theoktistos the Stoudite* [Brookline, Mass., 1983]).

SPEROS VRYONIS, JR. is Alexander S. Onassis Professor of Hellenic Civilization and Culture, and Director of the Alexander S. Onassis Center for Hellenic Studies at New York University. His published works include *The Decline of Medieval Hellenism in Asia Minor and the Process of Islamization from the Eleventh through the Fifteenth Century* (Berkeley, 1971; 1986), *Byzantium and Europe* (London, 1968), *Studies on Byzantium, Seljuks, and Ottomans* (Malibu, 1981), and *Byzantine Cyprus* (Nicosia, 1990), and he has recently edited *Greece on the Road to Democracy. From the Junta to PASOK, 1974–1986* (New Rochelle, 1990). He is currently conducting research on the Battle of Mantzikert and on the ethnogenetic theories of the Turks, Greeks, Roumanians, Bulgarians, Albanians, and Slavo-Macedonians.

JOHN J. YIANNIAS, Associate Professor of Art History, University of Virginia, has recently examined the "art statute" in the *Acts* of Nicaea II (*BZ* 80 [1987], 348–59) and has edited and contributed to *The Byzantine Tradition after the Fall of Constantinople*, which will be published by the University Press of Virginia in 1991. His current research centers on Byzantine and post-Byzantine refectory art, and on the relationship between liturgical space and meaning in Byzantine Art.

List of Illustrations

Thalia Gouma-Peterson, The Frescoes of the Parekklesion of St. Euthymios in Thessaloniki: Patrons, Workshop, and Style (following p. 129)

John J. Yiannias, The Palaeologan Refectory Program at Apollonia (following p. 174)

Smiljka Gabelić, Diversity in Fresco Painting of the Mid-Fourteenth Century: The Case of Lesnovo (following p. 194)

Doula Mouriki, The Wall Paintings of the Pantanassa at Mistra: Models of a Painters' Workshop in the Fifteenth Century (following p. 231)

Slobodan Ćurčić, Late Byzantine Loca Sancta? Some Questions Regarding the Form and Function of Epitaphioi (following p. 261)

Abbreviations

AIPHOS	*Annuaire de l'Institut de Philologie et d'Histoire Orientales et Slaves,* Université Libre de Bruxelles
AnalBoll	*Analecta Bollandiana*
AnatSt	*Anatolian Studies.* Journal of the British Institute of Archaeology at Ankara
Ἀρχ.Ποντ.	Ἀρχεῖον Πόντου
ArtB	*Art Bulletin*
BHG³	*Bibliotheca hagiographica graeca,* 3rd ed., ed. F. Halkin (Brussels, 1957)
BIABulg	*Bulletin de l'Institut Archéologique Bulgare,* Académie Bulgare des Sciences
Bonn ed.	Corpus scriptorum historiae byzantinae, ed. B. G. Niebuhr et al. (Bonn, 1828–97)
BSA	*Annual of the British School at Athens*
BSHAcRoum	*Bulletin de la Section Historique, Académie Roumaine*
BSOAS	*Bulletin of the School of Oriental and African Studies*
ByzF	*Byzantinische Forschungen*
BZ	*Byzantinische Zeitschrift*
CahArch	*Cahiers archéologiques*
CahCM	*Cahiers de civilisation médiévale, X^e–XIIe siècles*
CorsiRav	*Corsi di cultura sull'arte ravennate e bizantina*
CRAI	*Comptes-rendus des séances de l'Académie des Inscriptions et Belles-Lettres*
Δελτ.Χριστ.Ἀρχ.Ἑτ.	Δελτίον τῆς Χριστιανικῆς ᾿ΑΑρχαιολογικῆς Ἑταιρείας
DOP	*Dumbarton Oaks Papers*
DOS	Dumbarton Oaks Studies
EI²	*Encyclopédie de l'Islam,* new edition, ed. J. H. Kramers et al. (Leiden, 1954–)
EO	*Echos d'Orient. Revue d'histoire, de géographie et de liturgie orientales*
᾿Επ.Ἑτ.Βυζ.Σπ.	᾿Επετηρὶς Ἑταιρείας Βυζαντινῶν Σπουδῶν
GRBS	*Greek, Roman, and Byzantine Studies*
IEJ	*Israel Exploration Journal*
IRAIK	*Izvestija Russkogo Arheologičeskogo Instituta v Konstantinopole*
IstMitt	*Istanbuler Mitteilungen,* Deutsches Archäologisches Institut, Abteilung Istanbul
JÖB	*Jahrbuch der österreichischen Byzantinistik*
JÖBG	*Jahrbuch der österreichischen byzantinischen Gesellschaft* (from 1969, *Jahrbuch der österreichischen Byzantinistik*)
Κρ.Χρον.	Κρητικὰ Χρονικά
MarbJb	*Marburger Jahrbuch für Kunstwissenschaft*

MedSt	*Mediaeval Studies*
OCA	*Orientalia christiana analecta*
OCP	*Orientalia christiana periodica*
PG	Patrologiae cursus completus, Series graeca, ed. J.-P. Migne
PLP	*Prosopographisches Lexikon der Palaiologenzeit*, E. Trapp et al. (Vienna, 1976–)
PO	Patrologia orientalis, ed. R. Graffin et al. (Turnhout, 1907–)
RA	*Revue archéologique*
RBK	*Reallexikon zur byzantinischen Kunst*, ed. K. Wessel (Stuttgart, 1963–)
RDAC	*Report of the Department of Antiquities, Cyprus*
REArm	*Revue des études arméniennes*
REB	*Revue des études byzantines*
RESEE	*Revue des études sud-est européennes*
RSBN	*Rivista di studi bizantini e neoellenici*
SOforsch	*Südostforschungen*
TM	*Travaux et mémoires*
WJKg	*Wiener Jahrbuch für Kunstgeschichte*
WZKM	*Wiener Zeitschrift für die Kunde des Morgenlandes*
ZVI	*Zbornik Radova Vizantološkog Instituta, Srpska Akademija Nauk*

THE TWILIGHT OF BYZANTIUM

Introduction

WHEN CONSTANTINOPLE fell to the Turks on May 29, 1453, the agonizing process of political, economic, and social decline which had ravaged the Byzantine Empire for at least two-and-a-half centuries came to its symbolic end. During the past two decades the process of the Empire's decline has come under the close scrutiny of scholars in many different disciplines. Their research has yielded numerous significant results, yet a comprehensive history of this period remains to be written.

The present volume offers a further contribution to the understanding of the Byzantine Empire under its last imperial dynasty, the Palaeologi (Palaiologoi) (1259–1453). With no pretensions of dealing with the period comprehensively, this is a collection of eleven essays on an equal number of subjects, written by eleven different authors. The subjects of these essays vary as widely as do their methods of investigation. What these essays have in common is the pursuit of relatively narrow problems in depth, which permits their authors to draw some broader conclusions. This approach is conceptually different from that embraced by an earlier generation of scholars who preferred broader topics and more sweeping general conclusions. Nonetheless, the reader of this volume will find that the eleven essays convey the richness and texture of the Late Byzantine historical and cultural fabric.

In contrast to the complex matrix of multi-cultural relations which characterized the earlier phases of the Byzantine Empire, territorially shrunken Palaeologan Byzantium, as Speros Vryonis demonstrates, became the oasis of clearly articulated Greek sentiments, a foundation for the subsequent emergence of the modern Greek nation. The inhabitants of the beleaguered Byzantine state commonly sought refuge within the spiritual shelter of the Orthodox faith. Alice-Mary Talbot and Angela Hero both address this issue, but from different vantage points. Talbot shows that interest in the past, and, more specifically, in the past of the Orthodox Church, kept alive hopes for the future. Deprived of actual heroes, military or civilian, the Byzantine populace found them in their saints, whose life stories, rich in fantasy, became an important source of inspiration. By examining the career of a single man, Hero demonstrates that religious mystics often assumed important roles in the political and social life of Palaeologan Byzantium. Moreover, religious virtues became the most trusted of weapons, best tested in confrontation with major adversaries, champions of another faith, as Stephen Reinert's essay clearly illustrates.

The political and economic decline of the Empire was not neatly paralleled by a similar cultural decline. The paradoxical relationship of these broad phenomena is explored within the monastic setting of Macedonia by Marcus Rautman in his essay on architectural patronage. Robert Ousterhout examines builders' practices and their activities through the evidence of Constantinople and related regions of the Empire. Similarly, Thalia Gouma-Peterson pursues the development of early fourteenth-century painting by examining the stylistic trends of fresco painters' workshops active in Thessaloniki. The programmatic function of painting in the decoration of monastic refectories is the subject of John Yiannias' paper on the refectory in the monastery at Apollonia. Smiljka Gabelić explores changes which occurred in religious painting around the middle of the fourteenth century by focusing on the work of different artists active in the monastery of Lesnovo. Perceived stylistic modifications around the middle of the fourteenth century give way to a completely new style by the turn of the century. The genesis of this new style of painting, as witnessed at the Pantanassa of Mistra, is characterized by Doula Mouriki as a reflection of the new intellectual climate, the liberation from strict religious canons, and the impact of the West and Islam. Slobodan Ćurčić considers the form and function of *epitaphioi*, in which he recognizes Late Byzantine surrogates for the Tomb of Christ. Preoccupation with death, induced by grim political realities, spurred Late Byzantine patrons and artists to invent new artistic formulas as vehicles of Christian salvation.

This volume as a whole provides the reader with a graphic cross section of the Late Byzantine world. Despite its shrunken territory, its ailing economy, and social turmoil, the world of Palaeologan Byzantium still had much to offer. Erudition, sophistication, splendor, imagination, if not realism, were all hallmarks of the Late Byzantine cultural achievement. In an age of bleak realities, the Byzantines sought refuge in the spiritual realm, in visions of their past, in the reaffirmation of their ideological and religious values, in the dreams of a world they once knew and desperately continued to seek to the very end.

SLOBODAN ĆURČIĆ

Byzantine Cultural Self-Consciousness in the Fifteenth Century

SPEROS VRYONIS, JR.

ALTHOUGH Byzantinists have dealt for a long time with this fascinating subject, have laid out the structure or established a general outline of the purported nature of Byzantine cultural self-consciousness in the Palaeologan period, and we have profited greatly from this, nevertheless neither the salient details nor the dynamics of this phase of Byzantine culture have been worked out in all important details.[1] In the first instance this is due to the fact that the subject is far more complex than the mere title might indicate. We are dealing with a highly variegated social organism with a very rich cultural past that in addition had accumulated a rich cultural expression in writing, art, music, medicine, and folklore. Accordingly, the phenomenon of cultural self-awareness has a variety of aspects and a lively development with elements of both continuity and change. In speaking of culture and cultural awareness I of course refer to the broad, holistic concept of culture that has been developed by anthropologists, and not to the narrow and impoverished understanding of many traditional historians.

Within the broad structure of Byzantine culture thus defined there are two powerful strands: Graeco-Roman antiquity and Christianity, and their constant and mutual readjustment to one another. Thus the evolution of Byzantine culture feeds on this double heritage, both at the formal and popular levels of culture. Further, it often reconciles or resolves these two cultural streams successfully, whereas at other times Greece/Rome and Jerusalem remain in irreconcilable opposition.

The historical circumstances of the fourteenth–fifteenth centuries constitute specifics which determine the motive force or movement of cultural evolution and cultural self-consciousness. These specifics and historical conditions include:

1. Severe territorial dismemberment of the state and the corresponding subjection of large Byzantine populations to a foreign state and alien religion.

2. Political impotence vis-à-vis the Ottoman state, and demotion to the level of a petty Balkan state with Bulgars and Serbs.

3. The collapse of the high degree of political centralization within the Byzantine state, with the corresponding rise of the indigenous feudal *pronoiarioi* and the absorption and subordination of Byzantine merchants, bankers, and craftsmen into the economic imperialism of Venice and Genoa. Thus even within the empire the Byzantine state found its

---

[1] H.-G. Beck, Theodoros Metochites, *Die Krise des byzantinischen Weltbildes im 14. Jahrhundert* (Munich, 1952); *Vorsehung und Vorherbestimmung in der theologischen Literatur der Byzantinern* = *OCA* 114 (Rome, 1937). F. Dölger, "Politische und geistige Strömungen im sterbenden Byzanz," *JÖBG* 3 (1954), 3–18. I. Ševčenko, "The Decline of Byzantium seen through the Eyes of its Intellectuals," *DOP* 15 (1961), 167–86.

control of regalian rights suffering fundamental erosion with the concomitant inability to assert its traditional authority in the fiscal, religious, and social life of the empire.

4. The glaring disparity between the older, traditional *Weltanschaung* and the imperial theory on the one hand, and the grim daily political realities on the other came increasingly to be an additional and powerful factor in the shaping of Byzantine cultural self-consciousness.[2] Theodore Metochites expressed this awareness of impotence in his lament on the loss of Asia Minor: "Woe to us who now remain! It [Anatolia] has departed from the Roman state! O this destruction! O this loss! We live in a few remnants and members of life and body (formerly so great and beautiful), as though the majority and most vital members have been severed. And we continue to live in shame and derision, wholly incapable in the means of existence and life."[3]

These historical conditions produced an atmosphere of deep crisis with the corresponding haunting anxieties throughout Byzantine society. In another study I have delineated these anxieties: anxieties over loss of lands, peoples, houses, families, religion and churches, education and learning, villages, towns, and finally the loss of the Greek language itself.[4] Thus the Byzantines became sharply aware of what it was that they were losing, that is, their culture.

With the accelerating loss of lands to the Muslim Turks and with the economic control and religious proselytization of the Catholic Italians, the Byzantines came to see their relations with these peoples and cultures in ever sharper and greater relief. The Byzantines saw in the Italians and Turks not only economic exploiters and political tyrants, but also enemies of their culture, indeed as the instruments of the destruction of their ancient and hallowed culture.

At the same time their double heritage, Graeco-Roman and Christian, untrammeled as a result of the disappearance of the strong restraining hand of a centralized state and also as a result of the shattering of the church structure pursuant to the Ottoman conquests, became strongly dissonant, revealing how deeply rooted much of the pagan past was.

Obviously the structure of institutional and political changes which determined the cultural evolution of the Palaeologan period, and, within that cultural evolution, Byzantine cultural self-consciousness, is vast and cannot be covered here. Inasmuch as much has already been written on aspects of this[5] I move on here to four interesting points: first I shall

---

[2] S. Vryonis, Jr., *The Decline of Medieval Hellenism in Asia Minor and the Process of Islamization from the Eleventh through the Fifteenth Century* (Berkeley-Los Angeles, 1971), 403–43.

[3] Theodore Metochites, *Miscellanea philosophica et historica*, ed. Ch. G. Müller and Th. Kiesseling (Leipzig, 1821), 241. Vryonis, *Decline of Medieval Hellenism* (note 2 above), 413.

[4] S. Vryonis, Jr., "Crises and Anxieties in Fifteenth Century Byzantium: the Reassertion of Old and the Emergence of New Cultural Forms," in *Islamic and Middle Eastern Societies, A Festschrift in Honor of Professor Wadie Jwaideh*, ed. R. Olson (Brattleboro, Vermont, 1987), 100–125.

[5] The best survey is still G. Ostrogorsky, *History of the Byzantine State*, revised edition (New Brunswick, 1969); *idem, Pour l'histoire de la feodalité byzantine* (Brussels, 1954). A. Laiou, "The Greek Merchant of the Palaeologan Period: A Collective Portrait," *Praktika tes Akademias Athenon* 57 (1982), 96–132; "The Byzantine Ecomony in the Mediterranean Trade System, Thirteenth–Fifteenth Centuries," *DOP* 34–35 (1982), 177–222; "The Byzantine Aristocracy in the Palaeologan Period: A Stage of Arrested Development," *Viator* 4 (1973), 131–52. N. Oikonomidès, *Hommes d'affaires grecs et latins à Constantinople (XIIIᵉ-XVᵉ siècles)* (Montreal, 1959). I. Djurić, *Sumrak Vizantije (vreme Jovana VIII Paleologa) 1392–1448* (Belgrade, 1984).

return to the ancient Byzantinist exercise of examining the ethnic nomenclature which Byzantines applied to themselves. Second, the discussion will pass briefly to the cultural definitions that emerge in the writings of certain Byzantine religious and secular authors, as these will mesh with the matter of ethnic nomenclature. Third, there will be a very brief word, but no more, as to the cultural definitions from the level of popular culture. Fourth, and finally, I shall examine briefly the personality and some of the writings of the Cypriot Gregory II, patriarch of Constantinople (second half of the thirteenth century) in order to give a broader chronological dimension to the development of cultural self-consciousness in the Palaeologan era.

Let us turn briefly to eight fifteenth-century authors and examine the epithets which they utilize in designating Byzantines, their state, culture and language. Symeon of Thessaloniki employs exclusively one term and its derivatives for anything and everything Byzantine (also utilizing the term χριστιανικόν): Ῥωμαϊκῶν πραγμάτων, Ῥωμαϊκοῦ φύλου.[6] Sphrantzes, who rarely uses such epithets, employs only Ῥωμαϊκόν.[7] Let us continue with the historian Critoboulos. Most often he refers to the Byzantines as Ῥωμαῖοι, to the emperor as Βασιλεὺς Ῥωμαίων, to their officials as τοῖς ἐν τέλει Ῥωμαίων, to the Byzantine Empire as τὴν Ῥωμαίων ἡγεμονίαν, to the Byzantine armed forces as αἱ τῶν Ῥωμαίων δυνάμεις κατά τε γῆν καὶ θάλασσαν, and to the Byzantine nation as τοῦ γένους Ῥωμαίων.[8] Critoboulos thus seems to utilize the word Ῥωμαῖοι and its derivatives to denote the Byzantines, their state, ruler, etc. There are, however, a few exceptions: Critoboulos speaks of the city of Ainos and of other cities as αὕτη μετὰ τῶν Ἑλληνίδων πόλεων,[9] of the entire Greek sea, καὶ πᾶσαν τὴν Ἑλληνικὴν θάλασσαν,[10] of the western Anatolian coast as πᾶσαν τὴν Ἑλληνικὴν παραλίαν,[11] of Boeotia and other areas as πάντας τε τοὺς Ἑλληνικοὺς τόπους,[12] and the Greek language as τὴν . . . Ἑλλήνων.[13] Finally, and most interestingly, he uses the term Ἕλλην to denote the Byzantines on one occasion where he describes the devastating effects of the Ottoman conquests on the Balkan peoples: "καταστρέφονται δὲ Μυσοὺς τοὺς ἐν τῇ μεσογείᾳ καὶ πρὸς τῷ Ἴστρῳ οἰκοῦντες, ἔτι δὲ Ἰλλυρίους, Τριβαλλούς, Ἕλληνας . . . "[14] Though Critoboulos conforms to the customary Byzantine usage of the word Ῥωμαῖος,[15] he is not completely consistent.

G. C. Soulis, *The Serbs and Byzantium during the Reign of Tsar Stephan Dušan (1331–1355) and his Successors* (Washington, 1984). J. W. Barker, *Manuel II Paleologus 1391–1425. A Study in Late Byzantine Statesmanship* (New Brunswick, 1969). Vryonis, *Decline of Medieval Hellenism* (note 2 above). For the literature on Byzantine ethnic nomenclature, S. Vryonis, "Recent Scholarship on Continuity and Discontinuity of Culture: Classical Greeks, Byzantines, Modern Greeks," in *The "Past" in Medieval and Modern Greek Culture* (Malibu, 1978), ed. S. Vryonis, n. 2 and passim.

[6] Symeon of Thessaloniki, *Politico-Historical Works of Symeon Archbishop of Thessalonica (1416/17 to 1429)*, critical Greek text with introduction and commentary by D. Balfour (Vienna, 1979), 45, 47.

[7] Georgios Sphrantzes, *Memorii, 1401–1477*, ed. V. Grecu (Bucharest, 1966), 114.

[8] *Critobuli Imbriotae Historiae*, ed. D. R. Reinsch (Berlin, 1983) (hereafter Critoboulos), passim.

[9] Critoboulos, II, 12, 8.

[10] Critoboulos, I, 6, 3.

[11] Critoboulos, I, 14, 3.

[12] Critoboulos, III, 9, 7.

[13] Critoboulos, Letter 1, pp. 3–5.

[14] Critoboulos, I, 14, 6.

[15] Critoboulos, passim.

Ducas similarly utilizes the traditional designation ʿΡωμαῖος, though he also employs the form Ἕλλην and derivatives to designate the ancient Greeks,[16] pagan education (ʿΕλληνικοῖς μαθήμασιν), and geographical regions.[17] Despite the fact that he generally uses the form ʿΡωμαῖος, there are two interesting exceptions. Attributing unnatural sexual desire to the Turks, he adds: "εἰ ʿΕλληνίδα ἢ Ἰταλὴν ἢ ἄλλην τινά ἑτερογενῆ προσλάβηται ἢ αἰχμάλωτον ἢ αὐτόμολον, ὡς Ἀφροδίτην τινὰ ἢ Σεμέλην ἀσπάζονται τὴν ὁμογενῆ δὲ καὶ αὐτόγλωτον ὡς ἄρκτον ἢ ὕαινα βδελύττοντες."[18] Here he employs as ethnic designation the term ʿΕλληνίδα in opposition to Ἰταλήν. In two other passages Ducas differentiates between the ancient Greeks, whom he describes as "ʿΕλλήνων λέγω τῶν ἡμιθέων ἡρώων ἀνδρῶν",[19] and their Byzantine descendants who have refused to take communion after the ecclesiastical union of 1452, whom he describes as "ὁ λαὸς ὁ ἀπηνὴς καὶ μισόκαλος, ἡ ῥίζα τῆς ὑπερηφανείας, ὁ κλάδος τῆς κακοδοξίας, τὸ ἄνθος τῆς ὑψηλοφροσύνης, ἡ τρυγία τοῦ γένους τῶν ʿΕλλήνων."[20] That is to say, Ducas refers to the contemporary Byzantines as "the dregs of the nation of the Hellenes." However, Ducas also refers to the Byzantines as Γραικοί, in one passage in opposition to Ἰταλοί, and indeed in the portion of his text where he speaks of the liturgy of the union in St. Sophia he uses all three terms to refer to contemporary Byzantines: ʿΡωμαῖος, Γραικοί, Ἕλληνες.[21] Again, as in the case of Critoboulos, we observe a certain inconsistency in the use of ʿΡωμαῖος and Ἕλλην.

Ioannes Chortasmenos (d. 1436/37) utilizes the word Hellene with two meanings: in his theological tract he uses the term synonymously with the idea of pagan. In his correspondence, Hellene refers to Byzantines, to the Greek language, and to the Byzantine mentality and virtues.[22]

George Gemisthos Pletho calls the Byzantines Ἕλληνες, as their language and customs are also ʿΕλληνικά, and the emperor is ruler of the Ἕλληνες.[23]

It is Laonicos Chalcocondyles who reverses completely the older Byzantine usage of ʿΡωμαῖος and Ἕλλην. The Byzantines are Ἕλληνες,[24] the Byzantine emperor is Βασιλεὺς ʿΕλλήνων,[25] Byzantine affairs of state are τὰ ʿΕλλήνων πράγματα,[26] their language and customs are τὰ ἤθη τε ἅμα καὶ τὴν φωνὴν προϊεμένους ʿΕλληνικήν.[27] The city of Philadelphia is described as Φιλαδέλφειαν πόλιν ἑλληνίδα,[28] and Constantinople is πόλιν

[16] Ducas, *Istoria turco-byzantina 1341–1467*, ed. and trans. V. Grecu (Bucharest, 1958) (hereafter Ducas), 31, 57, 95.

[17] Ducas, 267, 177.

[18] Ducas, 59.

[19] Ducas, 95.

[20] Ducas, 319.

[21] Ducas, 317–319.

[22] Johannes Chortasmenos (ca. 1370–ca. 1436/37), *Briefe, Gedichte und kleine Schriften, Einleitung, Regesten, Prosopographie, Text*, ed. H. Hunger (Vienna, 1969), 22, 168–69.

[23] Pletho, in S. Lambros, *Palaeologeia kai Peloponnesiaka* (Athens, 1926), III, 247–48.

[24] *Laonici Chalcocondylae historiarum demonstrationes*, ed. E. Darkó (Budapest, 1922–1927), 2 vols. (hereafter Chalcocondyles), passim.

[25] Chalcocondyles, I, 78.

[26] Chalcocondyles, II, 236.

[27] Chalcocondyles, II, 219.

[28] Chalcocondyles, I, 518.

βασιλίδα ῾Ελλήνων.[29] Not only does he describe everything Byzantine by some form of ῞Ελλην, but he reverses completely the meaning of ῾Ρωμαῖος and its derivatives. When he speaks of τῆς ἡγεμονίας τε καὶ ῾Ρωμαίων βασιλείας, he refers to the domain of the Hapsburgs,[30] and on another occasion he names its emperor βασιλέα ῾Ρωμαίων ῎Αλβερτον.[31] Further, the Pope of Rome is ῾Ρωμαίων ἀρχιερέα or οἱ τῆς ῾Ρώμης ἀρχιερεῖς, and it is he who crowns the Roman emperor ἐπὶ τοὺς Γερμανῶν ἡγεμόνας μετενήνεκται ψῆφος τοῦ ῾Ρωμαίων ἀρχιερέως.[32] Thus Chalcocondyles is completely consistent: ῞Ελλην is Byzantine, ῾Ρωμαῖος is German and papal.

Up to this point we have moved across the entire spectrum from authors who apply the traditional Byzantine nomenclature, such as Symeon and Sphrantzes, to those who employ the term Hellene, such as Pletho and Chalcocondyles, the latter of whom completely reverses the more ancient system of nomenclatures: Hellene equals the Byzantine east, *Rhomaios* the Latino-Germanic west. Of particular interest here, and it is to this which we should pay attention, is that in the case of three authors the lines between the usage of ῾Ρωμαῖος and ῞Ελλην (and even Γραικός) are not absolutely and clearly drawn. Critoboulos and Ducas, despite their preponderant usage of ῾Ρωμαῖος as the Byzantine ethnic epithet, also employ the form ῞Ελλην not only as a linguistic, geographical, and ancient epithet, but also as the sobriquet for contemporary Byzantines. And indeed Ducas uses the term Γραικός as well. Chortasmenos employs ῞Ελλην as an appellation both for pagans and for contemporary Byzantine Christians.

This brief survey suggests that in the fifteenth century the boundaries of ethnic terminology varied not only from author to author, but often within the writings of one and the same author. This would suggest that the term Hellene was more widespread than formerly asserted and that the lines between Hellene and Rhomaios had become blurred.

This is amply, and surprisingly, demonstrated in the voluminous writings of George Gennadios Scholarios, opponent of ecclesiastical union, firm defender of Byzantine Christianity against the Latin Church, Islam, and the reviving Hellenic paganism. Given Gennadios' strong religious and traditional orientation, one would expect him to adhere carefully to the traditional Byzantine nomenclature wherein Hellene signified pagan and *Rhomaios* Byzantine. As a sampling I have examined volumes I, IV and VII of the edition of his works,[33] and a rough tabulation of his use of ῾Ρωμαῖος and ῞Ελλην (I have ignored Γραικός) yields the following preliminary and rough results. In twenty-two instances where Gennadios uses an ethnic epithet to denote a Byzantine, fifteen passages utilize the ethnic ῞Ελλην and only seven employ the word ῾Ρωμαῖος. When he speaks of language and education he uses exclusively the form ῞Ελλην (five occurrences). In over twenty instances he utilizes ῞Ελλην for ancient Greek and pagan Greek. On four other occasions when he

[29] Chalcocondyles, I, 79.
[30] Chalcocondyles, I, 79.
[31] Chalcocondyles, II,189.
[32] Chalcocondyles, I, 68–69; see also I, 66–67.
[33] Gennadios Scholarios, *Oeuvres complètes de Gennade Scholarios*, ed. L. Petit, X. A. Sideridès, M. Jugie (Paris, 1928, 1935, 1936) (hereafter Scholarios).

employs Ῥωμαῖος it refers to the ancient Romans. Thus, and surprisingly, Gennadios for the most part employs the term Ἕλλην as an ethnic epithet for his contemporaries. We can dispense with the few instances in which he uses the form Ῥωμαῖος to indicate Byzantine phenomena as well as ancient Rome, as these instances present no deviation from the traditional usage: Byzantines, Byzantine emperors, affairs of the Byzantine state, Byzantine officials, Byzantine fortunes, and the ancient Romans.[34]

More remarkable are Gennadios' elaboration and use of the form Ἕλλην. In a sermon on the Nativity of Christ, dated 1467, we read the following statement in the clergyman's survey of the history of mankind prior to the Nativity: "ἡ πρὸς ἡμῖν αὕτη καὶ ἀρχαῖα πατρὶς ἡμῶν Ἑλλάς."[35] He informs his Christian flock that their ancient fatherland is Hellas. In speaking of Italians who have learned the Greek language in his own day, he refers to their Byzantine contemporaries as "τοὺς νῦν Ἕλληνας."[36] Significant in the same treatise, entitled "Justificatory Discourse of Scholarios accused of Latinism," is his retort to the critics that the Byzantines have neglected intellectual studies, in contrast to the Italians, so that "τοὺς δὲ παρ' ἡμῖν Ἕλληνας ὄνομα ὄντας καὶ πλὴν δυοῖν τινῶν ἢ τριῶν τοὺς ἄλλους οὐδὲ γραμματιστὰς εἶναί τε καὶ λέγεσθαι δυναμένους."[37] I leave the text without comment. In the same discourse he couples Ἰταλός and Ἕλλην as contrasting ethnic epithets.[38]

The term Ἕλλην receives further definition in Gennadios' polemic against Pletho on the subject of Aristotle as well as in his later references to Pletho's paganism. He begins by asserting that he has proper respect for Pletho: "δι' αἰδοῦς γάρ ἐστιν ἡμῖν ὁ ἀνὴρ τά γε ἄλλα ἐν τοῖς νῦν Ἕλλησιν."[39] In a later passage of the same discourse Gennadios reasserts his proper respect for the aged Pletho by stating that Pletho has written concerning Aristotle "ὅσα καὶ ὅπως οὐδενὶ τῶν νῦν Ἑλλήνων, ἐγὼ συνοῖδα δυναμένῳ."[40] Thus, according to Gennadios Pletho is the foremost of the Hellenes of his own day: ἐν τοῖς νῦν Ἕλλησιν. Early on in the same text he paraphrases Pletho as saying that the more ancient Greek and Roman wise men (philosophers) preferred Plato to Aristotle: "Ὁ μὲν δὴ Πλήθων Ἀριστοτέλους προτιμᾶν φησι Πλάτωνα τοὺς παλαιοτέρους Ἑλλήνων τε καὶ Ῥωμαίων σοφούς."[41] We see, accordingly, that Pletho differentiates between contemporary Hellenes and ancient Hellenes: τοῖς νῦν Ἕλλησιν, τοὺς παλαιοτέρους Ἑλλήνων. He brings the two together in his historical view of what has been said on Aristotle: "Ἐγὼ γὰρ ὑπὲρ μὲν Ἀριστοτέλους καὶ ἀληθείας αὐτῆς οὐδενὶ Ἑλλήνων, οὔτε τῶν παλαιοτέρων, οὔτε τῶν ἐπ' ἐμοῦ, τοσαῦτά τε καὶ τοιαῦτα πεπραγματευμένῳ σύνοιδα."[42] It is clear: Gennadios calls both the ancient Greeks and Byzantines Ἕλληνες, differentiating them by chronological indicators.

[34] Scholarios, IV, 426, 442, 457, 459, 510; VII, 2.
[35] Scholarios, I, 225.
[36] Scholarios, I, 382.
[37] Scholarios, I, 386.
[38] Scholarios, I, 388.
[39] Scholarios, IV, 2.
[40] Scholarios, IV, 114. He reports, conditionally, the same thought a few lines further down: "εἰ τῶν ἄλλων Ἑλλήνων νῦν πλεῖστα προέχει."
[41] Scholarios, IV, 3.
[42] Scholarios, IV, 10.

Is it possible that he employs Ἕλλην here in reference to Byzantines involved with classical texts and philosophy and is therefore not using the term ethnically?

In 1449/50 Gennadios addressed a letter to the ruler of Trebizond: "Κοσμεῖς δὲ ἄρα τοιοῦτος ὢν τὸ γένος ἅπαν τῶν Ἑλλήνων."[43] Here the term Ἕλλην is a more general ethnic appellation for the entire γένος or nation of the Byzantines. Certainly the most convincing evidence in this respect is his long pastoral letter (1455) on the fall of Constantinople and his first abdication from the patriarchal throne. Here he speaks of the sufferings of the city, which no longer exists, and of the suffering "τῶν ἐν τῷ κλίματι τῷδε Ἑλλήνων" (of the Hellenes in this region).[44] Looking back on the fall of the city and the decimation of the Greeks he laments: "I saw, o woe!, every hope of the wretched remnant of the Hellenes that was still stirring cut down in one city and in a few bodies with fewer virtues. I had lived on, wretched, nourished by the hope that at some time Hellenic superiority would flourish as a result of some unexpected transformation . . . But human existence shall no longer enjoy the noble qualities of the Hellenes or the monuments of ancestral virtue."[45] Prior to the seige of the capital he addressed a letter to Notaras (1451/2) in which he speaks of "ἡ κακὴ τῶν Ἑλλήνων τύχη."[46] These passages leave no doubt that Gennadios was applying the term ethnically to denote the Byzantines. In the writings of the traditionalist and patriarch we see a free, easy, and preponderant use of the term Hellene for his contemporary Greek-speaking Orthodox Christians. The mixed use of Ῥωμαῖος and Ἕλλην in Ducas and Critoboulos is much more developed in Gennadios, and so we are brought to an interesting conclusion. The use of Ἕλλην was probably so widespread by the time of the fall of Constantinople that even a religious traditionalist such as Gennadios found no difficulty or paradox in employing it and in differentiating between τῶν παλαιοτέρων and τῶν νῦν. As for the paganism (ἑλληνισμός) of both Pletho and the ancients, it constituted ληρήματα.

Within the rapidly moving vortex of military disasters and economic strangulation that was drawing the Byzantine Empire and its society irrevocably to destruction, the resultant anxieties are clearly manifested in the literary remains of the era. These writings enable us to extrapolate elements in the complex cultural self-consciousness of the Byzantines. The religious element in this self-definition was pervasive, though not always complete, for the Byzantines were beset by two hostile religions: Latin Christianity and Turkish Islam. Scholars have generally overemphasized the anti-Latin religious sentiment of the Byzantines, often implying that they preferred or welcomed the Ottomans and Islam. The standard text which they trot out is the famous statement attributed to Notaras by the historian Ducas: "It is better to see in the midst of the city the ruling turban of the Turks than the Latin tiara."[47] This text has thus often been brought forth as evidence for the purported preference of the Byzantines for Turkish rule. First it is instructive to ascertain the fate of Notaras: he was beheaded by the sultan when he refused to turn over his twelve-year-old

[43] Scholarios, IV, 453.
[44] Scholarios, IV, 213.
[45] Scholarios, IV, 220.
[46] Scholarios, IV, 292.
[47] Ducas, 329.

"The fatherland of the composer of this book is the island of Cyprus. His fathers, and the fathers of his fathers, and indeed the entire genealogical chain were foremost as to wealth and position until the Hellenic element there [in Cyprus] had as its fate to be enslaved to the barbarous Italians."[59] The relevant phrase reads: "ἕως οὔπω βαρβάροις ἔλαχεν Ἰταλοῖς τὸ ἐκεῖσε δουλεύειν Ἑλληνικόν."[60] Thus Gregory refers to the Cypriots as τὸ ἐκεῖσε . . . Ἑλληνικόν, i.e., the Hellenic population there (in Cyprus), thus implying that there is τὸ ἐδῶ Ἑλληνικόν (he was writing in Byzantine territory).

At the age of seventeen Gregory had left Cyprus because the system of Greek schools had so declined after 1191 that only the elementary schools existed. There were also the παιδευτήρια Ῥωμαίων, where, he says, "grammar was taught in the language of the Latin fathers,"[61] that is, in Latin. Inasmuch as he desired a higher Greek education, and as the Latin schools did not even teach Aristotle, he went to Ephesos where he had hoped to study with Blemmydes, "ἀνὴρ ὡς ἐλέγετο, οὐ μόνον Ἑλλήνων τῶν ἐφ' ἡμῶν, ἀλλὰ καὶ πάντων ἀνδρῶν σοφώτατος."[62] Once more he uses the term Ἑλλήνων to refer to contemporary Byzantines in the Byzantine Empire.

Already in the thirteenth century, and therefore two-hundred years before Chalcocondyles had completely reversed the meanings of Ἕλλην and Ῥωμαῖος to signify Byzantine and western Europeans respectively, we see in the writings of a provincial, a Cypriot, this reversal of meaning in connection with the terms Ἕλλην and Ῥωμαῖος.

This indicates that the variegated process of cultural identification in fifteenth-century Byzantium was a process in which there were already various and competing elements at least two-hundred years earlier.

---

[59] PG, vol. 142, 20. See S. Vryonis, *Byzantine Cyprus*, Fifth Annual Lecture on History and Archaeology Sponsored by the Cultural Foundation of the Bank of Cyprus (Nicosia, 1990). C. Constantinides, *Higher Education in Byzantium in the Thirteenth and Fourteenth Century (1204–c. 1310)* (Nicosia, 1982). W. Lamerre, *La tradition manuscrite de la correspondance de Grégoire de Chypre, patriarche de Constantinople (1283–1289)* (Brussels-Rome, 1937).

[60] PG 142, 21.

[61] PG 142, 21.

[62] PG 142, 22.

Old Wine in New Bottles: The Rewriting of Saints' Lives in the Palaeologan Period

ALICE-MARY TALBOT

THE SAINTS' lives written during the final two centuries of the Byzantine Empire have begun to attract more attention during the past decade. In 1980, for example, Angeliki Laiou analyzed nineteen lives of Palaeologan saints and extracted valuable information on social conditions in the Balkans in this period of the declining empire.[1] The following year, at the Birmingham symposium on the Byzantine saint, Ruth Macrides examined the cults of some holy men of the early Palaeologan period.[2] The present paper will focus not on the saints, but on some of the hagiographers of the Palaeologan period and, where possible, will examine the motivations which lay behind the composition of vitae and *enkomia* of saints, especially those of holy men and women from the distant past.

The Palaeologan period was an era of revival for the genre of hagiography; not only were substantial numbers of contemporary holy men commemorated in vitae and *enkomia*, but new versions of the vitae of saints of earlier centuries were also produced. This phenomenon is particularly striking in comparison with the twelfth century, when, as Paul Magdalino has pointed out, there was a marked decline in the numbers of holy men, and some indications of opposition to the ascetic lifestyle.[3]

My research to date has produced the following, no doubt incomplete, figures on the composition of hagiography in the Palaeologan period. Approximately thirty-six vitae were devoted to thirty-two contemporary holy men: the Patriarch Athanasios was eulogized in two vitae, and Maximos Kausokalybites in four. Most hagiographers of contemporary saints wrote about only one holy man, with the exception of Philotheos Kokkinos who wrote five such biographies. A much larger number of hagiographical works, approximately 125, by about forty-five different authors, was devoted to saints who lived before the thirteenth century. For the purposes of this survey, I have excluded from my calculations *enkomia* of New Testament personages and have included only saints of the post-apostolic period. The most active writers of vitae of older saints were Constantine Akropolites, Nikephoros Gregoras, and Philotheos Kokkinos.

Virtually all of the holy men who lived in the Palaeologan period were of monastic background; quite a few attained high ecclesiastic office. Three or four (like St. Michael, St.

[1] A. Laiou-Thomadakis, "Saints and Society in the Late Byzantine Empire," in *Charanis Studies. Essays in Honor of Peter Charanis*, ed. A. Laiou-Thomadakis (New Brunswick, N.J., 1980), 84–114.

[2] R. Macrides, "Saints and Sainthood in the Early Palaiologan Period," in *The Byzantine Saint*, ed. S. Hackel (London, 1981), 67–87.

[3] P. Magdalino, "The Byzantine Holy Man in the Twelfth Century," in *The Byzantine Saint* (note 2 above), 51–66.

George, and St. Niketas the Younger) were neo-martyrs who were executed by the Turks or other Muslims. Some of these holy men were noted for their opposition to the Union of Lyons; others were staunch supporters of Palamism. The wandering holy man, a prime example being St. Maximos Kausokalybites (the Hut-Burner),[4] is a common figure; many of these saints moved from one holy mountain to another, sometimes living in cenobitic monasteries, sometimes preferring an eremitic lifestyle. Many were praised for exploits of extreme asceticism. Holy women are conspicuous by their total absence; for reasons that are still obscure, not a single female saint is documented during the Palaeologan centuries. I have suggested elsewhere that women may have failed to achieve sanctity in this period because the nuns of this era almost always lived in cenobitic convents, and were not encouraged to engage in the ascetic exploits and mortification of the flesh which gave their male counterparts the reputation of holy men.[5] Like their heroes, the authors of these lives of contemporary saints were, with only a few exceptions, monks or churchmen, often disciples of the holy man whose life they recount. Examples are Theoktistos the Stoudite and Joseph Kalothetos, both monks who wrote vitae of the Patriarch Athanasios I; Makarios Chrysokephalos, metropolitan of Philadelphia, who wrote a life of Meletios of Galesios; and Philotheos, metropolitan of Selymvria, who composed an *enkomion* of Makarios of Constantinople. Usually a generation or so younger than the holy man they eulogized, the writers were eyewitnesses to some of the events they relate, and may have gathered much of their information first-hand from the lips of their master. These authors were motivated by a desire to record the exemplary lives of their spiritual masters and to document their prophecies and miracles. In some instances the accounts appear to have been designed to support the canonization of the holy man (Athanasios, Palamas).[6] Some of the vitae were intended, at least in part, to praise the foundation of a monastery, as in the vita of Athanasios of Meteora.[7] Some were written to promote the cause of hesychasm: one vita of Patriarch Athanasios, who was considered a precursor of hesychasm, was written by the Palamite monk Joseph Kalothetos, while Philotheos Kokkinos, the most distinguished Palaeologan hagiographer, wrote lengthy biographies of four hesychast saints, including Gregory Palamas.[8] It is also worthy of note that all four of Philotheos' subjects had some connection with Thessaloniki, his birthplace.

Let us now turn to the production of new vitae of old saints: what could be termed "old wine in new bottles". Since almost eighty percent of Palaeologan hagiography falls into that

---

[4] The most recent article on Maximos is by K. Ware, "St. Maximos of Kapsokalyvia and Fourteenth-Century Athonite Hesychasm," in *Kathegetria. Essays Presented to Joan Hussey for her 80th Birthday* (Camberley, 1988), 409–30.

[5] A.-M. Talbot, "A Comparison of the Monastic Experience of Byzantine Men and Women," *Greek Orthodox Theological Review* 30 (1985), 17f.

[6] A.-M. Talbot, *Faith Healing in Late Byzantium: The Posthumous Miracles of the Patriarch Athanasios I of Constantinople by Theoktistos the Stoudite* (Brookline, Mass., 1983), 21–29.

[7] N. A. Bees, "Συμβολὴ εἰς τὴν ἱστορίαν τῶν μονῶν τῶν Μετεώρων," *Byzantis* 1 (1909), 237–60.

[8] Besides Palamas, they were Sabas the Younger (*BHG*[3] 1606), Germanos Maroules (*BHG*[3] 2164), and Isidore I Boucheiras (*BHG*[3] 962). Palamas was a metropolitan of Thessaloniki, while the other three were born in that city.

category, it seems worthwhile to analyze this body of material in an attempt to ascertain the reasons for the great interest in this form of literary composition, especially in the late thirteenth century and first half of the fourteenth century.

The authors of these lives of earlier saints are a very different group of writers from the monks who wrote vitae of contemporary holy men. With few exceptions (like Philotheos Kokkinos) the authors of the reworked versions of vitae of older saints are literati, not monks. It should be noted further that the Palaeologan writers who tried their hand at this literary genre tended to be staunchly Orthodox and anti-Unionist; hagiography was not to the taste of pro-Western writers who had closer links with the Italian humanists and the papal curia than with the imperial court or patriarchate.

The most prolific writer of saints' lives during the Palaeologan period was Constantine Akropolites.[9] Eldest son of the historian George Akropolites, Constantine served Andronikos II for most of his long reign, first as *logothetes tou genikou* and then as *megas logothetes*, from 1294–1321. Constantine concentrated his literary efforts on writing new versions of the vitae of saints of past centuries. For this apparent emulation of Symeon Metaphrastes he earned the epithet ὁ νέος μεταφραστής, "the new translator". Of his twenty-nine hagiographical works, only one, a Logos on St. John Merciful the Younger,[10] most probably an early thirteenth-century saint, deals with a relatively contemporary holy man. The cult of St. John, who had a special reputation for curing diseases of the eyes, was limited to the region of Nicaea. Akropolites relates that he wrote the oration on St. John at the request of his teacher, who as a child had been healed of an eye affliction by going to the saint's shrine in Nicaea.[11]

But why did Constantine devote his twenty-eight other *enkomia* of saints to holy men and women of the distant past? Many were obscure figures martyred under the Roman emperors: Oraiozele, for example, was a disciple of St. Andrew; others died in the reigns of Vespasian and Hadrian; and at least six of the saints Constantine eulogized were martyred under Diocletian.

Some insight is provided by a number of Constantine's letters discussing his production of hagiographical works.[12] These letters, sent to members of his literary circle, reveal that Constantine was in the habit of circulating copies of his newly written vitae among his friends, asking for their opinion of his compositions. Sometimes one friend was asked to pass the manuscript on to another. Occasionally Constantine notes that he was urged by one of his acquaintances to write the vita of a certain saint. Perusal of this correspondence of Akropolites reveals that most of his hagiographical texts were designed to be read aloud in churches on the feastday of the given saint. One letter provides the otherwise unattested

---

[9] For a biographical sketch of Akropolites and list of all his hagiographical works, both published and unpublished, see D. M. Nicol, "Constantine Akropolites: A Prosopographical Note," *DOP* 19 (1965), 249–56.

[10] Ed. D. I. Polemis, "The Speech of Constantine Akropolites on St. John Merciful the Younger," *AnalBoll* 91 (1973), 31–54.

[11] *Ibid.*, 48f.

[12] H. Delehaye, "Constantini Acropolitae Hagiographi Byzantini epistularum manipulus," *AnalBoll* 51 (1933), 263–78.

information that Constantine had recently made a trip to Jerusalem. As a kind of thank-you present for his host, who is unnamed, he enclosed a eulogy of St. Prokopios, who was particularly venerated in the Holy Land, requesting that his composition be read at the local monastery named after the martyr.[13] In this case it is evident that a journey to the Holy Land stimulated his interest in a local martyr, St. Prokopios.

But why the twenty-seven other saints? In some cases, the texts of his *logoi* and *enkomia* reveal the motivation behind his selection. Consider his *enkomion* of Theodosia,[14] an iconodule martyr of the first iconoclastic persecution of Leo III. She was the nun who reportedly pulled the ladder out from under the soldier who had been ordered to destroy the mosaic image of Christ at the Chalke Gate. After merciless flogging she was executed with an animal's horn. At the end of his oration Akropolites describes some recent posthumous miracles of Theodosia, and thus demonstrates that he had very specific reasons for eulogizing this saint. In fact, he could personally bear witness to the efficacy of her relics in performing miraculous cures. Around the year 1300 Akropolites' son-in-law, Michael of Trebizond, was knocked unconscious in a riding accident and emerged from a coma in a deranged and delirious condition. The doctors bled him and tried other remedies, to no avail. Akropolites took the lad to the shrine of St. Theodosia where he was fully cured through contact with her relics and by being anointed with oil from the lamp over her sarcophagus.[15] Akropolites himself had also benefited from the healing power of the saint. He had incurred a leg injury as the result of being kicked by a horse, and suffered recurrent pain for years. Again the physicians were powerless to help, but he was cured by visiting the relics of St. Theodosia.[16]

In 1306 the miraculous healing of a deaf-mute boy at the church of St. Theodosia attracted the attention of the emperor himself, who favored the shrine with a visit.[17] It seems likely, then, that Akropolites' new oration on Theodosia was somehow connected with the growing reputation of her church as a shrine of miraculous healing, and was either written spontaneously in gratitude for his own cure and that of his son-in-law, or as a commissioned piece.

Constantine was similarly inspired to write an *enkomion* of St. Barbaros, because both he and his young daughter were healed by anointing themselves with μύρον from the saint's relics: Akropolites was cured of arthritis, his daughter of severe boils.[18]

Yet another *enkomion* by Akropolites, that of Athanasios, bishop of Adramyttium in the tenth or eleventh century, may also have been inspired by contemporary miracles, since in the fourteenth century his relics, which exuded healing μύρον, still attracted large crowds.[19]

---

[13] Constantine Akropolites, ep. 143, ed. Delehaye (note 12 above), 275f.

[14] PG 140:893–936.

[15] PG 140:925D–932A.

[16] PG 140:932A–933B.

[17] Pachymeres, *Historiae*, ed. I. Bekker, Bonn ed. (1835), II, 452.15–455.8.

[18] Ed. A. Papadopoulos-Kerameus, *Analekta Hierosolymitikes Stachyologias* 1 (St. Petersburg, 1891), 405–20.

[19] A. Papadopoulos-Kerameus, *Varia graeca sacra* (St. Petersburg, 1909), 141–47. The passage on the tomb is found on p. 145.

Another saint eulogized by Akropolites was Thomais,[20] who gained fame in the tenth century as a holy woman even though she never took monastic vows. Originally from Lesbos, she moved to Chalcedon with her parents. She lived somewhere in the region of the capital with her husband who became distressed by her charitable activities and beat her because she gave away so much to the poor. One might wonder what connection there could be between this saintly battered wife and Akropolites. The last paragraph of his *enkomion* provides the clue, for he prays to Thomais to bless "the pious and Christ-loving empress (ἄνασσα) who out of love for God restored this church and many others which were ruined and who built others from the foundations . . . "[21] This passage suggests that Akropolites delivered the oration on the occasion of the rededication of a church which either bore the name of St. Thomais or was somehow related to her. There is in fact such a church in Constantinople, at the convent bearing the curious name of the Theotokos ta Mikra Romaiou, where the mother of Thomais was superior and where Thomais was buried. Akropolites refers to this monastery in his oration (246A), although he does not specifically identify it as the site where he was speaking. In the mid-fourteenth century the Russian pilgrim Stephen of Novgorod visited this church and kissed the relics of Thomais.[22] As for the ἄνασσα who restored the church, it seems most likely that she was the Dowager Empress Theodora Palaeologina, widow of Emperor Michael VIII, who is also known to have reconstructed the convents of Lips and of Kosmas and Damian.[23] Since she died in 1303, it may be possible to date the vita of Thomais to the end of the thirteenth century or very beginning of the fourteenth century.

Akropolites may have intended several other of his hagiographical works for delivery on the feastdays of saints or at dedication ceremonies for newly restored churches in Constantinople or elsewhere. At least seven of the old saints commemorated by Akropolites, including the little-known martyrs Florus and Oraiozele, were either the patron saints of churches in Constantinople or their relics are known to have been deposited in churches in the capital. And in all seven cases, thanks to the testimony of the Russian pilgrims and other sources, we know that these churches were functioning in the fourteenth century or that the relics continued to be venerated.[24] Unfortunately many of the *enkomia* of these saints remain

---

[20] *Acta Sanctorum*, Nov. IV (Brussels, 1925), 242–46.

[21] *Ibid.*, 246F.

[22] R. Janin, *La géographie ecclésiastique de l'empire byzantin*, I, *Le siège de Constantinople et le patriarcat oecuménique, iii, Les églises et les monastères* (Paris, 1969), 197. G. Majeska, *Russian Travelers to Constantinople in the Fourteenth and Fifteenth Centuries* (Washington, D.C., 1984), 40, 321–25.

[23] Janin, *Églises* (note 22 above), 285f., 307–10. The only other woman who might have been described as ἄνασσα ca. 1300 would be Irene-Yolanda of Montferrat, wife of Andronikos II. Irene is better known, however, for her preoccupation with the marital alliances of her children than for her patronage of the arts.

[24] The seven saints and their related churches are as follows: 1) Eudokimos: his body was preserved at the monastery of St. Eudokimos; cf. Majeska, *Russian Travelers* (note 22 above), 148, 316–18. 2) Florus: his relics were at the Pantokrator Monastery; cf. Majeska, 42, 152, 162, 186, 293. 3) Leontios: his head was at the church of St. Nicholas at Blachernae; cf. Majeska, 44, 338. 4) Metrophanes: his stole and head were at a church in the Heptaskalon region at the beginning of the thirteenth century; cf. Janin, *Églises* (note 22 above), 336f. 5) Oraiozele: there was a church dedicated to her where healing miracles occurred; cf. *Propylaeum ad Acta Sanctorum Novembris*, ed. H. Delehaye (Brussels, 1902), 848.47–52. 6) Panteleimon: a convent had his

unpublished, so I am unable at this point to investigate further this line of argument. I hope, however, that future study of the unedited texts of Akropolites in combination with careful analysis of his relevant correspondence will provide more information on the genesis of his encomiastic and hagiographic works and their relationship to Constantinopolitan churches and monasteries.

A different motivation lay behind the hagiographic composition of Theodora Raoulaina,[25] a contemporary of Akropolites. Theodora wrote only one saint's life, that of the ninth-century iconodule brothers Theodore and Theophanes[26] who earned the sobriquet Graptoi because of the punishment allegedly inflicted upon them during the second period of Iconoclasm: having verses tattooed upon their foreheads. Raoulaina is one of the very few Byzantine women known to have written a hagiographical text, and the only such female author in the Palaeologan period. Clues to her reasons for choosing the iconodule brothers as the subject of her eulogy can be found in her own background and in the text of the vita. Although Theodora was the niece of Emperor Michael VIII Palaeologos, she stubbornly opposed his policy on the Union of the Churches at the Council of Lyons in 1274; both she and her mother were sent into exile as a result of their views and had their property confiscated. In her introduction to the vita, Theodora notes that she wrote the work while she was in exile, at the urging of her mother Eulogia. She refers to the "confusion which afflicts the church now on account of the agreement between the emperor and the bishop of Rome" and attacks the supporters of Union who "disregard holy doctrines; [and] boldly hasten to destroy not only their own souls, but to make everyone else share in spiritual death."[27]

It seems likely that Theodora, as a member of the imperial family who found herself in opposition to official government religious policy, saw a parallel between her own situation and that of her namesake, the Blessed Theodora, the iconodule wife of the iconoclast Emperor Theophilos, who figures in her vita. Just as the Empress Theodora urged the restoration of veneration of images after the death of her husband, so Raoulaina's mother was to urge Andronikos II to repudiate the Union of Lyons as soon as he ascended the throne. There is yet another point of resemblance between Raoulaina's family and the two iconodule brothers whom she praised in her work; for just as the Graptoi had been persecuted for their beliefs, so Raoulaina's brothers-in-law Manuel and Isaac Raoul were blinded and imprisoned by Michael VIII for their opposition to Union.[28]

---

head and blood; cf. Majeska, 44, 162, 333, 342, 383f. 7) Sampson: his xenon still functioned in the fourteenth century; cf. Janin, *Églises* (note 22 above), 561f.

[25] On Raoulaina, see A.-M. Talbot, "Bluestocking Nuns: Intellectual Life in the Convents of Late Byzantium," in *Okeanos. Essays Presented to Ihor Ševčenko on his Sixtieth Birthday = Harvard Ukrainian Studies*, 7 (Cambridge, Mass., 1983), 605f., 611f., 615f.

[26] Ed. A. Papadopoulos-Kerameus, *Analekta Hierosolymitikes Stachyologias*, 4 (Jerusalem, 1897), 185–223; 5 (Jerusalem, 1898), 397–99.

[27] *Ibid.*, 187.21–23, 197.22–25.

[28] This parallel was first noted by D. M. Nicol in his article "The Greeks and the Union of the Churches," *Proceedings of the Royal Irish Academy* 63 C, no. 1 (1962), 12, 14.

Since Raoulaina wrote this vita while she was in exile and Michael was still on the throne, she must have found comfort in the fact that after the death of Theophilos the iconodules were released from prison or their places of exile, while the iconoclasts were punished.

When we move further into the fourteenth century, the name of the polymath Nikephoros Gregoras stands out as one of the leading practitioners of hagiography.[29] As in the case of other Palaeologan literati, virtually all of his hagiographic works were dedicated to old saints. The one exception was his vita of his uncle John, metropolitan of Pontic Herakleia.[30] Gregoras, who was orphaned as a child, had particular reason to eulogize his uncle, who had raised him and been responsible for his education. This vita is of considerable interest not only for the biographical information it provides about John of Herakleia, who is otherwise unknown, but also for the details of Gregoras' own youth and education.

Gregoras also wrote full-scale vitae of four saints who lived in earlier centuries, and several other *enkomia*. Three of these vitae were of ninth-century saints. In one case at least, the vita of Michael Synkellos,[31] the iconodule who was a companion of the brothers Theodore and Theophanes, Gregoras' motive for composition seems clear. Both Michael Synkellos and Nikephoros Gregoras had strong ties to the Chora Monastery. At the end of his life, when icon veneration had been restored by Empress Theodora, Michael became hegoumenos of the Chora and his remains were buried there. Gregoras himself had a long association with the Chora: he had assisted Metochites with the restoration of its church ca. 1316, and later on was entrusted by Metochites with the supervision of the library he had deposited at the monastery.[32] So it is not surprising that Gregoras decided to write a new version of the life of this saint who was especially venerated at Chora and whose relics still worked healing miracles in the fourteenth century.

Another ninth-century saint eulogized by Gregoras was the Empress Theophano, the saintly wife of Leo VI.[33] Distinguished for her charitable works and ascetic life style, she died in 895 or 896 at the age of 30. She was first buried in a chapel which Leo built in her honor at the church of the Holy Apostles; later her remains were transferred to the convent of St. Constantine which Theophano herself had founded. Her relics were still there in the mid-fourteenth century when they are mentioned by the Russian pilgrim Stephen of Novgorod.[34] The relics of Theophano continued to perform healing miracles in Palaeologan

---

[29] For a still useful analysis of Gregoras' hagiographical production, see R. Guilland, *Essai sur Nicéphore Grégoras* (Paris, 1926), 170–92.

[30] Ed. V. Laurent, "La vie de Jean, métropolite d'Héraclée du Pont," Ἀρχ.Ποντ. 6 (1934), 3–67.

[31] Ed. F. I. Shmit in *Kakhrie-džami* = *IRAIK* 11 (Sofia-Munich, 1906), 260–79.

[32] I. Ševčenko, "Theodore Metochites, the Chora, and the Intellectual Trends of His Time," in *The Kariye Djami*, vol. IV, ed. P. A. Underwood (Princeton, N.J., 1975), 35f.

[33] *Zwei griechische Texte über die hl. Theophano, die Gemahlin Kaisers Leo VI*, ed. E. Kurtz (St. Petersburg, 1898), 25–45.

[34] Majeska, *Russian Travelers* (note 22 above), 42, 296–98. *Idem*, "The Body of St. Theophano the Empress and the Convent of St. Constantine," *Byzantinoslavica* 38 (1977), 14–21.

times; Gregoras comments that he planned to devote a second volume to a description of those posthumous miracles, but was prevented by his own terrible headaches.[35] He hoped that he, too, would be cured by the intervention of the saint, but as far as we know the second volume never appeared.

It seems likely that Gregoras wrote a life of Theophano in part because of his association with the nuns of the convent of St. Constantine and his hope of a cure from her relics. He also states in his introduction that he composed the vita at the request of friends[36] but this may be merely a conventional topos. With regard to his sources, Gregoras claims that he used fragments of previous vitae of the saint.[37] This might suggest that as a result of the passage of time and/or the devastation caused by the Latin occupation of Constantinople in the thirteenth century, the full text of the vita of Theophano had disappeared, and that Gregoras was asked to produce a new, complete version. As a matter of fact, however, Gregoras' reworked text closely duplicates the data of the earlier vita. In revising the old vita, Gregoras aimed to improve its style and to raise it to an even higher level, including lengthy disquisitions on the title of *patrikios*, Constantinople as the capital of the empire, and so forth.[38]

In the eyes of his contemporaries, the style and content of his vitae were appreciated, for in 1341/2 Gregory Akindynos wrote Gregoras a letter[39] praising this very vita of Theophano, of which the hagiographer had sent him a copy. Akindynos comments on the "fluent" Attic language of the text; of even greater interest, however, is his approving remark that in the vita Gregoras had attacked the Palamite theory that human eyes could perceive the uncreated light of the Transfiguration. Akindynos also stated that he particularly admired the concluding passage of the vita in which Gregoras denounced the current ecclesiastical disorder. Kurtz dated the composition of this vita to the 1320s,[40] but the letter of Akindynos shows that Gregoras must have written it considerably later, at the time when the Palamite controversy was just beginning.[41] As in the case of Theodora Raoulaina's vita of the iconodule Graptoi brothers, which can be read as a prefiguration of the persecution of opponents of the Union of Lyons, so the vita of Theophano seems to contain veiled anti-Palamite allusions.

The third vita by Gregoras dealing with the ninth century is an uninformative biography of the Patriarch Antony II Kauleas.[42] It is unclear why Gregoras should have devoted hagiographical works both to the wife of Leo VI, Theophano, and, shortly afterward, to the patriarch who served the emperor from 893–901. Gregoras' motivation for writing a vita of this obscure patriarch is puzzling; in fact, Antony is so little-known that this life by

---

[35] *Vita of Theophano*, ed. Kurtz (note 33 above), 44.6–10.

[36] *Ibid.*, 26.7–14.

[37] *Ibid.*, 26.14–18.

[38] I. Ševčenko, "Levels of Style in Byzantine Literature," *JÖB* 31 (1981), 302.

[39] A. C. Hero, *Letters of Gregory Akindynos* (Washington, D.C., 1983), ep. 17, and commentary, 339–41.

[40] *Vita of Theophano*, ed. Kurtz (note 33 above), viii.

[41] The editor, Angela Hero (*Letters*, note 39 above), p. 340, dates the letter to 1341–42; Gregoras must have written the vita of Theophano shortly before.

[42] A. Papadopoulos-Kerameus, *Monumenta graeca et latina ad historiam Photii patriarchae pertinentia*, 1 (St. Petersburg, 1899), 1–25.

Gregoras is virtually our only source of information about him. Gregoras provides few concrete facts: e.g., that Kauleas lost his mother when he was still a child, and became a monk at age twelve. Eventually he was ordained priest and became hegoumenos of a monastery where he was joined by his father. He then came to the attention of Emperor Leo the Wise who made him patriarch. He was remembered primarily as the founder of a Constantinopolitan monastery called τοῦ Καλλέως or τοῦ κῦρ Ἀντωνίου, where he was buried. We know from another fourteenth-century writer, Philotheos of Selymvria, that the Latins occupied this monastery after 1204 and destroyed its circuit wall;[43] it was restored to the Greeks after 1261, however, and in the first half of the fourteenth century, at the time when Gregoras wrote the vita of its founder, it was not only still functioning but was praised for its size and beauty. It seems possible then that Gregoras chose to eulogize Antony Kauleas either through some personal connection with the monastery or because he was commissioned to write the vita.

The authors examined thus far, Akropolites, Raoulaina, Gregoras, had a variety of reasons for penning hagiographic compositions on saints of olden days: gratitude for a miraculous cure and the wish to promote the relics of a particular saint, the commissioning of an oration to be delivered at the dedication of a new or restored church or monastery, the desire to improve the style of an earlier vita, or the opportunity to comment on current ecclesiastical policy.

In addition to these factors, civic loyalty was also a powerful stimulus for hagiographers: most of the Palaeologan authors who wrote eulogies of St. Demetrios (Makarios Makres, Symeon of Thessaloniki, Gregory Palamas, Nicholas Kabasilas, Constantine Harmenopoulos, Isidore Glabas, Makarios Choumnos, Demetrios Chrysoloras, to name a few) had spent at least part of their lives in Thessaloniki, where Demetrios was the patron saint. Kabasilas also wrote about Theodora of Thessaloniki, Makarios Makres about David of Thessaloniki. Since all three of these saints had churches in Thessaloniki, it seems likely that their *enkomia* were not composed merely as literary exercises, but as orations to be delivered at their churches on their feast days.

One of the best examples of an oration sparked by civic pride is the *enkomion* of St. Agathonikos by Philotheos, metropolitan of Selymvria in the fourteenth century.[44] Agathonikos, a martyr of the late third century, was supposedly born in Nikomedeia, and beheaded in Selymvria by order of Emperor Galerius. Philotheos, who was also born in Nikomedeia, and subsequently became metropolitan of Selymvria, thus had a double connection with the martyr. He devoted a substantial portion of his oration to praise of the two cities, noting that if Thessaloniki had the relics of Demetrios, Selymvria could boast of the head of Agathonikos.[45] Philotheos describes earlier miracles produced by the saint's relics, for example, the

---

[43] *Vita of Makarios*, ch. 6, ed. A. Papadopoulos-Kerameus, *Maurogordateios bibliotheke* = *Hellenikos Philologikos Syllogos*, suppl. 17.2 (Constantinople, 1886), 49. Cf. Janin, *Églises* (note 22 above), 39–41.

[44] PG 154:1229–40 (incomplete edition).

[45] PG 154:1237A.

healing of Emperor Manuel I in the twelfth century. Manuel, who had suffered head inju-
ries in a polo game, visited Selymvria in 1167, and was cured of his headaches by holding
the martyr's head above his own head for a considerable length of time. In gratitude the
emperor restored the cathedral of Selymvria.[46] Sometimes the head could be "loaned out", as
when it was sent to the imperial palace in Constantinople to cure Emperor John V
Palaeologos.[47] Philotheos also attributed his own vindication from charges of sacrilege to the
intercession of the martyr. The metropolitan had been accused by members of his own
clergy of removing the ambo from the cathedral and the marble paving stones from the
church of the martyr Alexander to the metropolitan palace, presumably for repairs to his
own residence. He was also charged with selling sacred vessels to ransom prisoners and to
help restore the city's fortifications. The synod in Constantinople, after long deliberation,
finally declared his innocence on August 22 of an unknown year, the feast day of Agathonikos.[48] It is clear that Philotheos delivered this oration to an audience in the cathedral of
Selymvria, no doubt on a subsequent feast day of Agathonikos; he claims that he had composed the *enkomion* at the request of the inhabitants of the city. Even though he realized he
was inadequate to the task, he agreed to accept the challenge because, he claims, no one else
had ever written an *enkomion* on the martyr.[49]

Another impetus for hagiographic composition by writers of monastic background was
pride in one's monastery, its distinguished superiors, and its relics. We have seen this factor
to be a determinant in Gregoras' vita of Michael Synkellos, hegoumenos of Chora. There
are other similar examples: Makarios Choumnos, who became hegoumenos of the Stoudios
monastery after leaving Nea Mone in Thessaloniki, wrote an *enkomion* of his predecessor
Theodore the Stoudite.[50] Gregory of Cyprus, who was a Galesiot monk at one point in his
career, wrote a vita of Lazaros of Mt. Galesios.[51] This factor also explains why Makarios, a
monk at the Mangana Monastery during the reign of Andronikos II, wrote a vita of Ia, a
little known female Persian saint of the fourth century, martyred under Shapur II.[52] A
church in Constantinople near the Golden Gate was originally dedicated to Ia and contained her relics, which performed numerous healing miracles. The church was restored by
Justinian, but after Constantinople fell to the Fourth Crusade in 1204 it was destroyed, and
Ia's relics were moved to the Mangana monastery, where they were a source of pride to the
monks.[53] Makarios notes that the passage of 900 years had not destroyed the martyr's relics,

---

[46] A section on the miracles worked by the head of Agathonikos, not included in PG 154, has been edited by
P. Magdalino, "Byzantine Churches of Selymbria," *DOP* 32 (1978), 309–15. The passage on Manuel is
found on p. 311.1–9.

[47] *Ibid.*, 311.18–24.

[48] *Ibid.*, 311.25–42.

[49] PG 154:1229D–1232A. Philotheos seems, however, to be mistaken in his claim, since *BHG*[3] lists several
hagiographical works on Agathonikos (*BHG*[3] 39–43).

[50] *BHG*[3] 1759m (unpublished).

[51] *Acta Sanctorum*, Nov. III (Brussels, 1910), 588–606.

[52] *Martyrion of Ia* by Makarios, ed. H. Delehaye, *Les versions grecques des actes des martyrs persans sous
Sapor II* = PO 2.4 (Paris, 1905), 461–73.

[53] Janin, *Églises* (note 22 above), 253.

but did obliterate the accounts of her life and passion; hence he felt compelled to compose a new martyrion for her.[54]

Still other motivations stimulated the composition of lives of saints from the distant past. John Eugenikos, for instance, wrote a vita of James the Persian because he possessed a relic of that saint.[55] Other authors chose to write about the saints after whom they were named. Constantine Akropolites devoted a vita to St. Constantine the emperor; Gregory of Cyprus, formerly named George, wrote about St. George; Demetrios Chrysoloras about St. Demetrios; Theodore Pediasimos composed an account of the miracles wrought by Theodore Stratelates and Theodore Teron, his namesakes and patron saints.

I would like to suggest yet another reason why Palaeologan literati may have found the composition of vitae of earlier saints a more congenial exercise than writing about contemporary holy men. Despite the undoubted piety of men like Metochites and Gregoras, there was a gulf between the literati, trained in the classical tradition, and the wandering eremitic monks who most often rejected secular literature and the ancient heritage. We learn from a vita of Maximos Kausokalybites that a certain logothetes, probably to be identified with Theodore Metochites, had an antipathy for monastic eccentricity and scorned Maximos because of his lack of formal education.[56]

I have endeavored in this study to demonstrate some of the reasons why Palaeologan writers decided to compose lives of saints of earlier centuries and the motivation which lay behind their choice of subject. For authors like Akropolites, Metochites, and Gregoras, surely the question of style was of great importance. They relished the challenge of trying to present old materials in new and different fashion. Gregoras, on the other hand, went so far in his *enkomion* of St. Merkourios as to omit all details of the saint's life which had previously been recounted by other hagiographers, and to include only those facts overlooked by his predecessors.[57] He followed the same procedure in composing his *enkomion* of St. Demetrios. Not surprisingly, however, in many other vitae the Palaeologan hagiographers were unable to present any new material, but only to recast well-known facts. For these writers satisfaction lay in appreciation by their contemporaries, as when Akindynos highly praised Gregoras' *enkomion* of Emperor Constantine, noting that "it was skillfully composed, . . . [with] powerful thoughts, elegant expression, graceful composition; the parts [were] perfectly arranged to make up the whole."[58] A task that remains for the future is to make a careful comparison of Palaeologan vitae with earlier versions of the life of the same saint.

In some cases, however, reworking of vitae of older saints by the literati may not have been merely the result of a desire to improve the style, but was rather a response to a genuine need to replace lost accounts. It is important to remember that these authors lived during

[54] *Martyrion of Ia*, ed. Delehaye (note 52 above), 472.40–45.

[55] C. Hannick, "L'éloge de Jacques le Perse par Jean Eugenikos," *AnalBoll* 90 (1972), 261–87.

[56] F. Halkin, "Deux vies de S. Maxime le Kausokalybe ermite au Mont Athos (XIVe s.)," *AnalBoll* 54 (1936), 70f. Cf. D. M. Nicol, "Hilarion of Didymoteichon and the Gift of Prophecy," *Byzantine Studies/Études Byzantines* 5 (1978), 187.

[57] Guilland, *Grégoras* (note 29 above), 185.

[58] Akindynos, ed. Hero (*Letters*, note 39 above), ep. 18, pp. 66.10–68.1.

the period following the Byzantine recovery of Constantinople from the Latins. Many Greek churches and monasteries in the capital had suffered damage during the conquest of the city by the Crusaders in 1204; some were handed over to Latin monks and may have undergone modification in structure or decoration, as in the well-known case of Kalender-hane Camii;[59] still others were abandoned and fell into ruin during the Latin occupation. Not only were buildings destroyed, but monastic libraries were looted and their contents dispersed. Evidence for the loss of monastic documents is found in the introduction to the typikon for the convent of Kosmas and Damian written by the Empress Dowager Theodora Palaeologina toward the end of the thirteenth century. She comments that when she re-stored the monastery which had fallen into ruins and had lost most of its estates as a result of the Latin occupation, she also found it necessary to write a new typikon.[60] We have seen a similar situation in the case of Ia and Theophano: their earlier vitae were lost or damaged and had to be replaced in the fourteenth century by new versions. Philotheos, in fact, seemed unaware that *enkomia* of Agathonikos had indeed been written in previous centuries; evi-dently no manuscripts of these works were to be found in Selymvria in the fourteenth cen-tury. This may also be true of a number of other vitae of saints from the distant past.

In closing I should like to stress that, although the reworked vitae of older saints may add little to our knowledge of the lives of these holy men and women, they can still be useful as historical sources, especially when they include accounts of recent miracles worked by the saints' relics. They can provide information on the continuity of the cults of these martyrs and saints, and sometimes shed light on the sanctuaries where the saints were venerated and their relics preserved. As in the case of Akropolites' vita of Thomais, a number of these vitae may have been specially commissioned for the dedication ceremonies of the churches and monasteries rebuilt during the reigns of Michael VIII and Andronikos II. It may eventually be possible to prove some sort of linkage between the spurt of construction and restoration activity in the years following 1261 and the marked increase in the production of hagiogra-phy in the first century of the Palaeologan period.

---

[59] C. L. Striker, Y. D. Kuban, "Work at Kalenderhane Camii in Istanbul: Second Preliminary Report," *DOP* 22 (1968), 190f.

[60] H. Delehaye, *Deux typica byzantins de l'époque des Paléologues* (Brussels, 1921), 137.11–21.

Theoleptos of Philadelphia (ca. 1250–1322):
From Solitary to Activist

ANGELA CONSTANTINIDES HERO

A LUMINARY of the reign of Andronikos II, the metropolitan Theoleptos of Philadelphia is known to students of the twilight of Byzantium through various studies highlighting various aspects of his career.[1] A synthesis of his life and work has yet to appear[2] and while such a monograph remains a desideratum for Byzantinists interested in the last centuries of the empire, I shall attempt within the limits of this paper to fill part of the gap by presenting, if not a full portrait, at least a snapshot of the multi-faceted personality: Theoleptos the solitary, the religious dissident, the prelate and successful defender of his beleaguered metropolis, and last, but not least, the spiritual director.

Information about Theoleptos and his career can be found in both narrative and epistolary sources.[3] Of the two eulogies dedicated to him[4] the one by Manuel Gabalas—a

---

[1] On such studies up to 1980, see *PLP* 3 (1980), 51 no. 7509. To these must be added A. Rigo, "Nota sulla dottrina ascetico-spirituale di Teolepto metropolita di Filadelfia (1250/51–1322)," *RSBN* 24 (1987), 165–200; and the recent editions and translations by H.-V. Beyer, "Die Katechese des Theoleptos von Philadelpheia auf die Verklärung Christi," *JÖB* 34 (1984), 171–97; A. C. Hero, "The Unpublished Letters of Theoleptos Metropolitan of Philadelphia (1283–1322). Part I," *Journal of Modern Hellenism* 3 (1986), 1–31; *eadem*, "The Unpublished Letters of Theoleptos Metropolitan of Philadelphia (1283–1322). Part II," *Journal of Modern Hellenism* 4 (1987), 1–7; R. E. Sinkewicz, "A Critical Edition of the Anti-Arsenite Discourses of Theoleptos of Philadelpheia," *MedSt* 50 (1988), 46–95.

[2] Shortly after the colloquium at Princeton University, I decided to include in my forthcoming edition of Theoleptos' correspondence a biography of the metropolitan based on the paper presented at the colloquium. Fr. Sinkewicz has also informed me that his edition of the monastic discourses, which will appear very soon, will include a lengthy chapter on the life and works of the metropolitan.

[3] The contemporary historians, in particular Nikephoros Gregoras, John Kantakouzenos, and George Pachymeres, contain important references to the activities of Theoleptos. Of the epistolary sources, the following yield significant bits of prosopographical interest: Nikephoros Choumnos, letters to Theoleptos, ed. J. F. Boissonade, *Anecdota nova* (Paris, 1844; repr. Hildesheim, 1962), especially letters 88–92, 94, 99, 100–104, 116, 128; Irene-Eulogia Choumnaina, letter to her director and the director's answer to that letter, ed. A. C. Hero, *A Woman's Quest for Spiritual Guidance* (Brookline, 1986), letters 15 and 16; Manuel Gabalas, letters to Patriarch John Glykys and to the *Megas Dioiketes*, ed. J. Gouillard, "Après le schisme arsénite: la correspondance inédite du pseudo-Jean Chilas," *BSHAcRoum* 25 (1944), letters 1, 2, 6; *idem*, letter to Patriarch Niphon I, ed. D. Reinsch, *Die Briefe des Matthaios von Ephesos im Codex Vindobonensis Theol. Gr. 174* (Berlin, 1974), letter 62; *idem, Invective against Manuel Tagaris*, ed. Reinsch, *ibid.*, pp. 205–20; Michael Gabras, letters to Theoleptos, ed. G. Fatouros, *Die Briefe des Michael Gabras (ca. 1290–nach 1350)* (Vienna, 1973), letters 53, 63; Nikephoros Gregoras, letter to Theoleptos, ed. P. A. M. Leone, *Nicephori Gregorae Epistulae* (Matino, 1982–83), letter 61; and finally Theoleptos' five letters to Choumaina. The first of these letters was published by S. Salaville, "Une lettre et un discours inédits de Théolepte de Philadelphie," *REB* 5 (1947), 116–36. I have edited the second and third letters: Hero, "Unpublished Letters" (note 1 above); the remainder will appear shortly in my monograph *The Correspondence of Theoleptos of Philadelphia*, which will include all five letters.

[4] Gabalas, Τῇ βασιλίσσῃ παραινετικὸς ἐξ αὐτοσχεδίου συντεθειμένος ἐπὶ τῇ τελευτῇ Φιλαδελφείας

subordinate of Theoleptos in Philadelphia and later metropolitan of Ephesos—is a purely rhetorical piece, whereas its counterpart by the imperial chancellor Nikephoros Choumnos contains some important prosopographical details regarding the man who had influenced both the spiritual and material fortunes of the Choumnos family.

According to his encomiast, Theoleptos was a native of Nicaea.[5] He must have been born ca. 1250, since he was twenty-five years old when Patriarch John Bekkos ordered the persecution of the opponents of the Union of Lyons in 1275.[6] His origins were undoubtedly humble, or Choumnos would not have avoided discussing his parentage on the pretext that the metropolitan had nothing but scorn for the things of this world and would have preferred to be praised for his spiritual rather than his earthly forefathers. Theoleptos, declares his encomiast, was the progeny of Nicaea, the Zion of Orthodoxy, and his ancestors were the holy fathers of the ecumenical councils held in that city.[7]

As for his educational background, while Choumnos dwells on Theoleptos' early penchant for the study of the Scriptures, he has nothing to say about his secular education.[8] However, the metropolitan's own writings argue against this *paraleipsis*, for although they are considerably free of rhetorical artifice and display scarcely any classical allusions, their faultless grammar and syntax indicate that their author was not without literary training. Choumnos attributes Theoleptos' success as a writer to divine inspiration,[9] but John Kantakouzenos remarks more realistically that the metropolitan of Philadelphia possessed "no little outer learning."[10]

Be that as it may, Theoleptos did not make use of his literary gifts until he was catapulted into prominence as one of the leaders of the anti-unionist party. In the summer of 1275, his disagreement with the religious policy of Michael VIII forced the twenty-five-year-old Theoleptos—a married deacon—to abandon his wife and home in Nicaea and seek the safety and spiritual comfort of the wilderness, probably in the vicinity of Mount Saint

---

κυροῦ Θεολήπτου, ed. L. Previale, "Due monodie inedite di Matteo di Efeso," *BZ* 41 (1941), 26–31. Choumnos, *Epitaphios*, ed. J. F. Boissonade, *Anecdota graeca* (Paris, 1829–1833; repr. Hildesheim, 1962) (hereafter, Choumnos, *Epitaphios*), 5, 183–239.

[5] Choumnos, *Epitaphios*, 188.

[6] Choumnos, *Epitaphios*, 200; see also note 11 below.

[7] Choumnos, *Epitaphios*, 188. Neither the name of his family nor his own baptismal name is known. The name Theopemptos appears in certain manuscripts which preserve the names of the signatories of the tome of the Second Synod of Blachernae, and Laurent assumed it to be the monastic name of the metropolitan, but it is undoubtedly a scribal error, since the oldest manuscript of the tome shows the reading Theoleptos. See V. Laurent, "Les signataires du second synode des Blakhernes (1285)," *EO* 26 (1927), 143, 147. For Laurent's view regarding the form Theopemptos, see *idem, Les regestes des actes du patriarcat de Constantinople, I. Les actes des patriarches, fasc. IV, Les regestes de 1208 à 1309* (Paris, 1971), no. 1490, critique, 4.

[8] Choumnos, *Epitaphios*, 188–89.

[9] Choumnos, *Epitaphios*, 217–20. Choumnos recounts how Theoleptos, who previously had "neither the training nor the ability to be a writer," became the author of spiritual works (p. 220) after his recently deceased spiritual adviser and companion, a venerable ascetic named Neilos, offered him a drink of miraculous water. This incident allegedly occurred while Theoleptos was still living as a hermit (p. 217). On Neilos, see note 11 below.

[10] Kantakouzenos, ed. L. Schopen, Bonn ed. (1828), I.14, l. 67. Choumnos himself solicited Theoleptos' comments on his own works; see his letter to Theoleptos, ed. Boissonade (note 3 above), letter 92.

Auxentios, not far from Chalcedon.[11] While there, he attached himself to a venerable but unidentified ascetic who initiated him into monastic spirituality.[12] Theoleptos became immediately a zealous practitioner of spiritual vigilance and contemplation, and years later Gregory Palamas—whom Theoleptos is said to have instructed in hesychasm[13]—acclaimed the metropolitan of Philadelphia as one of the leading hesychasts of the end of the thirteenth century.[14]

While devoting himself to his ascetic exertions, Theoleptos did not forget the cause for which he had fled from the world. Even if he was not the leader of the anti-unionists, as his encomiast implies, he was sufficiently prominent to merit the attention of the emperor, who summoned him to his presence in the capital, as well as the solicitude of Patriarch Athanasios II of Alexandria, who endeavored to win him over to the unionist camp. Choumnos' account of the confrontation between the dissident Theoleptos and Michael VIII bears the traits of a hagiographical *topos*: the holy man's courageous defiance of the ruler so enraged his interrogators that they subjected him to all sorts of verbal and physical abuse, including flogging, before throwing him into jail.[15] It was probably during his incarceration that Theoleptos became acquainted with Nikephoros the Hesychast, a distinguished Athonite of Italian origin, who in the early spring of 1276 was exiled from the Holy Mountain because of his repudiation of Latin theology and, after appearing before the imperial tribunal, spent five and one half months in prison in Constantinople.[16] According to Gregory Palamas, the future metropolitan of Philadelphia associated with Nikephoros during the latter's exile and learned from him the hesychast method of prayer.[17]

[11] Theoleptos left Nicaea as soon as Patriarch John Bekkos ordered the persecution of the anti-unionists (Choumnos, *Epitaphios*, 198–200). On the date of John Bekkos' election (26 May 1275), see V. Laurent, "La chronologie des patriarches de Constantinople au XIIIe siècle (1208–1309)," *REB* 27 (1969), 145. Choumnos does not name the place of Theoleptos' retirement, but it is highly improbable that he went directly to Mt. Athos and became there the disciple of Nikephoros the Hesychast. Palamas assigns Theoleptos' association with that prominent Athonite to the period of the latter's exile, that is, after the spring of 1276; see notes 16 and 17 below. Furthermore, Theoleptos' spiritual adviser, the ascetic Neilos, is undoubtedly to be identified with Neilos the Italian, a monk from Mount Saint Auxentios; see *PLP* 8 (1986), 110 no. 20051; J. Meyendorff, *Introduction à l'étude de Grégoire Palamas* (Paris, 1959), 40–41; and A. Rigo "Nota sulla dottrina" (note 1 above), 173–74. On Mount Saint Auxentios as a contemporary center of spiritual revival, see Meyendorff, *Introduction*, 40–42.

[12] Choumnos, *Epitaphios*, 201.

[13] Philotheos, *Encomium Gregorii Palamae* = PG 151, 561A; Palamas, *Triad*, 1.2.12, ed. J. Meyendorff, *Grégoire Palamas, Défense des saints hésychastes*, 2nd edition (Louvain, 1973), 99. For Theoleptos' influence on Palamas' theology, see R. A. Sinkewicz, "Saint Gregory Palamas and the Doctrine of God's Image in Man According to the *Capita 150*," Θεολογία 57 (1986), 857–81.

[14] *Triads*, 1.2.12, 2.2.3, ed. Meyendorff, *Défense* (note 13 above), 99, 323.

[15] Choumnos, *Epitaphios*, 204–206.

[16] Nikephoros, *Dialexis*, ed. V. Laurent and J. Darrouzès, *Dossier grec de l'Union de Lyon (1273–1277)*, Archives de l'Orient Chrétien 16 (Paris, 1976), 486–91, 505, and, on the chronology, 84–85. Following his imprisonment in the capital, Nikephoros was expelled to Ptolemais (St. John of Acre) in Palestine, where he was tried by the Latins and sentenced to exile in Cyprus. Ten months later, he was released by imperial *prostagma* and, although we have no information regarding his subsequent activities, the possibility of his having met Theoleptos after his return from Cyprus cannot be dismissed.

[17] *Triads*, 2.2.3, ed. Meyendorff, *Défense* (note 13 above), 323. There can be no doubt that the reference is to the hesychast method of prayer. In this and the preceding paragraph (2.2.2), Palamas defends Nikephoros' writings on the hesychast prayer against the criticism of the Calabrian monk Barlaam.

When Theoleptos was released from prison and allowed to go wherever he wished, he chose to return to his native Nicaea, where he shut himself in a hut at a remote spot in the suburbs.[18] It was there that the young ascetic experienced his last temptation. The comely and loving wife whom Theoleptos had abandoned appeared suddenly at his door and pleaded with him to let her share his hut. Threatening to make that hut her grave if he chased her away, the despondent woman cried out: "Why are you turning away from a union of your choice? What slanderer of matrimony claims that only those who remain single can attain salvation whereas the others who enter into marriage and remain married are damned?"[19] One is tempted to detect in this passionate plea, which Choumnos puts in the mouth of Theoleptos' wife, the author's veiled criticism of Theoleptos' zeal for the monastic life. Choumnos had personal experience of the effects of that zeal. His own beloved daughter Irene, the widow of the despot John Palaiologos, had defied her parents and at the advice of the metropolitan had embraced monasticism at the age of sixteen. And when Choumnos was writing this encomium, late in his life, he himself and his wife had separated from each other at the behest of the dying Theoleptos and had retired to the double monastery which their daughter had established in Constantinople against their wishes.[20]

Theoleptos was subjected for an entire year to the temptation of having to resist his wife's amorous advances by means of gentle persuasion, but in the end he came out of his ordeal unscathed.[21] The repudiation of his wife enhanced his reputation for holiness, which, together with his well-known adherence to the Orthodox doctrines, began to draw large crowds to his hermitage, seeking his spiritual guidance.[22] Nevertheless, he remained an anchorite until the end of the persecutions; the entire period of his retirement from the world lasted eight years.[23]

With the restoration of Orthodoxy immediately after the death of Michael VIII in December 1282, Theoleptos, who is said to have been on Mount Athos at that time,[24] returned to Constantinople. Reports of his moral integrity and learning in theology had reached the new emperor, Andronikos II, who sought him out as an adviser, and Theoleptos became a leading spokesman for his party.[25] The reward for his exertions in behalf of Orthodoxy was his appointment to the metropolitan see of the populous city of Philadelphia.[26]

---

[18] Choumnos, *Epitaphios*, 209.

[19] Choumnos, *Epitaphios*, 210–11.

[20] On Irene, see A. C. Hero, "Irene-Eulogia Choumnaina Palaiologina, Abbess of the Convent of Philanthropos Soter in Constantinople," *ByzF* 9 (1985), 119–47. On her monastery, see R. H. Trone, "A Constantinopolitan Double Monastery of the Fourteenth Century: the Philanthropic Savior," *Byzantine Studies/Études Byzantines* 10 (1983), 81–87. On Choumnos, see J. Verpeaux, *Nicéphore Choumnos, homme d'état et humaniste byzantin (ca. 1250/1255–1327)* (Paris, 1959). On Theoleptos' final instructions to Irene's parents, see his last letter (letter 5 in Hero, *The Correspondence of Theoleptos of Philadelphia* [forthcoming]).

[21] Choumnos, *Epitaphios*, 211.

[22] Choumnos, *Epitaphios*, 212–13.

[23] See Choumnaina's letter to her director and the latter's answer, Hero, ed., *A Woman's Quest* (note 3 above), letter 15, ll. 83–84; letter 16, ll. 20–21.

[24] Philotheos, *Encomium Gregorii Palamae* = PG 151, 561A.

[25] Choumnos, *Epitaphios*, 215.

[26] On the history of Philadelphia during this period, see H. Ahrweiler, "La région de Philadelphie au XIVe

The correspondence of Irene-Eulogia Choumnaina establishes beyond doubt the year 1283 as the date of his elevation to the episcopate. At the time of his ordination, she writes, her spiritual father was thirty-three years old.[27] He was also most probably still a deacon, for, according to Choumnos, when Theoleptos returned to Nicaea from prison he was neither a priest nor a monk, having hesitated to assume the monastic habit until he was sufficiently prepared.[28]

It is not certain whether the new metropolitan took immediate possession of his see or remained in Constantinople to continue his polemical activity against the former Patriarch John Bekkos and his partisans. It is possible, judging from his later record, that he resided from the beginning in his diocese and visited the capital whenever the patriarch or the emperor required his presence. For during those turbulent times, when the Church was torn by internal strife, Theoleptos found himself involved in more than one controversy.

In the summer of 1285, following the Second Synod of Blachernae, Theoleptos signed the tome registering the condemnation of John Bekkos and his partisans.[29] The author of the tome, Patriarch Gregory II of Cyprus, had included in this document his own interpretation of a passage from John of Damascus which had been used by the unionists in support of the Latin doctrine of the *filioque*.[30] This provoked the objections of several patriarchal officials and the lower clergy—among others—who promptly accused Gregory of falling into the same trap as his predecessor by postulating the "eternal manifestation" of the Holy Spirit through the Son. By 1287, the patriarch's opponents were joined by the metropolitans John Cheilas of Ephesos, Daniel of Kyzikos, and Theoleptos. The latter disapproved not so much of Gregory but of a monk named Mark who claimed the patriarch's approval for a commentary he had written on the tome, proposing a meaning for the term "procession" contrary to Orthodox teaching. In the end, Gregory followed Theoleptos' advice and, after disassociating himself from Mark, he submitted his resignation. In June of 1289, at the recommendation of the metropolitan of Philadelphia, the patriarch's Orthodoxy was publicly acknowledged.[31]

Theoleptos' other disagreement with the Church, his schism from Patriarch Niphon I, was due to the latter's reconciliation with the schismatic Arsenites on 14 September 1310. Followers of Patriarch Arsenios, who had been deposed by Michael VIII in 1265 for refusing to sanction the blinding of the legitimate heir, John IV Laskaris, the Arsenites were among the protagonists in the struggle against union with Rome. After the restoration of Orthodoxy, therefore, they strove for control of the Church, and when they failed to achieve that objective they resumed their disruptive activities, particularly in Asia Minor.

---

siècle (1290–1390), dernier bastion de l'Hellénisme en Asie Mineure," *CRAI* (janvier–mars 1983), 175–97; *eadem*, ed., *Philadelphie et autres études*, Byzantina Sorbonensia 4 (Paris, 1984), 9–125.

[27] See Hero, ed., *A Woman's Quest* (note 3 above), letter 15, ll. 84–85; letter 16, l. 21.

[28] Choumnos, *Epitaphios*, 210, 213.

[29] Laurent, "Les signataires" (note 7 above), 147.

[30] Gregory of Cyprus, *Scripta apologetica* = PG 142, 240A.

[31] See Pachymeres 2.1–10: ed. I. Bekker, Bonn ed. (1835), II, 108–33; and A. Papadakis' excellent study *Crisis in Byzantium. The "Filioque" Controversy in the Patriarchate of Gregory II of Cyprus (1283–1289)* (New York, 1983).

Theoleptos' two surviving discourses against the Arsenites date from the period between 1285 and 1310 and, as Father Sinkewicz points out, the image they paint of these
religious and political agitators does not differ from that of other anti-Arsenite writers.[32]
The metropolitan describes the Arsenites as a seditious element, who even after the restoration of Orthodoxy continued to oppose the Church, not for any valid dogmatic reasons but
out of sheer arrogance, and he accuses them of spreading discord among families, encour-
aging the faithful to abstain from the sacraments and trying to extract money from the
people.[33]

Theoleptos' opposition to the healing of the Arsenite schism is known to us from the
contemporary correspondence of Manuel Gabalas, whom Kourouses has now corectly identified as the author of the correspondence formerly attributed to Pseudo-Cheilas.[34] Gabalas
had started his career as a protégé of the metropolitan and was a *protonotarios* at the metropolis of Philadelphia when his harmonious relationship with his superior was disrupted
due to their disagreement over the resolution of the Arsenite schism. Whereas Gabalas
bowed to the decision of the Church, Theoleptos resented the fact that this important matter
was decided without his knowledge and consent and he separated himself from Constantinople for nearly a decade.[35] During this period, Gabalas, who found himself not only without work but also excommunicated by his superior, appealed repeatedly to the emperor and
the patriarch, pleading with them to take disciplinary action against Theoleptos.[36]

His earnest representations brought no results. Andronikos II summoned the metropolitan to his presence, but Theoleptos defied the order and dismissed the imperial emissary
with a stern reminder that it was not the emperor's prerogative to discipline a priest. The
Church, on the other hand, made no attempt to excommunicate Theoleptos despite his own
refusal to communicate with both Patriarch Niphon I and his successor John XIII Glykys.

[32] Sinkewicz, ed., "Anti-Arsenite Discourses" (note 1 above), 47–49. On the history of the Arsenite schism
and its resolution, see V. Laurent, "Les grandes crises religieuses à Byzance: la fin du schisme arsénite,"
BSHAcRoum 26 (1945), 225–313.

[33] Sinkewicz, ed., "Anti-Arsenite Discourses" (note 1 above), *Philadelpheia Discourse 1*, ll. 42–67; *Philadelpheia Discourse 2*, ll. 230–39.

[34] S. Kourouses, Μανουὴλ Γαβαλᾶς εἶτα Ματθαῖος μητροπολίτης Ἐφέσου (1271/2–1355–60) (Athens,
1972), 122–34. The identification of the bishop against whom Gabalas inveighs anonymously in his correspondence is due to Laurent, "Les crises religieuses à Byzance. Le schisme anti-arsénite du métropolite de
Philadelphie Théolepte († c. 1324)," *REB* 18 (1960), 45–54.

[35] These are the reasons cited in the appeal which Arsenios of Tyre addressed to John Kantakouzenos in
1351. See the latest edition of the pertinent excerpt from this appeal in Kourouses, Μανουὴλ Γαβαλᾶς (note
34 above), 137–38. Gabalas also remarked that Theoleptos claimed the principle of ἀκρίβεια (canonical rigor-
ism) as the reason for his disagreement with Constantinople; see his second letter to Patriarch John Glykys,
ed. Gouillard, "Correspondance inédite" (note 3 above), letter 2, ll. 27, 79.

[36] Gouillard, ed., "Correspondance inédite" (note 3 above), letter 1 (to Patriarch John Glykys), ll. 74–85,
letter 2 (to the same), ll. 69–77, letter 6 (to the *Megas Dioiketes*), ll. 59–60; Reinsch, ed., *Briefe* (note 3 above),
letter 62 (to Patriarch Niphon), ll. 4–13. In addition to their disagreement over the resolution of the Arsenite
schism, the other reasons for Theoleptos' quarrel with his subordinate were the latter's support of Manuel
Tagaris, the military governor of the province, as well as Gabalas' antipathy for Theoleptos' nephew, whom
he describes as a true rogue; see letter 6, ll. 20–98. According to Gabalas, this young man embezzled the funds
destined for the relief of the poor, the administration of which Theoleptos had entrusted to him, and in the end
he was expelled from Philadelphia by his own uncle for having committed adultery.

Arsenios of Tyre—a representative of the patriarch of Antioch to the Palamite council of 1351—asserts that due to the exceptional regard in which he was held, not only was the metropolitan of Philadelphia spared the canonical penalties prescribed for insubordination, but he was even received with honor when he visited the capital in 1318.[37]

Theoleptos' temporary separation from Constantinople was a personal rift without any wider repercussions, but his anti-Arsenite zeal had unfortunate consequences for the defense of Asia Minor, which in 1298 was entrusted to a cousin of the emperor, John Palaiologos Tarchaneiotes. A leader of the moderate wing of the Arsenite faction, Tarchaneiotes was suspected of aspiring to the imperial throne. Nevertheless, Andronikos II respected John's ability as a soldier and did not hesitate to place him in command of one of the last attempts to stem Turkish expansion in Asia Minor. Tarchaneiotes showed himself worthy of his cousin's trust, but his success as a military commander and his hopes of carrying out land reform in Asia Minor foundered on ecclesiastical hostility. Patriarch John XII Kosmas denounced Tarchaneiotes to the emperor, and Theoleptos, due to his personal animosity towards the prominent Arsenite, became a tool in the hands of the pronoia-holders, who objected to Tarchaneiotes' reforms. The dramatic encounter of Theoleptos with Tarchaneiotes before the walls of the monastery, where the general had sought refuge, is recounted by Pachymeres. Although the historian was not an Arsenite sympathizer himself, he is critical of Theoleptos' interference in this matter, which put an end to one of the few successful campaigns in Asia Minor. He describes how the harrassed general, who feared for his life, bitterly reproached the metropolitan for allowing his personal bias to prevail over his judgement and also for consorting with the likes of the slanderous landowners who questioned his loyalty to the emperor.[38]

And yet, Theoleptos could at times demonstrate considerable political astuteness and flexibility. On one occasion, he shocked his fellow bishops when he advised Andonikos II that it was not wrong for a Byzantine emperor to address the Sultan of Egypt as his brother. With surprising casuistry, Theoleptos argued that even the demons are brothers of all human beings, including Christians, and he quoted patristic evidence in support of his view. Theoleptos pointed out that in his commentary on Song of Songs I:6—"The children of my mother quarreled with me"—Gregory of Nyssa declared that the children who quarreled with the Church were the demons, since they too were the creatures of God. This casuistic response to the emperor's query must have puzzled the pious Andonikos II, who, as Pachymeres observes, was not permitted to address the Pope of Rome as his brother.[39]

[37] Ed. Kourouses, Μανουὴλ Γαβαλᾶς (note 34 above), 138.

[38] Pachymeres 2.25: ed. I. Bekker, Bonn ed. (1835), II, 257–61. An incisive analysis of these events appears in A. E. Laiou, *Constantinople and the Latins: the Foreign Policy of Andronicus II, 1282–1328* (Cambridge, Mass., 1972), 86–89.

[39] Pachymeres 2.23: II, 246–49. I had assumed previously that this incident occurred in 1303, when the Byzantine emperor sent an embassy to the sultan al Nasir to protest against the latter's persecution of the Christians in Egypt: see M. Quatremère, *Histoire des sultans mamlouks de l'Égypte écrite en arabe par Taki-Eddin-Ahmed-Makrizi* (Paris, 1837–40), II, part 2, 177–80. However, Fr. Albert Failler, the editor of Pachymeres, believes that the latter's discussion of this episode in chapter 23 is a flashback to the period between October 1289 and October 1293, when there were some contacts between Andronikos II and the sultan that

Above all, it was his own metropolis of Philadelphia—an area in a chronic state of siege and suffering from frequent famines[40]—that afforded Theoleptos the best opportunity to exercise his talent for leadership. During the thirty-nine years of his tenure the sources record two sieges: one in 1304 and another which began shortly before the metropolitan's death at the end of 1322.[41] But the siege which marked Theoleptos' finest hour has only recently become known through Kourouses' exhaustive study of the letters of Manuel Gabalas and Michael Gabras, and has been dated by him to the year 1310.[42] In the previous year, Theoleptos had sent Gabalas to Constantinople to ask for the replacement of General Tagaris (the military governor of the province and a man he distrusted) and also probably to request military assistance against the impending attack by the Germiyan Turks.[43] When he failed to obtain his request, Theoleptos took personal charge of the defense of the city. Details of his activity during that blockade, which lasted from the early fall of 1310 until the following spring,[44] are given by his encomiast. Choumnos says that since famine was the most powerful ally of the enemy, Theoleptos not only supervised the feeding of the people, but with his own hands participated in the kneading, baking and distribution of bread to his flock. And at the end when he decided to go out and negotiate with the Turkish emir, he summoned the people and extracted from them a solemn oath that if he were taken prisoner they would not surrender the city in exchange for his life. Choumnos claims that the emir lifted the siege out of respect for the venerable figure of the metropolitan, and that he even provided him with supplies for his hungry flock,[45] but an inscription on a *medresse* in the Germiyan capital city of Kiutahia indicates that the metropolitan agreed to a payment of tribute.[46] There can be no doubt that Choumnos' account, which was up to now associated with the siege of 1304, refers to the events of 1310. In 1304 Philadelphia was saved by the timely intervention of the Catalan Company, whereas the siege discussed by Choumnos was lifted through the intervention of the metropolitan.[47] Theoleptos' decisive role during that

---

led to the discussion at the Permanent Synod. I wish to thank both Fr. Failler and Marie-Hélène Congourdeau (letter of December 1989) for this information.

[40] See Gregoras, 7.3: ed. L. Schopen, Bonn ed. (1829), I, 221.

[41] On these two blockades, see P. Schreiner, "Zur Geschichte Philadelpheias im 14. Jahrhundert (1293–1390)," *OCP* 35 (1969), 385–93.

[42] Kourouses, Μανουὴλ Γαβαλᾶς (note 34 above), 308–309 and 312–15.

[43] Gabalas, letter to the *Megas Dioiketes*, ed. Gouillard, "Correspondance inédite" (note 3 above), letter 6, ll. 20–25; Kourouses, Μανουὴλ Γαβαλᾶς (note 34 above), 308–309. On Tagaris see p. 37 below.

[44] Kourouses, Μανουὴλ Γαβαλᾶς (note 34 above), 314.

[45] Choumnos, *Epitaphios*, 230–34.

[46] According to this inscription, which bears the date 1314, the town of Alaşehir (Philadelphia) had been forced by Yakub b. Alishir to pay tribute (*djizya*); see *Encyclopedia of Islam* vol. II, col. 989. A. Ahrweiler convincingly argues that, since this inscription registers the date of the completion of the *medresse*, the reference is to the siege of 1310 and not to an allegedly later blockade in 1314, which is not known from any source; see "Région de Philadelphie" (note 26 above), 190. For the view that this inscription refers to an otherwise unknown siege in 1314, see Schreiner, "Geschichte" (note 41 above), 387, and Kourouses, Μανουὴλ Γαβαλᾶς (note 34 above), 312.

[47] This is another point correctly made by Ahrweiler, "Région de Philadelphie" (note 26 above), 190. During the earlier blockade in 1304, Theoleptos must have made every effort to sustain the morale of his flock. Gregoras (7.3: l. 221) says that God helped the Catalans to rescue Philadelphia because of the metropolitan's

crisis is further attested by Michael Gabras in a letter dating from 1311, in which he hails Theoleptos as the "savior of cities," meaning Philadelphia and its suburbs.[48]

In discussing other aspects of Theoleptos' administration of his diocese, Choumnos comments on the metropolitan's success in increasing church attendance by imposing discipline on both the clergy and the congregation and by inspiring his flock with his moving sermons and the hymns he composed himself.[49] But above all, Choumnos dwells on Theoleptos' concern for the poor. When church revenues, he says, were not sufficient for the needs of his populous and constantly beleaguered province, the metropolitan induced the rich to give generously. Quoting Matthew 25:24, Choumnos remarks—not without a touch of irony, perhaps—that Theoleptos "knew well how to reap where he did not sow and gather where he did not winnow."[50] The author is here speaking from experience. Part of his own vast fortune, which was given as dowry to his daughter Irene, was spent on the relief of the poor and the ransoming of prisoners. Irene was, of course, acting on the advice of Theoleptos, while her own father inveighed anonymously against those who encouraged children to disobey the wishes of their parents.[51] Theoleptos paid no attention to Choumnos' remonstrances and continued until the last year of his life to urge his spiritual daughter to divest herself of her remaining possessions regardless of the opposition of her family.[52]

And this brings us, finally, to Theoleptos' role as spiritual director, known to us primarily from his correspondence with Irene Choumnaina, who in 1307 was tonsured by Theoleptos himself, taking the name Eulogia and becoming the abbess of the monastery of Philanthropos Soter in Constantinople, which she rebuilt at her own expense.[53]

As a man deeply involved in the spiritual and political affairs of his time, Theoleptos must have corresponded with many of his prominent contemporaries; yet only his letters to his spiritual daughter have come down to us. It was she who preserved them together with the homilies that he addressed to the religious in her monastery and had them copied in a

---

"great virtue." As Beyer observes, however, the history of the Catalan expedition by Francisco de Moncada, which extols the role of Theoleptos, has no independent value. It is a later work based on Byzantine sources, such as Gregoras; see *The Catalan Chronicle of Francisco de Moncada*, trans. F. Hermandez and J. M. Sharp (El Paso, 1975), 44–45. Ramon Muntaner, a participant in the expedition, does not mention Theoleptos; see *The Chronicle of Muntaner*, trans. Lady Goodenough (London, 1921), and Beyer, "Die Katechese" (note 1 above), 185–86.

[48] Ed. Fatouros, *Die Briefe* (note 3 above), letter 53, ll. 33–34 and 37–38. For the date of this letter, see Kourouses, Μανουὴλ Γαβαλᾶς (note 34 above), 76.

[49] *Epitaphios*, 222–24, 227–29. See also D. Constantelos, "Mysticism and Social Involvement in the Late Byzantine Church: Theoleptos of Philadelphia—a Case Study," *Byzantine Studies/Études Byzantines* 6 (1979), 83–94. According to an inscription, Theoleptos also built a "splendid baptistry" in Philadelphia with money donated by the Palace; see H. Grégoire, *Les inscriptions chrétiennes de l'Asie Mineure* (Paris, 1922), no. 343bis, 125–26.

[50] *Epitaphios*, 228.

[51] See I. Ševčenko, "Le sens et la date du traité 'Anépigraphos' de Nicéphore Choumnos," *Bulletin de la Classe des Lettres et des Sciences Morales et Politiques, Académie Royale de Belgique*, 5th ser., 35 (1949), 473–88.

[52] See his second letter to Choumnaina from Philadelphia, Hero, ed., "Unpublished Letters" (note 1 above), ll. 119–25 (letter 3 in Hero, *The Correspondence of Theoleptos of Philadelphia* [forthcoming]).

[53] See Hero, "Irene-Eulogia" (note 20 above), 121–22.

manuscript which is now in the Vatican Library, the Ottobonianus gr. 405.[54] The margina-
lia in this manuscript preserve the comments that she scribbled as she read his writings and
show how carefully she studied them and how deeply she admired her mentor.

Of the metropolitan's five surviving letters, the first dates from the early months of his
association with the widowed princess, shortly before she took the veil; while the remaining
four were written during the last year of his life and are of particular interest, since, in
addition to their value as documents of spiritual guidance, they contain prosopographical
and historical information.[55]

It is a measure of Theoleptos' success as a spiritual director that this young and gifted
woman, who was no stranger to marital bliss, wealth, and power, not only embraced monasticism at his advice, but remained faithful to his precepts for nearly half a century. For
many years after his death the scholarly princess had difficulty finding a director who combined the metropolitan's spiritual and literary gifts. She even confessed that she missed him
more than her own father.[56]

Theoleptos saw his spiritual daughter for the last time in 1321 when he was called to
act as a mediator in the dispute between Andronikos II and his rebellious grandson.[57] In the
fall of the same year he returned to his see and died there a year later, at the end of 1322.[58]
His last days were troubled by his continuing quarrel with General Manuel Tagaris, the
military governor of the province, by the onset of yet another Turkish siege, and by deterio-
rating health. He was by that time approaching his seventy-second year.

The reasons for Theoleptos' prolonged dispute with Tagaris are not clear. Manuel
Gabalas—our only source of information in this case—is not a very reliable witness. Gabalas was a supporter of Tagaris at the beginning and he accused Theoleptos of treating the
general as a subordinate.[59] After the death of Theoleptos, however, when he clashed personally with Tagaris for reasons which are hard to determine, Gabalas compared the general to
the most vile characters in Greek history and mythology, and he admitted that he had made
a mistake by not helping the metropolitan to chase that "wolf away from his flock."[60] In his

---

[54] On this manuscript, see E. Feron and F. Battaglini, *Codices mss. graeci Ottoboniani Bibl. Vaticanae*
(Rome, 1903), 216.

[55] On the dates of these letters, see Kourouses, Μανουὴλ Γαβαλᾶς (note 34 above), 336–39.

[56] See the letter to her spiritual director, ed. Hero, *A Woman's Quest* (note 3 above), letter 7, l. 25.

[57] Gregoras, 8.6: ed. L. Schopen, Bonn ed. (1829), I, 320–21; Kantakouzenos, I.14, 19: ed. L. Schopen,
Bonn ed. (1828), I, 67–71, 93–97.

[58] On the date of his death, see Kourouses, Μανουὴλ Γαβαλᾶς (note 34 above), 339.

[59] Gabalas wrote that the metropolitan demanded from the general the same obedience that the general
demanded from his troops; see his letter to the *Megas Dioiketes*, ed. Gouillard, "Correspondance inédite" (note
3 above), letter 6, ll. 20–22. For the view that Theoleptos and Tagaris were representatives respectively of a
"local" and a "pro-Turkish" party in Philadelphia, see Ahrweiler, "Région de Philadelphie" (note 26 above),
193. On Gabalas' support of Tagaris in 1309, see his letter to the *Megas Dioiketes*, ll. 23–25, and his *Invective*
against Tagaris, ed. Reinsch, *Briefe* (note 3 above), ll. 221–35. On Tagaris, see D. M. Nicol, "Philadelphia
and the Tagaris Family," *Neohellenika* 1 (1970), 10–13. As Kourouses, Μανουὴλ Γαβαλᾶς (note 34 above)
suggests (339–43), the reasons for Gabalas' quarrel with Tagaris might have been the general's attempts to
prevent Gabalas from succeeding Theoleptos on the throne of Philadelphia.

[60] See his *Invective*, ed. Reinsch, *Briefe* (note 3 above), ll. 232–34.

long invective against the general, Gabalas accuses him of military incompetence, coward-
ice, rapacity, and treachery, and blames him for causing the latest siege by violating the
formal agreements which the Philadelphians had made with the Turks.[61] The siege in
question was the blockade of Philadelphia by the emirs of Germiyan and Aydin which
began in the summer of 1322 and did not end until 1324, when the aged and blind Alexios
Philanthropenos was sent from Constantinople to take command of the defense of the city.[62]

The need to replace Tagaris, who was proven an inept commander, and his later attempts to regain his position by attacking Philadelphia and subjecting that city to further
hardships[63] lend credence to Gabalas' accusations and thus help to explain Theoleptos'
hostility towards that man. The metropolitan, however, did not live to see himself vindi-
cated. Gabalas writes that Tagaris, who had threatened to have the aging prelate driven out
of Philadelphia on the back of a donkey, finally killed Theoleptos with the innumerable
insults that he hurled like arrows against his venerable head.[64]

When the Turkish siege started, the metropolitan was already seriously ill. The nature
of his illness cannot be determined, but in the last letter he wrote to his spiritual daughter
from his deathbed, he mentioned that he had been bedridden for five months.[65] His end is
described in detail by Choumnos, who writes that on the eve of his death Theoleptos summoned to his presence various groups representing the people of Philadelphia and, after
giving the appropriate advice to each one, he blessed them and bid them farewell. Afterwards he asked the monk who attended him to shut the gate of his modest dwelling and died
in the company of that one attendant. At the news of his death, says Choumnos, the large
city of Philadelphia swelled with grief like a vast sea. Men and women of all ages mourned
the loss of the man who had been not only their spiritual shepherd, but also their ambassa-
dor to the emperor, the feeder of the poor, and the defender of their city, willing to do and
suffer anything in their behalf.[66]

Was Theoleptos a typical member of the episcopate during the reign of Andronikos II?
Regrettably, the answer is no. Patriarch Athanasios I of Constantinople, in one of his letters
to the emperor, singles out Theoleptos and the metropolitan of Nymphaion as two prelates
who remained in their sees and did not, like the rest, seek the safety and comfort of the
capital.[67] In fact, although it may seem strange to compare the austere Athanasios with the
more gentle and charismatic Theoleptos, the two had several traits in common. Both started
out as solitaries, but instead of leading a contemplative existence, they became involved in

[61] *Invective*, ed. Reinsch, ll. 1–10 and 35–180.

[62] Schreiner, "Geschichte" (note 41 above), 389–95.

[63] On the activities of Tagaris after his replacement by Philanthropenos, see Kourouses, Μανουὴλ Γαβαλᾶς (note 34 above), 285–89.

[64] Gabalas, *Invective*, ed. Reinsch, *Briefe* (note 3 above), ll. 190–93.

[65] See letter 5 in my forthcoming edition (note 3 above), ll. 4–6.

[66] Choumnos, *Epitaphios*, 234–38.

[67] A.-M. Talbot, ed., *The Correspondence of Athanasius I Patriarch of Constantinople* (Washington, D.C.,
1975), letter 25, ll. 20–21. On Athanasios, see *ibid.*, xv–xxxi; *eadem*, "The Patriarch Athanasius (1289–1293;
1303–1309) and the Church," *DOP* 27 (1973), 11–28; and J. Boojamra, *Church Reform in the Late Byzantine Empire* (Thessaloniki, 1982).

the spiritual and political affairs of their time. Both were firm in their opposition to the Arsenites and to union with Rome. Both could be inflexible and at times their interference in imperial policy was ill-advised. But they also shared a lofty view of the social role of the Church. Their moral integrity, their strict adherence to the monastic vows of chastity and poverty, and above all, the pains they took to alleviate the suffering of their flocks during those critical times earned them the love and respect of the ordinary people.

Manuel II Palaeologos and His Müderris

STEPHEN W. REINERT

I

AFTER attaining the throne as sole emperor in March 1391, the learned Manuel II Palaeologos reconfirmed the pact of tributary alliance which his father, John V, had originally concluded with the Ottoman ruler Yıldırım Bāyazīd—Bāyazīd "the thunderbolt."[1] In so doing, Manuel persevered with a status of *de facto* submission to the sultan. As his subordinate or vassal, Manuel rendered Bāyazīd regular tribute, provided him with military aid on demand, and attended his court as summoned. Otherwise, the emperor retained a relative freedom of action, and hence autonomy, within the walls of Constantinople and the little which remained of the "empire of the Romans." From Bāyazīd's viewpoint, this arrangement established Manuel among his tributary princes and implied that he was assimilated, if precariously, within the framework of the expanding Ottoman state.[2] For Manuel, the liason was a strategy to ensure the survival of Constantinople, and not incidentally his own regime. It was also the accepted formula for coexistence with the Ottomans since 1372 or 1373, when his father John V inaugurated the policy vis-à-vis Murād I, Bāyazīd's father.[3]

Between spring 1391 and summer 1394, Manuel served as Bāyazīd's military ally—so far as we know—on only one campaign. From early June through late December of that year, Bāyazīd conducted operations in Anatolia initially against Süleymān Pāšā, the emir of

---

[1] This essay is nothing more than an exploratory sketch from a book in progress, tentatively entitled *The Emperor and the Sultan: Manuel Palaiologos' Encounter With Yıldırım Bāyazīd and the Early Ottoman World*. The editions of Manuel's works cited throughout are as follows: for his letters (abbreviated "*Ep.*"), that of G. Dennis, *The Letters of Manuel II Palaeologus. Text, Translation, and Notes* (Washington D.C., 1977); for the "Dialogue With a Persian" (abbreviated "*Dial. Pers.*"), that of E. Trapp, *Manuel II Palaiologos. Dialogue mit einem "Perser"* (Vienna, 1966); for the funeral oration (abbreviated "*Epitaph.*"), that of J. Chrysostomides, *Manuel II Palaeologus. Funeral Oration on His Brother Theodore. Introduction, Text, Translation and Notes* (Thessaloniki, 1985); and for the celebratory oration on John V's restoration to health, that of J. Boissonade, in *Anecdota Nova* (Paris, 1844; reprinted Hildesheim, 1962), 223–38.

For the wider context, I. Ševčenko's "The Decline of Byzantium Seen Through the Eyes of Its Intellectuals" remains authoritative (originally published in *DOP* 15 [1961] 169–86; reprinted in *idem, Society and Intellectual Life in Late Byzantium* [London, 1981], no II).

[2] On this liaison, see in general G. Ostrogorsky, "Byzance, état tributaire de l'empire turc," *ZVI* 5 (1958), 49–53; O. Iliescu, "Le montant du tribut payé par Byzance à l'empire ottoman en 1379 et 1424," *RESEE* 9 (1971), 427–32. On the Ottoman view of this relationship, see H. Inalcık, "Ottoman Methods of Conquest," *Studia Islamica* 2 (1954), 103–104, along with his review of J. Barker, *Manuel II Palaeologus* (note 4 below) in *Archivum Ottomanicum* 3 (1971), 272–73.

[3] Manuel himself refers to this relationship in standard diplomatic parlance as an alliance (συμμαχία) or friendship (φιλία). Cf. *Ep.* 14.27–28 (ed. Dennis, note 1 above); *Dial. Pers.* (ed. Trapp, note 1 above), 5.10; and *Epitaph.* (ed. Chrysostomides, note 1 above), 143.2.

Kastamonu, and subsequently the Qāḍī Aḥmad Burhān al-Dīn, the sultan's major antago-
nist in eastern Asia Minor, and Süleymān's brother Mubāriz al-Dīn of Sinope.[4] Manuel
was present with his contingent of troops (drawn, it seems, partly from the city garrison) for
the full duration of this campaign.[5] Moreover, he found time to dispatch at least eight letters
from Asia Minor to friends in Constantinople, which we may compare with related letters
(initiatory or reply) of Demetrios Kydonēs and Nicholas Kabasilas.[6] The exact sequence of
this long campaign is problematic. It is certain that in June the Ottoman forces defeated
Süleymān Pāšā, and Kastamonu and its dependencies were annexed.[7] Thereafter, according to Prof. Zachariadou, Bāyazīd moved towards Sinope (intending to subordinate or elim-
inate Mubāriz al-Dīn), but then engaged in a desultory clash with Burhān al-Dīn on the
plateau, ending up at Ankara for the final month, i.e., December.[8] Alternatively, one might
read the admittedly meager indicia in Manuel and Kydonēs' letters to deduce that Bāyazīd
proceeded from Kastamonu to his encounter with the qāḍī; that he stationed his troops
around Ankara in late October through November; and that he proceeded thereafter to his
fruitless tentative against Mubāriz al-Dīn.[9] Whatever the precise sequence, Bāyazīd apparently ceased operations by late December 1391, since Manuel had returned to Constantinople by the following January 7.

The experiences which Manuel had from June 1391 through January 1392 affected
him deeply, as is evident from several of the campaign letters as well as the writings he
composed soon after returning to Constantinople. The emperor was hardly indifferent, first
of all, to the realities of change—to the fact that the "tychē" of his ancestors had taken a
serious turn for the worse, that much had been lost, perhaps irrevocably lost. In his circuit
from Bithynia through Galatia, he observed with keen interest as well as melancholy the
ethnic and toponymic metamorphosis of Asia Minor. In numerous places he saw with his
own eyes the ruins of buildings and monuments which evoked memories of Roman rule, and

---

[4] The fundamental study of this campaign is E. Zachariadou's "Manuel II Palaeologos on the Strife between Bāyezīd I and Ḳāḍī Burhān al-Dīn Aḥmad," *BSOAS* 43 (1980), 471–81. Here, for the first time, the
material in ʿAzīz ibn Ardašir Āstarabaddī's *Bazm u Razm* is collated with Manuel's campaign letters, in a
strikingly original manner. Zachariadou's conclusions are followed most recently by C. Imber, *The Ottoman
Empire 1300–1481* (Istanbul, 1990), 38–40. The treatment of this episode in J. Barker's *Manuel II Palaeologus (1391–1425): A Study in Late Byzantine Statesmanship* (New Brunswick, 1969), 87–98, is little more
than a translation of the pertinent campaign letters.

[5] In a letter to Theodore Palaeologos dated autumn or winter 1391, Kydonēs remarks on the absence of
guards in the capital (*Ep.* 442.49–51, ed. R.-J. Loenertz, *Démétrius Cydonès Correspondance*, II [Vatican
City, 1960]).

[6] Manuel's *Ep.* 14 (ed. Dennis, note 1 above) (to Kydonēs), 15 (to Nicholas Chamaëtos Kabasilas), 16 (to
Kydonēs), 17 (to [Manuel?] Pothos), 18 (to Kydonēs), 19 (to Kydonēs), 20 (to Kydonēs), 21 (to Kydonēs);
Demetrios Kydonēs' *Ep.* 429 (to Manuel), 431 (to Manuel), 432 (to Manuel, in reply to the latter's *Ep.* 16),
442 (to Theodore Palaeologos), 444 (to Manuel, possibly in reply to the latter's *Ep.* 14), 445 (to Manuel); and
a letter of Nicholas Kabasilas to "an emperor," perhaps Manuel (ed. Dennis, *Letters* [note 1 above], 221–22
[Greek text with English translation]).

[7] See Zachariadou, "Manuel II Palaeologos on the Strife" (note 4 above), 472–73.

[8] *Ibid.*, 473–78. Cf. Trapp, *Manuel II. Palaiologos* (note 1 above), 54*–55*, who conjectures that Manuel's stay in Ankara extended from October to December.

[9] A full discussion of the evidence will appear in my book.

the greatness of the Romans.[10] In cities like Ankara he met the descendants of the Rhomaioi who spoke Turkish as well as Greek, and who thus could mediate his conversations with those who knew no Greek.[11] In the same way, the realities of his relationship with Bāyazīd underscored the retreat of "tychē" for the worse. Safe within the fortress of Constantinople Manuel was truly the βασιλεὺς καὶ αὐτοκράτωρ, but within Bāyazīd's military retinue he was unquestionably the sultan's subordinate. The emperor obviously regarded this surrender of autonomy as a contradiction in terms, an inversion of the right order of earthly powers and authorities. Moreover, he saw himself as categorically superior to Bāyazīd by virtue of his religion, his Hellenic culture and his divinely-ordained political status.[12] Perhaps most embittering, however, was Manuel's nagging awareness that by acting as Bāyazīd's ally he was in fact contributing to the further weakening of his own political and military situation.[13] All in all, the emperor's experiences on the 1391 campaign represented a harsh confrontation with the realities of Byzantine political and military decline. We may presume, moreover, that they frequently provoked him to agonize over the causes of the situation, as well as the prospects for the future.

These concerns form the immediate background to a text Manuel wrote shortly after the 1391 campaign, namely his *Dialogue Held With A Certain Persian, the Worthy Mouterizes, in Ankyra of Galatia*.[14] Addressed to his brother Theodore, the despot of Mistra, this is one of Manuel's most sophisticated works, and likewise one of the last great outpourings of Byzantine anti-Islamic polemic, and conversely Christian apology. It might be dated anywhere between early 1392, when Manuel returned from the long campaign, and 1407, when Theodore died. Most likely, however, Manuel wrote it between early 1392 and his break with Bāyazīd in 1393/1394.[15] Throughout the dialogue, Manuel alleges a number of his campaign experiences which are either scarcely or not at all evident from the dossier of campaign letters. He indicates, first of all, that Bāyazīd stationed his army in and around Ankara for approximately twenty days in the early winter of 1391 (extending into late November by my reckoning, or alternatively late December, following Trapp and others), implying that the onset of winter made further military manoeuvers west of the Halys impractical or impossible. He depicts the sultan occupying himself on clement days largely

---

[10] *Ep.* 16.22–49 (ed. Dennis, note 1 above).

[11] *Dial. Pers.* (ed. Trapp, note 1 above), p. 79, ll. 34–37.

[12] On Manuel's sense of his cultural superiority, see in particular *Ep.* 16.68–70, with Kydonēs' sympathetic affirmation in his *Ep.* 432.47–63. George Dennis has translated the pertinent passages of Kydonēs' letter (*Letters*, note 1 above) p. 50, in note 16 continuing from p. 49.

[13] *Ep.* 19.32–42 (ed. Dennis, note 1 above).

[14] Διάλογος, ὃν ἐποιήσατο μετά τινος Πέρσου τὴν ἀξίαν Μουτερίζη ἐν 'Αγκύρα τῆς Γαλατίας. On the dialogue in general, see Trapp's introductory remarks (*Manuel II. Palaiologos* [note 1 above], 54*–56*), and likewise A.-T. Khoury's remarks in *Manuel II Paléologue, Entretiens avec un musulman, 7e controverse* (Paris, 1966), 18–55.

[15] Trapp, *Manuel II. Palaiologos* (note 1 above), 54*–56*, but especially 56*. According to Khoury, Manuel composed the *Dialogue* ca. 1394–1399, i.e., amidst the Ottoman siege, but prior to departing for Europe (*Manuel II Paléologue, Entretiens avec un musulman* [note 14 above], 27–28). As Trapp notes, however, Manuel himself intimates that he wrote rather shortly after returning from the campaign (cf. *Dial. Pers.* [ed. Trapp, note 1 above], 5.8–9)

with hunting, and likewise suggests that he and his comrades spent their evenings in banquets, where the accent was on lively entertainment and certainly not sobriety.[16] We learn,
moreover, that Manuel not only joined Bāyazīd in the hunts and banquets,[17] but also became absorbed—or so he claims—in discussions on religious matters with a small group of
pious and learned Muslims, apparently members of the *ulema* residing in Ankara. Manuel
refers to the leader of this group as ὁ Μουτερίζης, and characterizes him as an elderly
gentleman who had recently arrived from "Babylon" (a term which might designate either
Cairo or Baghdad). "Mouterizes" is not, of course, an actual name but rather a helleniza-
tion of the Arabo-Turkish "müderris"—the term for a theological teacher, or in İnalcık's
words "a man of recognized authority in the religious and spiritual sciences."[18] According to
Manuel, he met with these Muslims largely at their initiative, at various times of the day
according to his convenience, and usually at the emperor's quarters. They pursued such
discussions for twenty consecutive days. On ten particularly cold and snowbound days,
when Bāyazīd forsook the pleasures of hunting, they lasted from morning to night.[19] As
depicted by Manuel, these involved a series of vigorous disputes over the basic precepts of
Christianity and Islam—discussions in which Manuel invariably proved his contentions,
and which culminated in the müderris's inner conversion.

The *Dialogue* Manuel composed in 1392/1394 purports to be a memoir or reconstruction of these discussions. Indeed, by presenting what transpired between himself and the
müderris in dialogue form, Manuel imparts to the text a lively "documentary" flavor. As
with many of Manuel's more intriguing compositions, however, one presumes it to be an
amalgam of fact *and* fantasy—a structure, in other words, which very likely embodies elements of actual experience, but much else as well. Admittedly, no independent evidence has
thus far emerged to establish that these dialogues actually took place, or clarify the identity
of the müderris.[20] It would be excessive, however, to suppose that Manuel's dialogue was
entirely a product of his imagination. After all, debates of this sort were by no means unknown in fourteenth century Anatolia, and Manuel clearly had a consuming interest in

---

[16] Zachariadou, "Manuel II Palaeologos on the Strife" (note 4 above), 473–478.

[17] In the letters, Manuel is silent regarding Bāyazīd's hunts, but alludes on one occasion to pre-prandial
wine-drinking (*Ep.* 16.99–101; ed. Dennis, note 1 above). For references to Bāyazīd's hunts in the *Dial. Pers.*
(ed. Trapp, note 1 above), see 26.1–2 50.1–4; 120.1–8; 121.1–2; 189.1–2; 250.7–8, 17. Regarding banquets
and festivities, see in particular 6.33–34, and 121.2–5. All these activities Manuel professes to find distasteful,
indeed morally reprehensible (see in particular *Dial. Pers.* [ed. Trapp, note 1 above], 121.1–14).

[18] H. İnalcık, *The Ottoman Empire, The Classical Age 1300–1600*, tr. N. Itzkowitz and C. Imber (New
York-Washington, 1973), 166, where he discusses the general characteristics of a müderris, and cf. 223.

[19] See Trapp, *Manuel II. Palaiologos* (note 1 above), 54*–55*, for the timetable implied within the *Dialogue*. We cannot, however, exclude the possibility that Manuel's presentation is literary artifice, and that in
point of fact the discussions transpired through fewer, perhaps far fewer, than twenty sessions. We simply do
not know.

[20] According to Fuat Bayramoğlu, this was none other than Hacı Bayram-ı Veli, the founder of the Bayra-
miyya order (cf. *Hacı Bayram-ı Veli, Yaşamı-Soyu-Vakfı*, vol. I [Ankara, 1983], 17–18). One of the central
difficulties in accepting Bayramoğlu's identification is the uncertainty over Hacı Bayram's age in 1391.
Throughout the dialogue, Manuel continually refers to the müderris as an old man. In 1391, however, Hacı
Bayram was either thirty-eight or fifty-one, depending on whether one dates his birth to 753 (1352/1353) or

theology, and theological polemic.[21] I am content to believe that the face-to-face encounters Manuel depicts indeed transpired, and moreover am sympathetic to the speculation that Manuel compiled a set of notes as they unfolded, exploiting these subsequently to depict the setting and protagonists, establish the basic repertoire of themes, and reconstruct some of the müderris's unusual arguments.[22] Clearly, however, in crafting much of the content as well as the course of the dialogues, Manuel proceeded beyond the underpinnings of actual experience. The text as a whole has a heavy overcoating of the high-style classicism characteristic of Manuel's writings—and this even extends to the dialogue parts he constructs for the müderris.[23] Furthermore, the speaking parts Manuel provides for himself and his opposites are sculpted as polished literary compositions, embodying considerable post-debate research done in the library.[24] Perhaps most importantly, the course and climax of the dialogue, in other words its basic drama, is arguably a piece of fiction, or at least to some extent. In what follows, I shall attempt to probe the dynamics of Manuel's imagination, exploring three simple questions: how did Manuel depict his encounter with Mouterizes; why did he portray their exchange as he did; and what does this representation reveal about the emperor's central concerns ca. 1391/1394, when presumably he was composing the text?[25]

II

Throughout the *Dialogue*, Manuel delineates himself and the müderris as rather idealized types whose encounter leads to a seemingly predictable conclusion. In the discussions per se, Manuel is not the basileus or the sultan's vassal, but rather the Christian philosopher and teacher par excellence. In a deeper sense, he emerges as an apostle of Christian Hellenism, with a mission to convert. Conversely, the müderris progressively unfolds as the exact opposite of what his title designates. He teaches Manuel nothing, but functions instead as the ideal pupil. In this regard, he is fully capable of logical reasoning from mutually

---

740 (1339/1340) (see Bayramoğlu, 12, and cf. V. Ménage, "Ḥadjdjī Bayrām Walī," *EI*[2], vol. III, 43b). While Manuel could certainly have regarded a man in his fifties as "old," it is difficult to suppose that he would have done so if Hacı Bayram was in fact a decade or so younger. Moreover, Manuel's other clues regarding the müderris' identity are not at all decisive. The identification is not crucial for the purposes of this paper, however, and I reserve a fuller discussion of the problem for my book.

[21] See in general S. Vryonis, *The Decline of Medieval Hellenism in Asia Minor and the Process of Islamization from the Eleventh through the Fifteenth Century* (Berkeley-Los Angeles, 1971), 425–26.

[22] Trapp, *Manuel II. Palaiologos* (note 1 above), 55*.

[23] On Manuel's language and stylistics, see E. Trapp, "Der Sprachgebrauch Manuels II. in den Dialogen mit einem 'Perser'," *JÖBG* 16 (1967), 189–97.

[24] In the dialogues devoted primarily to refuting Islamic precepts, Manuel fashions the discussions with consistent reference to parallels in Kantakouzenos' polemic. In those outlining the essentials of Christian doctrine, Manuel's lines often amount to miniature treatises, securely anchored in the key patristic authors (notably Gregory of Nazianzus and Basil of Caesarea), and replete with the emperor's personal exegeses of biblical texts.

[25] I shall not, therefore, focus intensively on Manuel's view of Islam, the basic outlines of which are apparent from Trapp's synopsis of the dialogue (*Manuel II. Palaiologos* [note 1 above], 63*–95*). In any case, Manuel's views do not radically depart from traditional Byzantine stereotypes. On the latter, the key syntheses

accepted premises, and often has the intellectual integrity to acknowledge his errors once they have been "demonstrated" to him. Here the juncture between artifice and reality is not, of course, necessarily absolute. We can hardly dispute Manuel's depiction of himself as an erudite scholar and theologian, and the müderris may indeed have possessed the intelligence and charm Manuel imparts to him in the *Dialogue*. The problem, however, lies in Manuel's depiction of their overall performance in the discussions—in other words, the underlying action of the text.

More than anything else, Manuel crafted the *Dialogue* as an ἄθλος or contest in twenty-six major rounds, and he indicates at every juncture who won and who lost. Victory, here, means the decisive proof of a proposition—polemical or apologetic—and the consequent reduction of the opposite side to agreement, confusion, or awkward pauses of embarrassed silence. As Manuel tells the story, by the final encounter the imperial track record was impressive indeed. On the polemical side, Manuel succeeded at the outset in silencing the müderris' criticism that the Septuagint is riddled with falsifications—a coup which naturally enables the emperor to invoke its authority, *in toto*, without fear of contravention.[26] As for the central phenomenon, Muhammad, the müderris is helpless in combatting Manuel's armamentarium of proofs establishing him as a false prophet, and unmasking his life and teachings as the essence of depravity. The emperor smashes the müderris' feeble efforts to defend Muhammad's law as a middle ground between the severe law of Moses and the too-lenient law of Christ, and demonstrates conclusively that the prophet's law is little more than a plundering of Mosaic precepts. The müderris is forced to concede, furthermore, that the reference to the paraclete in John 15:26 could hardly designate Muhammad. Manuel even succeeds in wringing from him a shamed confession that the prophet's view of paradise as a garden of sensual delights is immoral, and that his promise of it is deceptive.[27] In the process, Manuel also debunks some of the müderris' favorite notions—i.e., that the angels are immortal, that Enoch and Elias occupied themselves in paradise as tailors, and that animals are endowed with quasi-rational souls.[28] Manuel's exposition of the true faith occupies the last seventeen dialogues of the text, and these unfold largely at the promptings of the curious müderris. Here the müderris is ineffective in replying to the emperor's abstruse and verbose demonstrations of the Trinity, and the nature and necessity of Christ's saving work. Unlike his colleagues, moreover, he is moved to tears by Manuel's account of the apostles as witnesses for Christ, and as the worthy vessels of God's grace.[29] The foregoing,

---

are by Eichner, "Die Nachrichten über den Islam bei den Byzantinern," *Der Islam* 23 (1936), 135–244; S. Vryonis, "Byzantine Attitudes toward Islam during the Late Middle Ages," *GRBS* 12 (1971), 263–86; and A.-T. Khoury, *Polémique byzantine contre l'Islam (VIIIe–XIIIe s.)* (Leiden, 1972).

[26] *Dial. Pers.* (ed. Trapp, note 1 above), 9.28–10.28.

[27] Manuel's attack on Muhammad effectively begins at 72.23 and continues, with various pertinent digressions, through the eighth dialogue (ending at 104.18). For a general overview, see Trapp, *Manuel II. Palaiologos* (note 1 above), 62*–76*.

[28] *Dial. Pers.* (ed. Trapp, note 1 above), 11.7–14.36 (immortality of angels); 17.8–18.7 (occupations of Enoch and Elias in paradise—a discussion, Manuel affirms, which had once occurred between Murād I and John V); 38.6–43.42 (souls of animals).

[29] *Ibid.*, 298.20–22.

needless to say, are simply the major imperial triumphs. Manuel's minor victories along the way are too numerous to catalogue here. By the end of the *athlos*, the müderris is so overwhelmed by these continuous glimpses of the true light that he hovers at the frontier of embracing Manuel's Christianity, and abandoning his own religion.

Manuel's portrait of the müderris expressing his change of heart is a rhetorical tour de force. The müderris' experience occurs during the discussion on the apostles—the διδάσκα-λοι τῷ κόσμῳ—and the context, of course, is most apt.[30] This, of all moments, is the one in which Manuel's role as διδάσκαλος, and the müderris' role as μαθητής, are in highest relief. Weeping effusively, the müderris begins with an outpouring of gratitude to Manuel for having, like one of the apostles, revealed to him what he otherwise would not have known. He expresses rapture over what Manuel has persuaded him to believe, with his bewitching and compelling arguments, and also scorns the foolishness of *his* erstwhile propositions and defenses. He openly marvels at the magnificence of the law [of Christ], and all the [Christians'] teachings—especially the incomprehensible mystery of the Incarnation. He proclaims his readiness, in principle, to come to Constantinople and study more deeply with the priests and theology teachers there. He curses the fact that he cannot leave at once—since this would mean abandoning his household (wives, sons, daughters, grandchildren, beloved slaves), and leaving his fields and flocks without provisions. Nonetheless, he promises that as soon as he can make proper arrangements, he will come with one of his sons and pursue what now means more to him than anything else. In conclusion, the müderris bows deeply before Manuel, and casts his eyes to the ground. The emperor, in return, expresses his happiness, but groans with fear that in delaying his departure the müderris may run the risk of extinguishing the newly kindled flame of spiritual desire. Without further ado, the müderris now troubles Manuel for information on the Eucharist.[31]

With the müderris' inner conversion and his promise to Manuel, the drama of the *Dialogue* is effectively finished. Any assessment of what it all means is necessarily subjective. For those who believe that Manuel could neither deceive nor be deceived, there is little difficulty. The *Dialogue* records what actually happened, or a close facsimile thereof. For doubting Thomases and sceptical historians, making an evaluation is more troublesome.

As previously indicated, we cannot determine what fully transpired in the discussions of November or December 1391 without supplementary testimony—and here we are at a loss, both on the Byzantine and Turkish sides. Still, given Manuel's a priori conviction of the truth and superiority of Christianity, we are justified in suspecting that his version of events is, to say the least, somewhat filtered. The sections of the dialogue turning on Manuel's critique of Islam probably mirror the basic thematics of the original discussions with the least distortion. It is difficult, however, to suppose that the müderris responded to Manuel's trinitarian and christological disquisitions as sympathetically as Manuel alleges. In these passages the müderris dwindles to little more than a sounding board for Manuel, and we no longer detect a genuine exchange behind the text. As for the müderris' alleged conversion, it

[30] *Ibid.*, 298.10–11.
[31] *Ibid.*, 298.20–301.23.

is strange that such a noted figure would reveal such a sensitive decision literally within earshot of Bāyazīd, and in the presence of kinsmen and colleagues not quite so convinced of the errors of Islam. These observations, however, are little more than suspicions, and one is ultimately compelled to suspend the question of "what actually happened" between the emperor and the müderris.

One may, alternatively, consider why Manuel felt compelled to represent his encounter with Mouterizes as he did. His grandfather, John VI Kantakouzenos, and his teacher, Demetrios Kydonēs, had respectively formulated and translated "objective" treatises against Islam.[32] Why then did Manuel opt to write what is effectively a drama, a work in which the boundary between the literally true and the literally false is permissibly elastic, with himself as the star performer in a highly personalized duel? Was this perhaps a vehicle by which the emperor, in 1392/1394, sought to cope with his profoundly painful experiences of 1391, his ongoing status of subordination to Bāyazīd, and the sultan's continued military successes? In approaching these questions, let us return once again to the political context.

The apprehensions and tensions which Manuel experienced at the end of the 1391 campaign did not impel him to dissolve, at that time, his pact of tributary alliance with Bāyazīd. Within three months of Manuel's return to Constantinople, the sultan was planning to attack Sinope by land and sea. His objectives, it seems, were to deal summarily with the emir of Sinope (Mubāriz ad-Dīn Isfendiyāroğlu), and then embark on a more decisive confrontation with Qādī Aḥmad Burhān al-Dīn. According to Venetian intelligence, Manuel was designated to lead the naval assault, and in late April ships were being readied for the undertaking in Constantinople, Thessaloniki and other ports. Bāyazīd probably aborted the enterprise, and evidently spent the summer and autumn of 1392 campaigning in Rumili—specifically, in northwestern Serbia and parts of Albania.[33] Virtually nothing is known of Manuel's connections with Bāyazīd throughout most of 1393. The emperor was apparently not involved in Bāyazīd's major enterprise of that year—the campaign in Bulgaria—but it presumably affected Manuel deeply. That operation was conducted by Bāyazīd's son, Süleymān Čelebi, and resulted in the conquest of Tŭrnovo (July 13, 1393) and the incorporation of Bulgaria as an Ottoman province.[34] From Bāyazīd's perspective the action was fully justified, but Manuel—sitting in Constantinople—could not have regarded this latest triumph of the sultan with anything but melancholy and anxiety.[35] The rapport between Manuel and Bāyazīd deteriorated markedly in late 1393 or early 1394, the point of

---

[32] See generally Vryonis, *Decline of Medieval Hellenism* (note 22 above), 424–25.

[33] Zachariadou, "Manuel II Palaeologos on the Strife" (note 4 above), 478–81.

[34] Cf. C. Jireček, *Geschichte der Bulgaren* (Prague, 1876), 346–50, of enduring value because of its close reliance on Patriarch Euthymius' account; P. Schreiner, *Die byzantinischen Kleinchroniken. 2. Teil, Historischer Kommentar* (Vienna, 1977), 350–51.

[35] Admittedly we have no direct information regarding Manuel's reaction to the fall of Tŭrnovo. Let us note, however, that soon thereafter the relics of St. Hilarion of Moglen were removed from Sophia to the custody of Manuel's father-in-law, Konstantin Dragaš (see Schreiner, *ibid.*, with the chronicle text in *Die byzantinischen Kleinchroniken. 1. Teil, Einleitung und Text* (Vienna, 1975), notice 11, on p. 562). It is difficult to imagine that Manuel and his wife (Helena Dragaš) were not apprised of this melancholy event, and hence of the ravages Sophia suffered when Süleymān Čelebi stormed the city.

no return being the assembly at Serres.[36] Subsequently Manuel steadily progressed towards an open breach with the sultan, which occurred most likely in the summer of 1394. By September at the latest Bāyazīd had begun the first Ottoman siege of Constantinople.[37] This was to last, with varying degrees of intensity, down to 1402, when the situation was reversed by Timur's victory over Bāyazīd on the Čabuq Ovası outside of Ankara.

Let us return, now, to Manuel, the *Dialogue*, and the müderris. As previously indicated, the emperor very likely began the work sometime in 1392 and completed it by the latter part of 1393—certainly before Bāyazīd assembled his vassals at Serres in the late autumn 1393, or early winter 1393/1394. Considered against the political events between 1391 and 1393, the *Dialogue* exhibits Manuel privately reaffirming the bases of his identity vis-à-vis the friends/enemies, allies/antagonists with whom he had been and still was so deeply entangled. First of all, the content and drama of the *Dialogue* constitute a formal declaration of faith. Faced inescapably with the realities of Ottoman military and political encirclement, and indeed enmeshed within it, we see the emperor steadfastly refusing to curse his God, and—as happened with others—desert his religious traditions. Throughout the apparently lengthy process of composing the dialogue, Manuel reassured himself that his world view, at its very heart, was not only intrinsically superior to any other but also unassailable, regardless of external circumstances. The "Christ-hating" barbarians might seize land and cities, extort tribute, and even compel emperors to perform humiliating services—but they could never conquer the fortress of belief. This extended proclamation of basic faith doubtless provided Manuel with the strength and solace he needed to persevere in an ambiguous and depressing situation.

The emperor's depiction of his conversion of the müderris, moreover, is a complementary expression of imagined power, combined with hope. It exhibits, of course, an abiding confidence in the superior ability of the apostles of Christ, in whatever generation, to persuade the unbeliever—especially the virtuous pagans, who despite their ignorance are already halfway to the mark. As we've seen, Manuel has carefully sculpted himself and the müderris according to these prototypes. The conversion scene also underscores Manuel's specifically imperial view of the implications of conversion, revealing as well a dimension of hope. The true converts, whether individuals or nations, cannot dwell in isolation without bridges to the uppermost tier in the order of earthly powers. Converts, as individuals and groups, may cross the frontiers—dwelling among and mingling with the Rhomaioi. Converted peoples will assimilate within a family of Christian nations, hierarchically descending from the Rhomaioi and their basileus. All will acknowledge the superior status of the emperor, and their proper subordination to him. This political interpretation of conversion is one of the defining features of traditional Byzantine political ideology, and its assimila-

---

[36] H. İnalcık supports K. Hopf and M. Silberschmidt in locating this meeting not at Serres, but rather Berrhoia (Veroia), the Ottoman Kara Ferye. Cf. İnalcık's review of J. Barker's *Manuel II Palaeologus* (note 4 above) in *Archivum Ottomanicum* 3 (1971), 276, and most recently his essay "The Ottoman Turks and the Crusades, 1329–1451," in H. Hazard and N. Zacour, eds., *A History of the Crusades*, vol. VI, *The Impact of the Crusades on Europe* (Madison, 1989), 294.

[37] Barker, *Manuel II Palaeologus* (note 4 above), 110–22; Schreiner, *Die byzantinischen Kleinchroniken. 2. Teil* (note 35 above), 352–53.

tionist quality goes far to explain the extraordinary vitality of that state.[38] We can still feel the heartbeat of that mentality in what Manuel expects of the converted müderris, explicitly as well as implicitly. He will of course abandon the wilds of the non-Christian barbarians, and come to dwell in Constantinople. There he will not only receive instruction and baptism, but will come to comprehend the right order of authority in the world. He, too, will regard the emperor as his *despotēs*, and the simple bow of respect he accorded Manuel in his dwelling in Ankara will become, in Constantinople, a ritual act of proskynesis. Perhaps we can detect behind this Manuel's wildest hopes and dreams—the conversion and proper subordination of the group which the müderris represents.

Manuel's theological drama, however, does not end with the müderris fulfilling all the emperor's hopes. He does not come to Constantinople, after all, as Manuel admits. If Manuel had indeed succeeded in converting the müderris, this certainly must have disappointed him. In any case, we can at least see in the emperor's portrait of their encounter an ideal fantasy of how the plight of the Rhomaioi might be solved—i.e., through the traditional and time-honored means of taming the βάρβαροι through conversion, followed by gradual assimilation or subordination. We may doubt, of course, that Manuel—away from his writing desk—entertained realistic hopes of converting the Turks and somehow diminishing thereby the threats they posed. His sense of the ultimate solution takes us back again to his faith, and his fantasies.

The famous fifth dialogue provides us with the deepest insights into Manuel's hopes and expectations regarding the present state of affairs. The topic of debate, here, is the validity of Muhammad's claim to be a prophet. The müderris argues that the spread of Islam at the expense of the Roman Christians (i.e., Byzantines) proves the truth of the claim—for Muhammad himself had prophesied eternal victory over the unbelievers. Manuel responds with a two-pronged attack. He claims, first of all, that is was inevitable for the good fortune (ἀγαθὴ τύχη) of the Romans to suffer a reversal, to change for the worse, because in principle "fortune delights in changes" (χαίρει γὰρ αὕτη ταῖς μεταβολαῖς). A sentence later, he defines "tychē" as synonymous with "metabolē" (change)—i.e., "fortune" refers to shifts or changes of human circumstances.[39] Muhammad, therefore, merely proclaimed the predictable—which does not constitute prophesy at all. Alluding to one of his favorite metaphors for "life" in general, Manuel says that this is no more prophetic than proclaiming that calm will follow the storm.

At this point, he turns the tables on the müderris and warns him that all nations have experienced shifts of fortune, positive and negative alterations in circumstance, and specifically cites the Romans, Persians, Assyrians, and Macedonians. Manuel's point is clear: the Persians of today, i.e., the Turks, may well experience the same. Then he proceeds with

---

[38] One of the finest overviews of this general theme is D. Obolensky's chapter "Factors in Cultural Diffusion," in his *The Byzantine Commonwealth. Eastern Europe, 500–1453* (New York-Washington, 1971), 272–90.

[39] *Dial. Pers.* (ed. Trapp, note 1 above), 57.27–28 (Μᾶλλον δὲ τὴν τῶν ἀνθρωπίνων πραγμάτων μεταβολὴν τύχην, οἶμαι, κεκλήκασιν ἄνθρωποι).

examples of the reversals of individual rulers, and expatiates at length on Xerxes and his expedition against the Hellenes. Xerxes, says Manuel, advanced against the Hellenes puffed up with confidence in the might of his army and navy, and insolent because of his numerous trophies. When his forces were defeated, however, he himself instantly changed into the opposite of what he had been—and now proved himself a coward. Specifically, he fled as fast as he could to escape the Hellenes. Manuel concludes this part of his discourse with the time-honored tag from Isokrates—nothing in human life is certain or secure.[40]

In what follows, Manuel does not, of course, directly link Xerxes with Bāyazīd, and prophesy a parallel future fate. His talk with the müderris takes place, after all, in close proximity to the sultan. The implied analogy is nonetheless clear, since the terms Manuel uses to describe Xerxes' character are in their essentials precisely those he applies to Bāyazīd. It would seem, therefore, that in 1391–1392 Manuel was privately conceptualizing Bāyazīd according to the "barbarian tyrant" type, exemplified in Xerxes, and moreover expecting that "tychē" would change, and the tyrant would topple.

Manuel's association of Bāyazīd with the Xerxes type is of course fascinating, reflecting not only a reading of Aeschylos and Herodotos, but more importantly Aelius Aristides, who developed the metamorphosis motif quite vividly in the *Panathenaic Oration*.[41] One is puzzled, however, by Manuel's conception of "tychē" and its operations, particularly with reference to the future. His use of the term is of course archaizing, evoking an immediate "highbrow" association with the thought world of pagan Greek literature. Still, Manuel himself carefully controls the extent of the association by defining "tychē" simply as change (μεταβολή), denuding the term, so it would seem, of a theological reflex. Are we to understand, then, that he is telling the müderris that the Persians-Turks will experience a reversal, and that Xerxes-Bāyazīd will suffer a downfall, in the course of a natural rhythym or process, the dynamics of which are *not* connected with divine agency?

In an oration which he wrote two years before, in 1389, Manuel explained what he meant by τύχη. The occasion for this panegyric was his father John V's miraculous recovery from a serious illness. Throughout the oration, Manuel interprets this development as a sign of God's favor, as a good omen for the future. Midway through his speech, he reflects on the instability of prosperity and happiness, noting that it endlessly wanders now to one person, then to another; now to one nation or city, now to others. He sums it up by proclaiming what he will tell the müderris in the *Dialogue*—"Fortune delights in changes." For his court audience, however, Manuel elaborates further. Regarding these oscillations in prosperity he says: "The Hellenes call this tyche, and we too call it tyche. But for them it was a god, and for us who are pious [Christians] it has the glory of a mere word—with the sense of success (εὐπραγία) or failure (δυσπραγία)." He proceeds then to associate the "good fortune" of prosperity, and especially of peace, with God's benevolence—explicating these as

---

[40] *Ibid.*, 58.39–40.

[41] Eds. F. Lenz and C. Behr, *P. Aelii Aristidis opera quae exstant omnia*, vol. I (Leiden, 1976), 48.20–68.16, but especially 68.7–16. For the corresponding English translation, see C. Behr, trans., *P. Aelius Aristides, The Complete Works*, vol. I (Leiden, 1986), 28 (§115)–38 (§166), but especially p. 38 (§166).

benefactions given to the worthy, and predictably withdrawn from the unworthy.[42] Overall, however, the tone is optimistic. Manuel reminds his listeners that they partake of "prosperity" as baptized Christians, that they are the heirs to divine promises, and that God never overlooks those who pray to him in faith. He intimates, moreover, that the Rhomaioi hold a special status among the "people of God", that the covenant between God and the followers of Christ has a particular political corollary, namely the endurance of the Roman (i.e., Byzantine) state. John V's recovery, he reiterates throughout, is living proof of God's loyalty to his people —and reason for all to look forward with good hopes, believing that, through God, they shall again enjoy the "good fortune of their ancestors."[43]

Manuel declaimed the foregoing at the Constantinopolitan court in 1389. Let us return now to his debate with the müderris in Ankara in 1391, as portrayed in his *Dialogue* of 1392/1394. First of all, there is no reason to assume that Manuel had changed his views about $\tau\acute{u}\chi\eta$ since 1389. His hopes were as yet unfulfilled, but he still believed that God would aid the Rhomaioi—answering their prayers, restoring their old "fortune." But that remained for the future, and faced with the müderris' harshest argument he could not convincingly counter with a simple declaration of faith. Consequently, Manuel replies with a theory of history which *seemingly* transcends polemic (Allah vs. $\dot{o}$ $\Theta\epsilon\acute{o}s$, the promise of Muhammad vs. the promise of Christ), and mechanistically prophesies doom for the Turks and the sultan. In reality, however, Manuel's reply merely reiterates his faith (since Manuel knows perfectly well what he really means by "tychē")—affirming that his God determines the ebb and flow, fervently convinced that the storm will pass, and the Rhomaioi will be sailing on calm waters, rather than perishing like the Egyptians or Macedonians. In short, Manuel's parry turns on a semantic trick which supposedly silences the müderris, who, we are led to believe, lacks the presence of mind to insist that the emperor explicate his terms, or swiftly rejoin that the will of Allah is indistinguishable from "tychē" (the Turkic equivalent being "baht").[44]

---

[42] "χαίρει πως ἡ τύχη ταῖς μεταβολαῖς καὶ σφόδρα γε δυσκάθεκτόν τι χρῆμα ἡ εὐδαιμονία μοι φαίνεται, τούτου τε ἀφισταμένη καὶ ἐπ' ἄλλον μεταπηδῶσα, καὶ ἀεὶ περινοστοῦσα, οὐκ εἰς ἔθνη μόνον καὶ πόλεις, ἀλλὰ καὶ καθ' ἕκαστον ἄνθρωπον· κἂν μὴ τὸν ὑποδεξόμενον ἀξίως εὕρῃ, εὐθὺς ἐπειχθεῖσα χαίρειν τε τοῦτον ἐρεῖ, καὶ ἐκζητήσειεν ἂν παρ' ᾧ κεχαρισμένην ἑαυτῇ καὶ καλλίστην εὑρήσει ξενίαν τε καὶ ὑποδοχήν. Κἀκεῖνο δὲ πρὸς τούτοις οὐ περίεργον ἴσως οὐδέ τι φαῦλον εἰπεῖν· τύχην λέγουσιν Ἕλληνες, τύχην ὀνομάζομεν καὶ ἡμεῖς· ἀλλὰ θεὸς ἐκείνοις αὕτη νενόμισται, παρὰ δὲ εὐσεβέσιν ἡμῖν ψιλοῦ τινος ὀνόματος δόξαν ἔχει, εὐπραγίας ἢ καὶ δυσπραγίας ἔσθ' ὅτε σημαντικοῦ· τύχης τοίνυν λέγεται μετέχειν πᾶς ἀγαθῆς, ὅστις εὖ πράττων διατελεῖ· πράττει δὲ πᾶς τις εὖ καὶ εὐδαίμων ἐστὶν ἀληθῶς, ὃς τυγχάνει ἔχων τὸν Θεὸν εὐμενῶς διακείμενον εἰς αὐτὸν τῷ τὰ κεχαρισμένα πράττειν αὐτῷ· ὃς δ' αὖ τοιοῦτος ἐστὶ τὴν διὰ τῶν ἀποστόλων ἀπὸ τοῦ Σωτῆρος εἰρήνην, ὥσπερ τινὰ κλῆρον εἰς ἡμᾶς κατιοῦσαν, καθάπερ τινὰ πολυτελῆ στέφανον ἀτεχνῶς ἀναδήσεται" (*Log. Pan.*, 235).

[43] *Ibid.*, 236-38, and cf. 228-29.

[44] Turner considered Manuel's argument inconsistent and illogical: "The thought behind [Manuel's] arguments . . . is not that human prosperity is governed by a fickle Hellenistic $\tau\acute{u}\chi\eta$ . . . , but that it is governed by the regular 'laws of nature'; the conclusion to be drawn is that there is no connection between human prosperity and divine providence, except in so far as the laws of nature themselves are set by divine providence. Manuel is thus inconsistent when in his final arguments . . . he is prepared to perceive providence . . . behind human adversity. He appears to be marshalling as many arguments as he can to meet his immediate problem without being too careful to see that they are logically consistent: under stress of circumstances he wants to

Equipped with this theory of history, Manuel bided his time, convinced that God would inevitably intervene and strike down Bāyazīd, simultaneously the new Xerxes and the new pharaoh. It was doubtless this faith which emboldened Manuel to cut his ties with the sultan in the spring or summer of 1394, following the crisis at Serres—at a time when his military and even political resources were negligible. It sustained him, as we know from his letters, througout the years of the siege.[45] In 1402, finally, he had the pleasure of interpreting Timur's victory as a vindication of his faith, and a confirmation that the processes of Christian Roman history were as constant as ever.

Manuel's writings after 1402 are in many respects a program of victory celebrations.[46] In the *Dialogue*, we see at once the realities of Manuel's situation ca. 1391–1393, his strategies for coping, and a sample of his visions for a solution to his plight, and that of his people. In essence, Manuel's construction of the müderris, whoever he was, is largely an expression of the emperor's belief in the inevitability of victory: the triumph of Christ over Muhammad, the survival of the Rhomaioi, and the demise of the sultan. Licking his wounds from the long campaign, and oppressed by Bāyazīd's continuing successes, Manuel represented Mouterizes as an intellectual and spiritual aggressor striving to prove why such victory could not and would not occur, but failing in the attempt. Depicting himself vanquishing this opponent, dismantling the fortress of *his* belief, Manuel fortified his own faith and imagined the future victory. Writing the *Dialogue* was thus a propaideia to his open warfare with Bāyazīd, a battle the emperor expected to win, naturally with the help of his God.

---

exclude divine providence from the question of human prosperity and adversity, but where it suits him he is prepared to admit the traditional Christian belief that the affairs of man are subject to the hand of God" ("Pages from Late Byzantine Philosophy of History," *BZ* 57 [1964], 352–53). I differ from Turner in regarding Manuel's defense not as inconsistent or illogical, but rather calculating and devious—a manoeuver to deceive the müderris into assuming that Manuel has convincingly "atheized" the discussion of causality, when in point of fact the emperor's fundamental presumptions have not altered (and hence are still vulnerable to attack).

Beck, in his *Vorsehung und Vorherbestimmung in der theologischen Literatur der Byzantinern* = *OCA* 114 (Rome, 1937), did not address the fifth dialogue in any detail (cf. pp. 58–63).

[45] Exemplary is *Ep.* 31 (ed. Dennis, note 1 above), addressed to Kydonēs following the defeat of the crusaders at Nikopolis. See in particular lines 100–14.

[46] Notably his piece "On the Defeat of Bāyazīd in the form of a Psalm" (ed. E. Legrand, *Lettres de l'empereur Manuel Paléologue* [Paris, 1893], 104), and the companion ethopoiia "What Tamerlane Might Have Said to Bāyazīd" (*ibid.*, 103–104). Cf. also his treatment of Bāyazīd in *Epitaph.* (ed. Chrysostomides, note 1 above), notably 139.1/157.19.

Aspects of Monastic Patronage
in Palaeologan Macedonia

MARCUS RAUTMAN

FROM Byzantium's early hours through its long medieval twilight, monasticism stood near the cultural center as one of its most distinctive institutions. Encouraged by the generational accumulation of law and tradition and the echoed exhortations of churchmen, the monastic impulse was felt across the empire and on all levels of society by people who sought to define their place in the world and express their hopes for the next. The means of their aspirations, in human and material resources assigned to monastic purposes, constituted a major feature of the late Byzantine landscape, both social and geographic.[1] The surviving documents of the period provide isolated glimpses of this important chapter in the cultural history of the late Byzantine empire.

The social dynamics of Byzantine monasticism have been much discussed, from the varied personal motivations for undertaking a hermitic career to the legal and financial arrangements needed to support it.[2] The actual process of establishing a monastery was throughout the Byzantine period a peculiarly social undertaking that summoned the efforts and cooperation of many individuals. The donor's will and resources provided only the occasion for a complex συνεργασία that involved secular and clerical authorities as well as considerable physical labor and financial investment. Recent exploration of Byzantine monasticism has focused on its legal and proprietary dimensions, which are well documented by surviving texts. The availability of written material for the late empire has slowed the search for supplementary evidence from other, especially physical sources. On few occasions has this primarily documentary perspective been broadened to include such material aspects of monastic donation as church construction and decoration, despite the fact that buildings are especially sensitive witnesses to social factors in their conception, construction, and transformation through time. The late Byzantine period, with its relative abundance of both textual and tangible sources, offers an especially good opportunity to study the interactions of monastic authorities, patrons, and artisans on the socio-architectural plane. Rejoining these two participants in the same monastic moment allows special insight into this central facet of late Byzantine life.

---

[1] P. Charanis, "Monastic Properties and the State in the Byzantine Empire," *DOP* 4 (1948), 53–118 (repr. in *Social, Economic and Political Life in the Byzantine Empire* [London, 1973]); A. M. Bryer, "The Late Byzantine Monastery in Town and Countryside," in *The Church in Town and Countryside*, Studies in Church History 16 (Oxford, 1979), 219–41.

[2] Among the vast literature on Byzantine monasticism see H.-G. Beck, *Kirche und theologische Literatur im byzantinischen Reich* (Munich, 1959), 120–40; J. P. Thomas, *Private Religious Foundations in the Byzantine Empire*, DOS 24 (Washington, D.C., 1987), both with further sources.

Palaeologan Macedonia offers an important example of these dynamics at work in a setting removed from both the bureaucratic peculiarities of the imperial capital and the textual poverty of the more remote provinces. The area has remained ill-defined since antiquity; in order to focus on the late Byzantine province the term is used here geographically to refer to those parts of Macedonia and greater Thessaly that came under the control of the Palaeologan court between 1261 and 1453.[3]

On two sides the province is bounded by mountains (Map 1). To the west stands the Kandavian range of the lower Balkan ridge, whose lakes of Ohrid, Prespa, and Mikra Prespa drain through Albania to the Adriatic; to the south, beyond the Kamvounian range of Mount Olympos, lie the plains of δευτέρα Θετταλία.[4] Administratively, the province extended eastward across Chalkidiki to the Thracian frontier, which in the early 1300s stood near Christoupolis (present Kavala) and Philippi.[5] The province's northern border was the least clearly defined, moving progressively southward in the mid-fourteenth century under pressure by the ascendant Serbian state. The mountainous uplands of Macedonia are gathered into the three great catchments of the Aliakmon, Vardar, and Strymon rivers, which form broad agricultural plains as they reach toward the Thermaic and Strymonic gulfs. Projecting southward into the Aegean is the three-pronged peninsula of Chalkidiki, intensively cultivated from classical times. The easternmost spur is occupied by the monastic community of Mount Athos, the fullest expression of a way of religious life that still flourishes across the province.[6]

[3] Contemporary writers are inconsistent in referring to the province; see the sources collected in T. L. F. Tafel, *De Thessalonica ejusque agro dissertatio geographica* (Berlin, 1839); M. G. Demitsa, Ἀρχαία γεωγραφία τῆς Μακεδονίας συνταχθεῖσα κατὰ τὰς πηγὰς καὶ τὰ βοηθήματα I–II (Athens, 1870–1874); O. Tafrali, *Thessalonique au quatorzième siècle* (Paris, 1913), 53–57; P. Lemerle, *Philippes et la Macédoine orientale a l'époque chrétienne et byzantine. Recherches d'histoire et d'archéologie* (Paris, 1945), 191 n. 2, cf. 122 n. 3. For the physical geography see W. M. Leake, *Travels in Northern Greece* I–IV (London, 1835); N. G. L. Hammond, *A History of Macedonia* I (Oxford, 1982), 3–211; and more generally *Macedonia. 4000 Years of Greek History and Civilization*, ed. M. B. Sakellariou (Athens, 1983), 12–26. For the eastern province in Ottoman times see J. Lefort, ed., *Paysages de Macédoine. Leurs caractères et leur évolution à travers les documents et les récits des voyageurs*, TM monographies 3 (Paris, 1986). Specialized studies of parts of the late Byzantine province include G. I. Theocharides, Κατεπανίκια τῆς Μακεδονίας (Thessaloniki, 1954); C. Asdracha, *La région de Rhodopes aux XIIIᵉ et XIVᵉ siècles. Étude de géographie historique* (Athens, 1976); J. Lefort, *Villages de Macédoine* I. *La Chalcidique occidentale*, TM monographies 1 (Paris, 1982); and V. Kravari, *Villes et villages de Macédoine occidentale*, TM monographies (forthcoming).

[4] A. P. Avraméa, Ἡ βυζαντινὴ Θεσσαλία μέχρι τοῦ 1204. Συμβολὴ εἰς τὴν ἱστορικὴν γεωγραφίαν (Athens, 1976); J. Koder and F. Hild, *Hellas und Thessalia*, Tabula Imperii Byzantini I (Vienna, 1976), 37–41, 61–62 for the province's geographic delimitation.

[5] Macedonia's fourteenth-century border with Thrace is known by Gregoras, *Byzantina Historia* VIII, 6: ed. L. Schopen, Bonn ed. (1829), I, 312–21, at 321; and Kantakouzenos, *Historia* I, 23: ed. L. Schopen, Bonn ed. (1828), I, 113–19, at 115.

[6] S. Kokkine, Τὰ μοναστήρια τῆς Ἑλλάδος (Athens, 1976), 47–81. Mount Athos constitutes a special case that merits separate discussion. For the setting and early development of monastic Athos see E. A. de Mendieta, *Mount Athos* (Berlin-Amsterdam, 1972); and D. Papachryssanthou, *Actes de Prôtaton* (Paris, 1975). Chalkidiki, where Athos held extensive possessions, may not be fully representative of the larger empire either; see Lefort, *La Chalcidique occidentale* (note 3 above); and V. Dimitriades, "Ottoman Chalkidiki: An Area in Transition," in *Continuity and Change in Late Byzantine and Early Ottoman Society*, eds. A. Bryer and H. Lowry (Birmingham-Washington, D.C., 1986), 39–50.

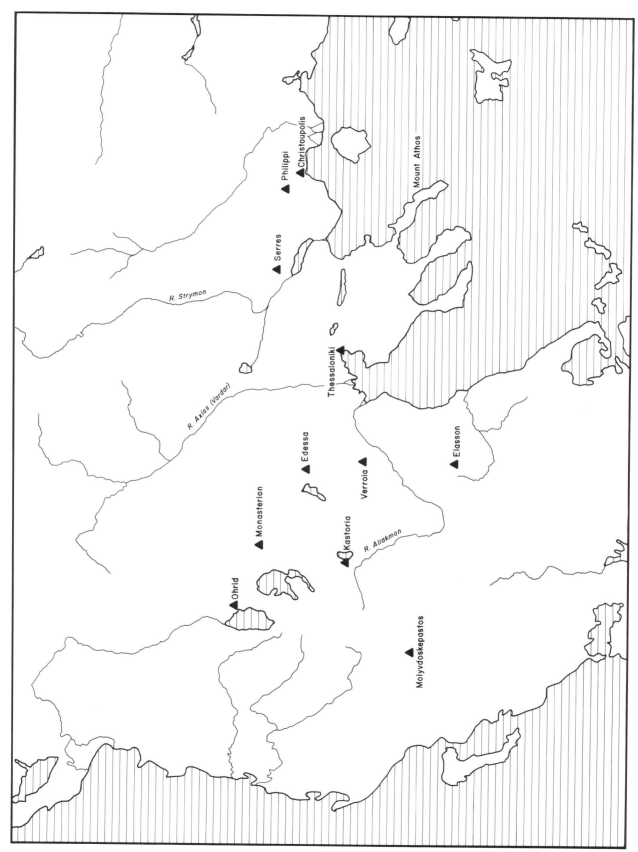

Map 1. Palaeologan Macedonia. Cities and documented monastic foundations

With its mountain villages and coastal settlements, Macedonia offers a representative example of the physical geography of late Byzantium. Small medieval cities like Serres, Christoupolis, Ohrid, and Veroia provided markets for the surrounding countryside as well as centers of local government; several of these settlements still retain their episcopal status. In the late Middle Ages a total of twelve neighboring bishoprics comprised the metropolitan see of Thessaloniki, that celebrated megalopolis that had been the regional focus of population, industry, and trade since Roman times. Thessaloniki's economic strength and urban character distinguished it among its Palaeologan counterparts as the second great city of the empire and even a cultural rival to Constantinople in the eyes of both residents and visitors. The thirteenth-century seat of two independent governments—the Crusader kingdom of Boniface of Montferrat and the equally short-lived Epirot domain of Michael II Angelos— Thessaloniki remained at the political, cultural, and religious center of Palaeologan Macedonia until its absorption into the Ottoman empire. The ministry of northern Greece is still based in the city.[7]

The increasing availability of literary and physical testimonia reinforces the potential of Macedonia in exploring late Byzantine monastic history. Best known are the Palaeologan historians, who recorded the tumultuous course of local political events from the Catalan incursions and the outbreak of civil war in the 1320s and again in the 1340s to the steady advance of the Serbian and Ottoman frontiers.[8] Less well explored are other sources that deal with the monasteries of the province. The indispensable Athonite material has not yet been fully published, much less systematically analyzed, and previous study of the physical monuments has focused primarily on individual buildings. The present survey offers an interim assessment of both literary and material evidence for monastic patronage in late Byzantine Macedonia. Its focus on the individuals and circumstances that attended a monastery's creation seeks to clarify a crucial chapter in the life of these institutions. Certain foundations are well-known from literary sources and some are even physically extant; others are attested by only a passing reference or fragmentary inscription. In order to compensate for this documentary disparity, this overview employs a geographic approach that treats monasteries as interrelated points on a continuous ecclesiastical landscape in order to discern deeper patterns of contemporary monastic behavior.[9] Since the primary goal is to explore the Byzantine monastery within its immediate social setting, contemporary foundations at Mount Athos and in Serbia are left to separate treatment. The meager record of

[7] O. Tafrali, *Topographie de Thessalonique* (Paris, 1913), 1–29; *idem, Thessalonique au quatorzième siècle* (note 3 above); A. Papagiannopoulos, *History of Thessaloniki* (Thessaloniki, 1982); for the province see Lefort, *Paysages de Macédoine* (note 3 above).

[8] For the political narrative see G. I. Theocharides, Ἱστορία τῆς Μακεδονίας κατὰ τοὺς μέσους χρόνους *(285–1354)* (Thessaloniki, 1980), 360–417. The extent to which these political conflicts affected rural settlement patterns is unclear; see Lefort, *La Chalcidique occidentale* (note 3 above); *idem,* "Population and Landscape in Eastern Macedonia during the Middle Ages: The Example of Radolibos," in *Continuity and Change* (note 6 above), 11–21.

[9] For similar approaches see the ongoing survey of Byzantine geography sponsored by the Fondation Européenne de la Science; see H. Ahrweiler, ed., *Géographie historique du monde méditerranéen*, Byzantina Sorbonensia 7 (Paris, 1988).

previous work in this area does not yet allow firm conclusions, but an initial gathering of evidence offers a new perspective on religious patronage in the late Byzantine period.

The present survey focuses only on pious foundations of demonstrably monastic intent for two reasons. The first concerns textual evidence. The complex legal setting of monasteries is more fully documented than are the many small churches and chapels erected in Byzantine times. The preserved sources comprise primarily *praktika* or tax inventories, synodal acts, and chrysobulls; more rarely, typika or foundation charters have survived to spell out the specific terms of an individual endowment. A second consideration is that late Byzantine monasteries posed special problems of organization, funding, and design that remained constant among themselves. For example, typika frequently address such administrative matters as the number of monks and their daily routine, sources of revenue and their management, and the nature of services celebrated at a monastery. In order better to control the available data this survey considers only initial foundations or refoundations, and not the large number of votive gifts, minor donations, sales, and miscellaneous acquisitions known from various sources. This selectivity rests on the assumption that there existed a special bond between the primary donor and her or his establishment, a relationship that was embodied in the expense of physically constructing and protecting the foundation from its many late Byzantine hazards and providing for its financial support.[10] Presumably this investment in a monastery's physical infrastructure preserved for a while the donors' wishes and names; in fact, the existence of a typikon expressing this order was a legal condition for the act of foundation.[11] Even if this close association of patron and foundation is not always verifiable, these criteria narrow the relevant sources from potentially hundreds to a more manageable number. Within these limits this sample of documented foundations is highly selective, yet its testimony suggests patterns of monastic patronage that distinguish Macedonian practices from those found in other parts of late Byzantium. These observations take on particular significance in light of the surviving monuments and suggest the presence of certain unrecognized processes of monastic finance and construction in the Palaeologan period.

In order to approach the Palaeologan monastery on its own terms it seems useful to proceed deductively from its Middle Byzantine ancestors and define by exception its salient characteristics. One can begin with several assumptions about the role of patronage derived from earlier practices noted across the empire. While monasticism was supported by all levels of Orthodox society, as a rule the establishing or refounding of a monastery required of the donor considerable responsibilities. These obligations not only included the construc-

---

[10] In general see Bryer, "The Late Byzantine Monastery" (note 1 above), 228; Thomas, *Private Religious Foundations* (note 2 above), 253–58. Physical threat to monasteries could be both internal and external; see A. K. Orlandos, Μοναστηριακὴ Ἀρχιτεκτονική, 2nd ed. (Athens, 1958); P. Charanis, "Piracy in the Aegean during the Reign of Michael VIII Palaeologus," *AIPHOS* 10 (1950), 127–36, repr. in *Social, Economic and Political Life* (note 1 above); N. Oikonomidès, "Monastères et moines lors de la conquête ottomane," *SOforsch* 35 (1976), 1–10.

[11] P. de Meester, *De monachico statu iuxta disciplinam Byzantinam* (Vatican City, 1942), 12, 150 n. 7; cf. C. Galatariotou, "Byzantine Ktetorika Typika: A Comparative Study," *REB* 45 (1987), 77–138, at 87. The writing of a typikon by the donor seems to have become increasingly common in the later empire; certainly the opportunity for authorship would have been a principal attraction of such patronage.

tion of a foundation's physical apparatus but extended to properties or funds donated for its future support. For these reasons, patrons in the eleventh and twelfth centuries tended to be members of the royal family, urban aristocrats, or major provincial landowners.[12] As is well-known, the motive forces of this monastic *ktētoreia* could involve considerations of personal, religious, and financial nature as well as pious philanthropy, and such bequests took on special urgency for the citizen confronting great sin, political disfavor, or poor health. Monastic endowment was usually directed to securing personal salvation through good works, which a foundation's contemplative, worshipful, and philanthropic missions all supported.[13] According to the stipulations of many typika, a monastery offered both shelter to members of a family while living and prayers on their behalf after death. The frequent provisions made for family members stress the importance of kinship definition in religious patronage, for relationships were clarified and renewed by the terms of endowment. Equally important, monastic patronage often reinforced ties that joined a family with a specific place, bonds that effectively linked the provincial aristocracy with their lands and local settlements. This relationship between patron and monastery found its fullest expression in the occasional donation by a benefactor of her or his tomb.[14] Despite important changes that occurred in the proprietary monastery's legal status in the thirteenth century, these fundamental motive forces continued to function into the late empire.[15]

These traditional mechanisms of monastic patronage suggest one expectation for Palaeologan Macedonia: since the province was dominated by landed magnates in the thirteenth and fourteenth centuries, one would expect to find the countryside littered with their religious foundations. Wealthy families like the Angeloi, Devlitzenoi, Synadenoi, Tornikioi, Tzamplakoi, Kantakouzenoi, and Choumnoi comprised a well established aristocracy in

[12] J. Darrouzès, "Le mouvement des fondations monastiques au XIe siècle," *TM* 6 (1976), 159–76; R. Morris, "The Byzantine Aristocracy and the Monasteries," in *The Byzantine Aristocracy, IX–XII Centuries*, ed. M. Angold (Oxford, 1984), 112–37; *idem*, "Monasteries and their Patrons in the Tenth and Eleventh Centuries," *ByzF* 10 (1985), 185–231; C. Galatariotou, "Byzantine Ktetorika Typika" (note 11 above), 89–107; Thomas, *Private Religious Foundations* (note 2 above), 143–48, 214–18.

[13] D. J. Constantelos, *Byzantine Philanthropy and Social Welfare* (New Brunswick, N.J., 1968), 88–110; Morris, "Monasteries and their Patrons" (note 12 above), 215–25; C. Galatariotou, "Byzantine Ktetorika Typika," (note 11 above), 91–106; *idem*, "Byzantine Women's Monastic Communities: The Evidence of the Τυπικά," *JÖB* 38 (1988), 263–90, at 277–84.

[14] Concerning monastic burial procedures see J. von Zhishman, *Das Stifterrecht in der morgenländischen Kirche* (Vienna, 1888), 63; D. de F. Abrahamse, "Women's Monasticism in the Middle Byzantine Period: Problems and Prospects," *ByzF* 9 (1985), 35–58, at 38–39; Galatariotou, "Byzantine Ktetorika Typika" (note 11 above), 96–97.

[15] A recent overview is offered by Thomas, *Private Religious Foundations* (note 2 above), 244–62. Concerning the analogous role of gift exchange in medieval England see J. T. Rosenthal, *The Purchase of Paradise. Gift Giving and the Aristocracy, 1307–1485* (London, 1972).

[16] The term is employed in an inclusive sense to refer to those landowning families that contemporary sources place at the upper end of the Palaeologan social scale; these examples are representative but by no means exhaustive. In general see P. Charanis, "The Aristocracy of Byzantium in the Thirteenth Century," in *Studies in Roman Economic and Social History in Honor of Allen Chester Johnson*, ed. P. R. Coleman-Norton (Princeton, 1951), 336–55; *idem*, "On the Social Structure and Economic Organization of the Byzantine Empire in the Thirteenth Century and Later," *Byzantinoslavica* 12 (1951), 94–153; *idem*, "Town and Country in the Byzantine Possessions of the Balkan Peninsula during the Later Period of the Empire," in *Aspects of the Balkans. Continuity and Change*, eds. H. Birnbaum and S. Vryonis (Mouton, The Hague, 1961), 117–37

the province, with extensive holdings in its cities as well as across the countryside.[16] Among the province's hereditary landowners, Manuel Angelos still retained villages near Thessaloniki and Serres in the early fourteenth century.[17] The Devlitzenoi, a family apparently of Serbian origin, included a number of military men who are known to have lived in Thessaloniki and to have owned property there and in Chalkidiki, especially near Hermeleia.[18] Members of the Armenian-Georgian family of Tornikioi held various administrative posts in Palaeologan Macedonia, especially in Thessaloniki and Serres.[19] The family of Theodore Synadenos held lands in the Strymon valley and near Serres.[20] The Tzamplakoi are known to have owned properties in Thessaloniki, the Serres-Zichnai region, and around Christoupolis.[21] Since the twelfth century the Kantakouzenoi retained vast territories in Thrace and Macedonia, especially in Thessaloniki and around Serres-Zichnai.[22] Resident in Macedonia since Middle Byzantine times, the Choumnos family constituted one of the most venerable aristocratic houses in the province, with extensive properties in and around Thessaloniki, Serres, and Zichnai, including a village Χούμνικον located on the banks of the Strymon river.[23]

Despite their tangible interests throughout the province, very few of these landed families can be linked with local monasteries in Palaeologan times. Tradition identifies John Tornikios with the tenth-century founding of the Iviron monastery on Mount Athos, but the only late Byzantine monastery closely associated with the family is ἡ τοῦ Τορνικίου μονή that stood near Nicaea at the end of the thirteenth century.[24] A single text mentions a

---

(the latter two reprinted in *Social, Economic and Political Life* [note 1 above]); G. Ostrogorsky, "Observations on the Aristocracy in Byzantium," *DOP* 25 (1971), 1–32; A. E. Laiou, "The Byzantine Aristocracy in the Palaeologan Period: A Story of Arrested Development," *Viator* 4 (1973), 131–51, at 143–44; Lefort, *La Chalcidique occidentale* (note 3 above); Galatariotou, "Byzantine Ktetorika Typika" (note 11 above), 89–91; and cf. Rosenthal, *The Purchase of Paradise* (note 15 above).

[17] L. Petit and B. Korablev, *Actes de Chilandar* (St. Petersburg, 1911), 50–51 no. 23 (1306).

[18] N. Oikonomidès, "The Properties of the Deblitzenoi in the Fourteenth and Fifteenth Centuries," in *Charanis Studies. Essays in Honor of Peter Charanis*, ed. A. E. Laiou-Thomadakis (New Brunswick, N.J., 1980), 176–98; *idem, Actes de Docheiariou* (Paris, 1984), 160, 253–55, 258–61.

[19] G. Schmalzbauer, "Die Tornikioi in der Palaiologenzeit. Prosopographische Untersuchung zu einer byzantinischen Familie," *JÖB* 18 (1969), 115–35.

[20] L. Maksimović, "Poslednje godine protostratora Teodora Sinadina," *ZVI* 10 (1967), 177–85; Ch. Hannick and G. Schmalzbauer, "Die Synadenoi. Prosopographische Untersuchung zu einer byzantinischen Familien," *JÖB* 25 (1976), 125–61.

[21] G. I. Theocharides, "Οἱ Τζαμπλάκωνες," Μακεδονικά 5 (1959), 125–83; P. Lemerle, "Un praktikon inédit des archives de Karakala (Janvier 1342) et la situation en Macédoine orientale au moment de l'usurpation de Cantacuzène," Χαριστήριον εἰς 'Αναστάσιον K. 'Ορλάνδον I (Athens, 1965), 278–98.

[22] D. M. Nicol, *The Byzantine Family of Kantakouzenos (Cantacuzenus), ca. 1100–1460. A Genealogical and Prosopographical Study*, DOS 11 (Washington, D.C., 1968), 32; G. Weiss, *Joannes Kantakuzenos—Aristokrat, Staatsmann, Kaiser und Mönch—in der Gesellschaftsentwicklung von Byzanz im 14. Jahrhundert* (Wiesbaden, 1969), 91–92; *PLP* 5 (1981), 86–98.

[23] J. F. Boissonade, *Anecdota Nova* (Hildesheim, 1844), 29, let. 24; J. Verpeaux, "Notes prosopographiques sur la famille Choumnos," *Byzantinoslavica* 20 (1959) 252–66; *idem, Nicéphore Choumnos, homme d'état et humaniste byzantin (ca. 1250/55–1327)* (Paris, 1959), 45 n. 4.

[24] For the family's role in the Iviron's foundation see J. Lefort, et al., *Actes de Iviron* I. *Des origines au milieu XIe siècle* (Paris, 1985), 9–10, 15–18. Theodore Mouzalon was buried at the Nicaean monastery in 1294; see Pachymeres, *De Andronico Palaeologo* 31: ed. I. Bekker, Bonn ed. (1835), II, 193; *PLP* 8 (1986),

monastery of the Virgin τῆς Καντακουζηνῆς (sic) that is thought to have stood in or near Thessaloniki around 1302.[25] Aristocratic donation of churches is only a little more evident and often took place on the Serbian frontier. Thomas Komnenos Prealympos (Preljoub) with his wife Maria Doukaina Palaeologina built the church of the Panagia Γαβαλλιώτισσα at Vodena (Edessa) in the 1360s, and the father of John Kappadox refounded a church of H. Georgios at Zintzos (Sitochorion, near Achinos) also around mid-century.[26] Private monasteries seem to have been offered almost as frequently by families of lesser renown.[27]

The imperial Palaeologoi similarly held material interests in the province and were active monastic donors in Asia Minor and the capital. Apart from Mount Athos, however, examples of their benefaction in Macedonia are as difficult to establish as for the aristocracy.[28] Most of Thessaloniki's imperial monasteries were apparently pre-Palaeologan foundations.[29] The Pantodynamos Monastery in that city was associated with Michael VIII, but any imperial support he may have offered was clearly secondary to the patronage of the metropolitan Theodore Kerameas, who founded and endowed the complex before 1284.[30] Within the larger context of ecclesiastical affairs, such isolated examples only reinforce the general absence of imperial foundations in the province.

44–45 no. 19439. The Pinkernissa Anna Tornikina later donated alienated lands to the Athonite Pantokrator: P. Lemerle, G. Dragon, and S. Ćirković, *Actes de Saint-Pantéléêmôn* (Paris, 1982), 100–105, no. 12 (1358).

[25] P. Lemerle, et al., *Actes de Lavra* II. *De 1204 à 1328* (Paris, 1977), 119–121 no. 93 (1302). The document, a *praktikon* of Demetrios Apelmene, concerns former properties of the monastery at Agathes and Karalevka, which suggests that the foundation may have been abandoned at this time. See F. Dölger, "Aus dem Wirtschaftsleben eines Frauenklosters in der byzantinischen Provinz," in *Festschrift für Heinrich Felix Schmid* (Vienna, 1956), 11–17, repr. in *idem*, ΠΑΡΑΣΠΟΡΑ (Munich, 1961), 350–57; Nicol, *The Byzantine Family of Kantakouzenos* (note 22 above), 23 associates the foundation with Anna Palaeologina Kantakouzena.

[26] P. Lemerle, et al., *Actes de Lavra* III. *De 1329 à 1500* (Paris, 1979), 100–107 nos. 146–47 (both 1375); J. Lefort, *Actes de Esphigménou* (Paris, 1973), 157–64 no. 27 (1365). For Kappadox see *PLP* 5 (1981), 105 no. 11051. Among the best-known examples of Middle Byzantine patronage is Alexios Komnenos' founding in 1164 of the church of H. Panteleimon at Nerezi.

[27] For example, in 1339 Ypomone gave to the Mount Menoikion Prodromos the small monastery of H. Georgios ὁ Κρυονερίτης that her husband had founded, together with lands, animals, vessels, and books; see A. Guillou, ed., *Les archives de Saint-Jean-Prodrome sur le mont Ménécée* (Paris, 1955), 110–113 no. 34.

[28] The parents of Theodora Palaeologina Philanthropene were known as *ktetores* of the Athonite Philotheos; see V. Kravari, "Nouveaux documents du monastère de Philothéou," *TM* 10 (1987), 261–356, at 315–23 no. 6 [1376]); for other examples of imperial patronage see Lemerle, et al., *Actes de Saint-Pantéléêmôn* (note 24 above), 96–100, no. 11 (1353), 115–17, no. 15 (1375).

[29] The Vasilikon apparently dates from before the early thirteenth century, when it was transformed by Epirot patronage into a convent for women; see P. Magdalino, "Some Additions and Corrections to the List of Byzantine Churches and Monasteries in Thessalonica," *REB* 35 (1977), 277–85, at 277–79. The βασιλικῆς μονῆς τοῦ Καίσαρος is now attested as early as 1300; see Lemerle, et al., *Actes de Lavra* II (note 25 above), 77–95 no. 90; cf. P. Schreiner, "Zwei unedierte Praktika aus der zweiten Häfte des 14. Jahrhunderts," *JÖB* 19 (1970), 33–49, at 34–35; Lefort, *La Chalcidique occidentale* (note 3 above), 183–85.

[30] For Theodore Kerameas and the Pantodynamos see *PLP* 5 (1981), 172 no. 11638; Lemerle, et al., *Actes de Lavra* II (note 25 above), 27–33 no. 75; cf. IV (Paris, 1982), 205. This inclusion of an imperial *ktetor* for honorific reasons anticipates the naming of John VI Kantakouzenos in the Serres Prodromos typikon (Guillou, ed., *Les archives de Saint-Jean-Prodrome* [note 27 above], 173–74). At Molyvdoskepastos, on the frontier

A second reasonable expectation could be drawn from earlier practice, i.e., that aristocratic monasteries should appear concentrated in the cities of Macedonia. While lacking clear urban criteria, the late Byzantine "city" can be understood as a residential, commercial, and administrative center which often served as the seat of a bishop. So defined, such settlements as Ohrid, Christoupolis, Serres, and Philippi offer few examples of aristocratic patronage.[31] The most extensive evidence comes from Veroia, located toward the southern edge of the Macedonian plain. In the 1320s the skouterios Theodore Sarantenos with his wife Eudokia founded a monastery of the Prodomos to represent this highest level of local nobility.[32] The nearby monastery of George Sphrantze, which is traditionally associated with the lost H. Nikolaos church, offers a second contemporary example.[33] Secular support otherwise appears mostly limited to votive foundations like the small church of the Anastasis endowed by Xenos Psalidas and Euphrosine in 1315.[34] Among other well-known surviving monuments is the church of the Bogorodica Peribleptos (the present St. Clement) in Ohrid, built by Progonos Sgouros with his wife Eudokia in the late thirteenth century.[35]

These apparent departures from an established Middle Byzantine tradition of aristocratic religious patronage raise certain questions. One obvious concern is methodological: the validity of this sample of known foundations depends on minimizing any distortions in its composition. The important factors which certainly affect any survey of Macedonian monasteries include variable survival rates for both documents and buildings. In addition, literary sources are naturally more abundant for the cities of the province while rural foun-

---

of Epiros, the Koimesis church preserves an inscription identifying its restoration by Andronikos (II?) Palaeologos; see D. Nicol, "The Churches of Molyvdoskepastos," *BSA* 48 (1953), 141–53.

[31] The problem of distinguishing cities from lesser settlements in late Byzantium is discussed in Charanis, "Town and Country" (note 16 above), 129–37; Bryer, "The Late Byzantine Monastery" (note 1 above), 221–23; *idem*, "The Structure of the Late Byzantine Town: *Diokismos* and the *Mesoi*," in *Continuity and Change* (note 6 above), 263–79; M. Angold, "The Shaping of the Medieval Byzantine 'City'," *ByzF* 10 (1985), 1–37, at 24–37; W. Müller-Wiener, "Von der Polis zum Kastron. Wandlungen der Stadt im Ägäischen Raum von der Antike zum Mittelalter," *Gymnasium* 93 (1986), 435–75, at 463–75.

[32] J. Darrouzès, *Les regestes des actes du Patriarcat de Constantinople* I. *Les actes des Patriarches*, Fasc. V. *Les regestes de 1310 à 1376* (Paris, 1977), 83 no. 2112 (1324), 110 no. 2150 (1329); G. Ch. Chionides, Ἱστορία τῆς Βεροίας τῆς πόλεως καὶ τῆς περιοχῆς II (Thessaloniki, 1970), 188–89. Eudochia supervised construction while Theodore was in Constantinople. The Sarantenoi also held family estates near present Tagarades; e.g., Lemerle, et al., *Actes de Lavra* II (note 25 above), 77–95 no. 90 (1300), 180–278 nos. 108–109 (both 1321); and in general G. I. Theocharides, Μία διαθήκη καὶ μία δίκη βυζαντινή (Thessaloniki, 1972).

[33] Chionides, Ἱστορία τῆς Βεροίας II (note 32 above), 184.

[34] Chionides, Ἱστορία τῆς Βεροίας II (note 32 above), 177–79, cf. 131; S. Pelekanides, Καλλιέργης, ὅλης Θετταλίας ἄριστος ζωγράφος (Athens, 1973); M. Panayotidi, "Les églises de Véria, en Macédoine," *Corsi-Rav* 22 (1975), 303–15, at 309–13. It remains uncertain whether this foundation is related to the local monastery of Christ Soter, of which rights of *ephoreia* were first given to the hieromonk Ignatios Kalothetos in 1314; see Lemerle, et al., *Actes de Lavra* II (note 25 above), 159–61 no. 103, renewed III (note 26 above), 13–14 no. 121 (1330) = Darrouzès, *Les regestes* V (note 32 above), 15 no. 2018, cf. 119–20 no. 2161.

[35] H. Hallensleben, "Die architekturgeschichtliche Stellung der Kirche Sv. Bogorodica Peribleptos (Sv. Kliment) in Ohrid," *Mélanges Dimče Koco* (= *Zbornik Arheološki musej na Makedonija* 6–7, 1975), 297–316, with earlier literature. Kastoria preserves several inscribed donations among its churches, including the H. Athanasios τοῦ Μουζάκη of 1383/84; see A. K. Orlandos, "Ὁ Ἅγ. Ἀθανάσιος," Ἀρχεῖον τῶν βυζαντινῶν μνημείων τῆς Ἑλλάδος 4 (1938), 147–58; and now S. Pelekanides and M. Chatzidakis, *Kastoria* (Athens, 1985), 106–107; cf. *PLP* 8 (1986), 43 no. 19425.

dations are significantly less well attested; historical texts, when preserved, tend to speak more often of catastrophe by fire or external attack than of endowment. The physical continuity of monuments is further conditioned by later historical factors: those structures which found adaptive reuse in Ottoman times were most likely to survive.[36]

Yet the paucity of aristocratic patronage is only half the story. Despite intrinsic limitations, the available evidence attests the relatively greater activity of patrons of non-aristocratic rank, especially those who were associated with the Church. The distinction between these two broad categories of donors is not always easy to maintain, especially in light of the fluid boundaries of a complex, socially mobile culture. Nevertheless, in monastic patronage one can usefully differentiate between individual or family enterprises marked by dynastic burials and typika structured to maintain kinship ties on the one hand, and on the other the foundations of clerics or career monastics, especially those who resided at one time or another on Mount Athos.[37] Abundant evidence attests the latters' activities in this area. The μονή Ταξιάρχου Τσούκας still stands in the remote fastness of western Macedonia, not far from Kastoria. An inscription links its foundation around the turn of the fourteenth century with the monks Nikephoros, Iakovos, and Andronikos, who may also have erected ἐκ βά-θρων the nearby church of H. Georgios at Omorphokklesia.[38] At Monasterion, in the northern district of Morihovon, John the deacon and chartularios of the archbishop dedicated the three-aisled katholikon of H. Nikolaos in 1271.[39] The Prodromos Monastery on Mount Menoikion outside Serres was founded ca. 1300 by the bishop of Ezora, Ioannikios: the *ktētor* was buried within the katholikon endowed by his nephew (later metropolitan of Zichnai), Ioakeim, in his typikon of 1324.[40] Two similar donations are known near Serres: the hieromonk Theodosios Melissenos founded the monastery of H. Nikolaos τῆς Καμενικαίας before 1304, and the hieromonk Hyakinthos established the Nea Mone before 1353.[41]

[36] Concerning the problems of source survival see Darrouzès, "Le mouvement des fondations monastiques" (note 12 above), 171–74. Conditions surrounding the reuse of certain Macedonian churches are discussed in M. Kiel, *Art and Society of Bulgaria in the Turkish Period* (Assen/Maastricht, 1985), 167–77.

[37] Darrouzès, "Le mouvement des fondations monastiques" (note 12 above), 174–76; Galatariotou, "Byzantine Ktetorika Typika" (note 11 above). The problem of differentiation is illustrated by the hieromonk Matthew Perdikarios' transfer of his H. Triados Monastery in Thessaloniki to his three sons, the monks Dionysios, Ioannikios, and Maximos (Lemerle, et al., *Actes de Lavra* II [note 25 above], 1–4 no. 70 [1240]); or Ioannitzes Vardas, also known as the hieromonk Joseph, who built and decorated with his own hands the Ἄσπρη Ἐκκλησία at Selada (*ibid.*, 43–45 no. 78 [1285]).

[38] P. Tsamisis, Ἡ Καστορία καὶ τὰ μνημεῖα της (Athens, 1949), 121; D. M. Nicol, "Two Churches of Western Macedonia," *BZ* 49 (1956), 96–105, at 99–100 (apparently dating to 1285 or 1301).

[39] D. Koco and P. Miljković-Pepek, *Manastir* (Skopje, 1958); V. J. Djurić, *Byzantinische Fresken in Jugoslawien* (Munich, 1976), 21, 239 n. 12 associates the church with John Pediasimos.

[40] *PLP* 4 (1980), 137–38 no. 8372; Guillou, ed., *Les archives de Saint-Jean-Prodrome* (note 27 above), 161–76, Appendix I; Darrouzès, *Les regestes* V (note 32 above), 91–92 no. 2121 (1324), 101–102 no. 2135 (1327); Lefort, *Paysages de Macédoine* (note 3 above), 208. For the building see H. Hallensleben, "Das Katholikon des Johannes-Prodromos-Klosters bei Serrai," *Polychordia. Festschrift Franz Dölger zum 75. Geburtstag* I (= *ByzF* 1, 1966), 158–73. Ioannikios had also granted the small monastery of H. Georgios Paryakos, located on the Strymon lake, to the Athonite Esphigmenou Monastery; see Lefort, *Actes de Esphigménou* (note 26 above), 153–55 no. 25 (1358).

[41] *PLP* 7 (1985), 198 no. 17815; Petit and Korablev, *Actes de Chilandar* (note 17 above), 150–51 no. 64 (1321), although the monastery of H. Nikolaos is known as early as 45–46 no. 20 (1304); *ibid.*, 295–97 no. 140 (1353) for the testament of Hyakinthos.

In Veroia the bishop Makarios has been credited with erecting the church of HH. Kyriakos kai Ioulitte, probably late in the thirteenth century.[42] All of these examples suggest that the Church played an active role in religious sponsorship across the province.

This evidence of clerical support for regional monasteries appears throughout Macedonia and especially at Mount Athos, but the sources are too thinly preserved and too poorly studied to clarify its source or direction.[43] The only opportunity to refine this pattern seems to be in Thessaloniki, which constitutes the best documented corner of the province. While not without certain deficiencies, the data from this primary urban center can be interrogated by direct and indirect means to shed light on local monastic affairs. Contemporary sources record at least twelve local foundations that were established or renewed between 1280 and 1400, and many other monasteries are first attested in fourteenth- and fifteenth-century documents. Several of these can be identified with structures that still stand in the city, including the Peribleptos, Vlatadon, and Nea Mone.[44] These monuments attest an age of monastic patronage that dawned in the early Palaeologan city after years of relative quiet, an efflorescence that appears distinctive within both its Macedonian context and the wider Palaeologan frame.

As observed in outlying parts of the province, the foremost class of monastic patron known in Constantinople and across the late empire is poorly represented in Palaeologan Thessaloniki. The city's best-known aristocratic monasteries apparently date from the eleventh and twelfth centuries.[45] The Akapnios was founded ca. 1018 by St. Photios of Thessaly, apparently with the support of this well-known Macedonian family.[46] The renowned monastery of Christ Παντοκράτορος τοῦ Φιλοκάλου is attested as early as 1112.[47] The

[42] Chionides, Ἱστορία τῆς Βεροίας II (note 32 above), 176–77; for the date cf. Ch. Mauropoulou-Tsioume, Ἑλληνικά 24 (1971), 465–67; Panayotidi, "Les églises de Veria" (note 34 above), 314–15; Ἀρχ.Δελτ. 27 Χρονικά Β′ 2 (1972), 553–54; 28 Χρονικά Β′ 2 (1973), 483–85.

[43] For examples of clerical patronage at Mount Athos see, e.g., P. Lemerle, Actes de Kutlumus² (Paris, 1988), 76–79 no. 16 (1330); Oikonomidès, Actes de Docheiariou (note 18 above), 133–38 no. 17 (ca. 1330/31, referring to events of ca. 1294/95), 248–50 no. 46 (1378); Lefort, Actes de Esphigménou (note 26 above), 160.

[44] The late Byzantine churches of Thessaloniki are discussed in Ch. Diehl, M. le Tourneau, and H. Saladin, Les monuments chrétiens de Salonique (Paris, 1918); P. L. Vokotopoulos, "Οἱ μεσαιωνικοὶ ναοὶ τῆς Θεσσαλονίκης καὶ ἡ θέση τους στὰ πλαίσια τῆς βυζαντινῆς ναοδομίας," Ἡ Θεσσαλονίκη μεταξὺ Ἀνατολῆς καὶ Δύσεως, Πρακτικὰ συμποσίου τεσσαρακονταετηρίδος τῆς Ἑταιρείας Μακεδονικῶν Σπουδῶν (Thessaloniki, 1982), 97–110. For the written sources see R. Janin, La géographie ecclésiastique de l'empire byzantin, II, Les églises et les monastères des grands centres byzantins (Paris, 1975), 341–456. An initial review of sources is offered by M. L. Rautman, "Patrons and Buildings in Late Byzantine Thessaloniki," JÖB 39 (1989), 295–315. The other monasteries of the Palaeologan city will be discussed elsewhere.

[45] Local churches also shared in this private beneficence, as is best illustrated by the construction by Christophoros, protospatharios and katepano of Langobardy, with his family of the present Panagia Chalkeon in 1028; see J.-M. Spieser, "Inventaires en vue d'un recueil des inscriptions historiques de Byzance. I. Les inscriptions de Thessalonique," TM 5 (1973), 145–80, at 163–64, no. 13. A related case may be a lost church built by the εὐγενέστατος Ἰωάννης Κομνηνός (P. N. Papageorgiou, "Ἀρχαία εἰκὼν τοῦ Ἁγίου Δημητρίου τοῦ πολιούχου Θεσσαλονίκης ἐπὶ ἐλεφαντοστέου," BZ 1 [1892] 479–87, at 485).

[46] V. Grumel, "Le fondateur et la date de fondation du monastère thessalonicien d'Acapniou," EO 30 (1931) 91–95; Janin, Grands centres (note 44 above), 347–49.

[47] Oikonomidès, Actes de Docheiariou (note 18 above), 60–73 no. 3 (1112); G. I. Theocharides, "Μία ἐξαφανισθεῖσα σημαντικὴ μονὴ τῆς Θεσσαλονίκης. Ἡ μονὴ Φιλοκάλλη," Μακεδονικά 21 (1981), 319–48.

Mastunes Theotokos is known from a colophon of 1185.[48] By contrast, in late Byzantine times secular donors seem to have played a less obvious role in monastic benefaction. Despite the enormous wealth, extensive urban properties, and social prominence of these families, local foundations preserve few traces of their material support. Local aristocratic interest in religious philanthropy was for the most part directed elsewhere, primarily to Constantinople and Mount Athos.

Several conspicuous examples illustrate this surprising tendency during a period of otherwise intensive monastic activity. Theodore Metochites, court minister and chancellor to Andronikos II, represented the emperor in Thessaloniki from 1303 to 1305 but turned to monastic sponsorship only after 1316 with his restoration of the celebrated Chora in Constantinople.[49] Nikephoros Choumnos was kephale of Thessaloniki in 1309–1310, but he also undertook support of a Constantinopolitan monastery at the Theotokos Gorgoepekoos.[50] Irene Choumnaina held properties in Thessaloniki, near Serres-Zichnai, and in Thrace, but refounded and lavishly endowed the Philanthropos Monastery in the capital.[51] Both Irene Palaeologina (Yolanda of Montferrat) and Anna Palaeologina (Anne of Savoy) resided in the city, but neither showed any interest in local monasteries.[52] The Kantakouzenos family, while possessing extensive holdings around Thessaloniki as well as Serres, similarly preferred to focus its patronage in Constantinople and on Mount Athos.[53]

[48] P. N. Papageorgiou, "Περὶ χειρογράφου εὐαγγελίου Θεσσαλονίκης," *BZ* 6 (1897), 538–46, at 542–43; Janin, *Grands centres* (note 44 above), 396.

[49] I. Ševčenko, "Theodore Metochites, the Chora, and the Intellectual Trends of his Time," in *The Kariye Djami* IV, ed. P. A. Underwood (Princeton, 1975), 19–91 at 90–91; R. G. Ousterhout, *The Architecture of the Kariye Camii in Istanbul*, DOS 25 (Washington, D.C., 1987). Metochites records that his work at the Chora was prompted by Andronikos.

[50] V. Laurent, "Une fondation monastique de Nicéphore Choumnos. Ἡ ἐν ΚΠ μονὴ τῆς Θεοτόκου τῆς Γοργοεπηκόου," *REB* 12 (1954), 32–44; I. Ševčenko, *Études sur la polémique entre Théodore Métochite et Nicéphore Choumnos* (Brussels, 1962), 278–79.

[51] Gregoras, *Byzantina Historia* XXIX, 21–22: ed. I. Bekker, Bonn ed. (1855) III, 237–39; Pachymeres, *De Andronico Palaeologo* IV, 7: Bonn ed. II, 287–90; V. Laurent, "Une princesse byzantine au cloître. Irène-Eulogie Choumnos Paléologine, fondatrice du couvent de femmes τοῦ Φιλανθρώπου Σωτῆρος," *EO* 29 (1930), 29–60; A. C. Hero, "Irene-Eulogia Choumnaina Palaiologina, Abbess of the Convent of Philanthropos Soter in Constantinople," *ByzF* 9 (1985), 119–47.

[52] Irene stayed in the city from 1303 to 1317 (Gregoras, *Byzantina Historia* VII, 5 [Bonn ed. I, 233–244]; Pachymeres, *De Andronico Palaeologo* V, 5 (Bonn ed. II, 378–79]), and Anna lived there from 1351 to ca. 1365 (R. J. Loenertz, "Chronologie de Nicolas Cabasilas, 1345–1354," *OCP* 21 [1955] 205–31, at 216–20); for the latter's secular building projects see Spieser, "Les inscriptions de Thessalonique" (note 45 above), 175–76 no. 28 (1356).

[53] Thessaloniki's monastery τῆς Καντακουζηνῆς may have been inactive at the time it was acquired by the Lavra monastery in 1302 (Lemerle, et al., *Actes de Lavra* II [note 25 above], 119–21 no. 93). The Kantakouzenoi held interests in the Constantinopolitan monastery of Kyra Martha, and during his retirement after 1354 John Kantakouzenos retired to the monasteries of H. Georgios at the Mangana and the Theotokos Peribleptos in the capital (Nicol, *The Byzantine Family of Kantakouzenos* [note 22 above], 94–95; R. Janin, *La géographie ecclésiastique de l'empire byzantin* I. *Le siège de Constantinople et le Patriarcat Oecuménique*, III, *Les églises et les monastères* [2nd edition, Paris, 1969], 218–22, 324–26). Theodora Kantakouzena gave the Eleousa monydrion near Serres to Kutlumus in 1338 (Lemerle, *Actes de Kutlumus²* (note 43 above), 82–87, 353–55 no. 18). This example was followed by others throughout the fourteenth century: e.g., Lefort, *Actes de Esphigménou* (note 26 above), 76–80 no. 10 (1301); Lemerle, *Actes de Kutlumus²*, 50–53, 330–32

When documented at all, examples of secular or aristocratic benefaction in Thessaloniki appear isolated and relatively modest by Palaeologan standards.[54] Demetrios Tzerigges, for example, is known to have rebuilt a monydrion of H. Ioannes Theologos in the third quarter of the fourteenth century, which he later gave to the Nea Mone.[55] It seems especially revealing that such donations frequently originated outside the city—indeed, beyond the boundaries of the province itself. The imperial protostrator Michael Glabas Tarchaneiotes with his wife Maria restored the small parekklesion of H. Euthymios by 1303.[56] The Serbian king Milutin maintained close ties with Irene's court in Thessaloniki, married her daughter Simonis, and established or renewed several local foundations between 1282 and 1321.[57] The only clear example of locally based monastic patronage occurs later in the century when Makarios Choumnos, himself apparently a member of the secular clergy, established the Nea Mone around 1360.[58]

This relative neglect appears striking within the larger Byzantine context, for the very evolution of the proprietary monastery had in many respects been directed by aristocratic interests. As in outlying Macedonia, in Thessaloniki the resulting vacuum was filled at least in part by patrons whose primary social identity was not with the secular, propertied elites but with the Church.[59] An early example is the hieromonk Matthew Perdikarios, who

no. 8 (1313), 97–99, 363–64 no. 24 (1362), 132–34, 382–84 no. 35 (1377); D. Papachryssanthou, *Actes de Xénophon* (Paris, 1986), 204–207 no. 28 (1348), 210–14 no. 30 (1364); Petit and Korablev, *Actes de Chilandar* (note 17 above), 216–17 no. 105 (1325); Kravari, "Nouveaux documents du monastère de Philothéou" (note 28 above), 315–23 no. 6 (1376). Antonios Kantakouzenos is credited with founding the monastery of H. Stephanos at Meteora before 1400; see in general D. M. Nicol, *Meteora. The Rock Monasteries of Thessaly*, 2nd edition (London, 1975); Koder and Hild, *Hellas und Thessalia* (note 4 above), 219–20. Like Athos, this important Thessalian enclave deserves further discussion.

[54] For lands, buildings, and monydria donated to local monasteries see, e.g., Alexios Angelos Philanthropenos' assignments to the Nea Mone (Lemerle, et al., *Actes de Lavra* III (note 26 above), 116–21 nos. 150–51 (1384, 1389).

[55] Lemerle, et al., *Actes de Lavra* III (note 26 above), 125–28 no. 153 (1392).

[56] Spieser, "Les inscriptions de Thessalonique" (note 45 above), 167–68 no. 19; T. Gouma-Peterson, "The Parecclesion of St. Euthymios in Thessalonica: Art and Monastic Policy under Andronicus II," *ArtB* 58 (1976) 168–83; H. Belting, C. Mango, and D. Mouriki, *The Mosaics and Frescoes of St. Mary Pammakaristos (Fethiye Camii) at Istanbul*, DOS 15 (Washington, D.C., 1978), 14.

[57] Milutin's building activities in Thessaloniki included churches of H. Nikolaos, H. Georgios, and a small monastery of Holy Jerusalem, as well as one or more residences; see Petit and Korablev, *Actes de Chilandar* (note 17 above), 53–55 no. 25 (1309); A. Xyngopoulos, "L'église de Saint Nicolas Orphanos et les constructions du kral Miloutine à Thessalonique," *Balkan Studies* 6 (1965), 181–85; Magdalino, "Some Additions and Corrections" (note 29 above), 283–84; L. Mavromatis, *La fondation de l'empire serbe. Le kralj Milutin*, Βυζαντινὰ κείμενα καὶ μελέται 16 (Thessaloniki, 1978), 59–62; S. Kissas, "Srpski srednjovekovni spomenici u Solunu," *Zograf* 11 (1980), 29–43.

[58] V. Laurent, "Une nouvelle fondation monastique des Choumnos: La Néa Moni de Thessalonique," *REB* 13 (1955), 109–27; G. I. Theocharides, "Ἡ Νέα Μονὴ Θεσσαλονίκης," Μακεδονικά 3 (1953–1955), 334–52; with further sources in Janin, *Grands centres* (note 44 above), 398–99. The Nea Mone has been identified with the present church of the Prophetis Elias; see G. I. Theocharides, "Δύο νέα ἔγγραφα ἀφορῶντα εἰς τὴν Νέαν Μονὴν Θεσσαλονίκης," Μακεδονικά 4 (1955–56), 315–51.

[59] Of course, some of these clerical donors may indeed have come from the great landed families of the province, e.g., Makarios Choumnos and the monk Arsenios Tzamplakon (Petit and Korablev, *Actes de Chilandar* (note 17 above), 256–58 no. 123 [1333]; cf. F. Dölger, *BZ* 31 [1931] 451). Several of the period's best-

founded a monastery of the Trinity in Thessaloniki sometime before 1240.[60] The monastery of the Theotokos τοῦ ʿΥπομιμνῄσκωντος was apparently founded by a metropolitan officer in the 1200s and is attested as late as the sixteenth century.[61] Theodore Kerameas, the former metropolitan of Thessaloniki, established the monastery of Christ Pantodynamos during his episcopate sometime before 1284.[62] The monastery of the Theotokos Peribleptos, whose katholikon still stands as the church of H. Panteleimon, is associated with Iakovos, metropolitan in the 1290s, who apparently retired there under the name Isaac.[63] The monk Laurentios Kladon erected a convent in honor of the Virgin near the Hippodrome before 1324.[64] The present church of the HH. Apostoloi once served a monastery in western Thessaloniki; epigraphic evidence suggests that it was a metropolitan initiative begun before 1310, continued until early 1314 by the Patriarch of Constantinople Niphon, and completed by its δεύτερος κτήτωρ the hegoumenos Paul.[65] Dorotheos and Markos Vlates founded or refounded a monastery of Christ Pantokrator in the upper city toward mid-century.[66] Makarios Choumnos' work at the Nea Mone was continued by the priest and later metropolitan Gabriel as its second donor.[67]

Significantly, most of these sponsors can be traced to the city's clergy. Local churchmen are also known to have commissioned manuscripts, as did the Philokalos monastery's skeuphylax of Theodore Hagiopetrites around 1291.[68] Such patronage of the liturgical arts by

known saints came from upper-class backgrounds, as discussed in A. E. Laiou-Thomadakis, "Saints and Society in the Late Byzantine Empire," in *Charanis Studies* (note 18 above), 84–114, at 87–88. In the realm of monastic patronage, however, the written sources preserve few such names.

[60] Lemerle, et al., *Actes de Lavra* II (note 25 above), 1–4 no. 70 (1240).

[61] J. Darrouzès, "Obits et colophons," Χαριστήριον εἰς ᾿Αναστάσιον Κ. ᾿Ορλάνδον I (Athens, 1965), 299–313, at 301, 308; Janin, *Grands centres* (note 44 above), 413–14.

[62] Note 30 above.

[63] *PLP* 4 (1980), 87 no. 7905; G. I. Theocharides, "ʿΟ Ματθαῖος Βλάσταρις καὶ ἡ μονὴ τοῦ κῦρ- ᾿Ισαὰκ ἐν Θεσσαλονίκῃ," *Byzantion* 40 (1970), 437–59; Janin, *Grands centres* (note 44 above), 386–88.

[64] *PLP* 5 (1981), 187 no. 11768; Papachryssanthou, *Actes de Xénophon* (note 53 above), 162–66 no. 20 (1324); cf. 197–200 no. 26 (1343) where this or a similar monastery is identified as a metropolitan foundation.

[65] Spieser, "Les inscriptions de Thessalonique" (note 45 above), 169–70 no. 22.

[66] *PLP* 2 (1977), 81 nos. 2818–2819; G. A. Stogioglou, ʿΗ ἐν Θεσσαλονίκῃ πατριαρχικὴ μονὴ τῶν Βλατάδων, ᾿Ανάλεκτα Βλατάδων 12 (Thessaloniki, 1971); and for further sources Janin, *Grands centres* (note 44 above), 356–58. Recent excavations conducted around the Vlatadon katholikon make it clear that the structure was rebuilt by the brothers Vlates in the third quarter of the fourteenth century. Their incorporation of foundations and parts of the floor and rising walls of the earlier church suggests that the donors refounded an earlier monastery. For reports see E. Chatzetryphonos, "Τὸ μαρμαροθετημένο δάπεδο στὸ νότιο παρεκκλήσι τοῦ καθολικοῦ τῆς μονῆς Βλατάδων," Κληρονομία 14 (1982), 375–406; Ch. Mavropoulou-Tsioumi, "Οἱ τοιχογραφίες τῆς Μονῆς Βλατάδων, τελευταία ἀναλαμπή τῆς βυζαντινῆς ζωγραφικῆς στὴ Θεσσαλονίκη," ʿΗ Θεσσαλονίκη 1 (1985), 231–54; D. Makropoulou, "᾿Από το ὑστεροβυζαντινό νεκροταφείο τῆς μονῆς Βλατάδων," ʿΗ Θεσσαλονίκη 1 (1985), 255–309.

[67] *PLP* 2 (1977), 134–35 no. 3416; V. Laurent, "Le métropolite de Thessalonique Gabriel (1397–1416/19) et le couvent de la NEA MONH," ῾Ελληνικά 13 (1954), 241–55; Janin, *Grands centres* (note 44 above), 398–99.

[68] A. Turyn, *Dated Greek Manuscripts of the Thirteenth and Fourteenth Centuries in the Libraries of Great Britain*, DOS 17 (Washington, D.C., 1980), 60–62; R. S. Nelson, "Theodore Hagiopetrites and Thessaloniki," *JÖB* 32/4 = *XVI. Internationaler Byzantinistenkongress. Akten II/4* (Vienna, 1982), 79–85.

Hypomimneskontos	founded	13th century	metropolitan official
Christ Pantodynamos	founded	before 1284	Metropolitan Theodore Kerameas
Theotokos Peribleptos	re-founded	1290s	Metropolitan Iakovos
Holy Jerusalem	founded	ca. 1310?	Milutin
HH. Apostoloi katholikon	(re-?)built	ca. 1310–14	(Metropolitan Malachias and ?) Patriarch Niphon
Dovrosontos	re-founded	ca. 1310–14	Patriarch Niphon
Taxiarchai katholikon	built	early 14th century	?
H. Nikolaos Orphanos katholikon?	built	early 14th century	? (Milutin?)
H. Aikaterini katholikon	built	early 14th century	?
Theotokos near Hippodrome	founded	before 1324	Laurentios Kladon
H. Ioannes Theologos	rebuilt	1352–76	Demetrios Tzerigges
Mone Vlatadon	(re-?)founded	1355–75	Markos and Dorotheos Vlates
Nea Mone	founded	ca. 1360	Makarios Choumnos; later Gabriel

Table 1. Thessaloniki, late Byzantine monastic foundations and their patrons

the Church establishment is known elsewhere in the Palaeologan state, but its prominence in Thessaloniki's monastic affairs appears unique in the late empire. In total, at least a dozen instances of monastic endowment can be identified in or near the city in the late thirteenth and fourteenth centuries (Table 1). Of these, over half were offered by clerical patrons, while only two or three enjoyed aristocratic support. The sources for other Palaeologan cities reveal a very different picture. Late Byzantine Constantinople saw the foundation or renewal of more than twenty-seven monasteries, but of this total at least twenty-five donations were imperial or aristocratic in origin. Only two were definitely clerical events: the double monastery of Xerolophos founded by the Patriarch Athanasios, and the monastery of the Theotokos τῆς Παυσολύπης, established in the mid-fourteenth century by the monk Kallinikos.[69] Similar patterns of primarily aristocratic and imperial monastic foundation can be noted in Arta, Mistra, and across the late empire.[70]

Despite its obviously approximate nature, the available evidence describes what seems to be an exceptional pattern of religious patronage in late Byzantine Macedonia. Of the nineteen Palaeologan foundations identified in the province, at least thirteen were estab-

[69] Janin, *Constantinople*[2] (note 53 above), 10–11, 217; clarified by A. C. Hero, *A Woman's Quest for Spiritual Guidance* (Brookline, Mass., 1986), 108–109. For the setting of patronage in Constantinople see I. Ševčenko, "Society and Intellectual Life in the Fourteenth Century," in *Actes du XIVᵉ Congrès International d'Études Byzantines, Bucharest 1971*, I (Bucharest, 1974), 69–92, at 80 n. 32.

[70] Bryer, "The Late Byzantine Monastery" (note 1 above), 224; Rautman, "Patrons and Buildings" (note 44 above), 308–309. For the minimal role of bishops in monastic foundation outside of Macedonia see Thomas, *Private Religious Foundations* (note 2 above), 249–50, cf. n. 23.

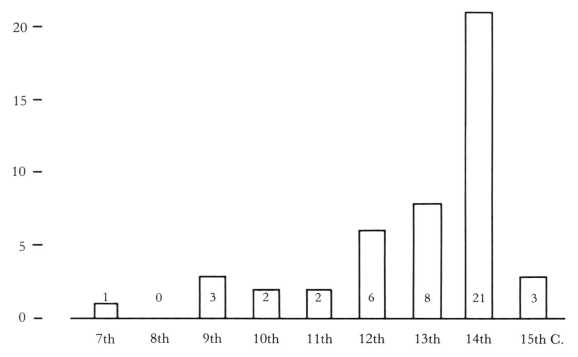

Table 2. Thessaloniki, attested Byzantine monasteries. Earliest testimonia for all identified foundations, by century

lished by clerical donors. In both town and countryside, secular support for regional monasteries tended more toward assigning additional lands to the holdings of previously established foundations. The potential scale of this reorientation in Macedonia's monastic history can be illustrated by tabulating the textual appearances of individual foundations in Thessaloniki (Table 2).[71] At least twenty-two monasteries are attested through the end of the thirteenth century; during the relatively stable period from the tenth through the twelfth century, an average of three new foundations occur among the sources each century. The fourteenth century alone, on the other hand, saw the appearance of over twenty new establishments. Obviously, the mere appearance of a name does not necessarily mean that it was founded at this time, and to some extent the distribution can be attributed to uneven archival conditions. Yet the substantial increase in monastic representation seems too great to ascribe entirely to source survival, especially since the number of extant monuments attributed to the late thirteenth and fourteenth century reflects a similarly sharp rise. Moreover, few of these late Byzantine foundations are known by proper family names. In sum, both textual and physical

---

[71] The patchwork of fragmentary surviving sources ensures that any attempt at quantified analysis will yield only approximate conclusions. As long as this selectivity is kept in mind, these approximations nevertheless can be instructive; see A. Kazhdan and G. Constable, *People and Power in Byzantium* (Washington, D.C., 1982), 176–77; Bryer, "The Late Byzantine Monastery" (note 1 above), 219–21; Abrahamse, "Women's Monasticism" (note 14 above), 36–38; A. E. Laiou, "Observations on the Life and Ideology of Byzantine Women," *ByzF* 9 (1985), 59–102, at 60–62, cf. 72.

evidence points toward the relative neglect of monasteries by the aristocratic families of the province and the prominence of clerical, especially episcopal patrons on their behalf.

Likely reasons for this regional anomaly in late Byzantine patronage lie in the historical setting of Macedonia itself. The absence of secular patrons may best be understood within the destabilized social frame of the province in the early fourteenth century. Its border with Serbia was rarely static: Milutin's southward expansion was continued by Stefan Dušan, whose empire by 1334 included Ohrid, Prilep, and Strumica, was soon extended to Vodena, Kastoria, Lerin, and Albania, and by 1345 included all of Macedonia except maritime Thessaloniki and Christoupolis. In eastern Macedonia and Chalkidiki the Catalan episode of 1308–1310 foreshadowed the greater devastation of civil war in the 1320s and 1340s, when the province's roads became impassable and its cities isolated.[72] These unsettled conditions would hardly have encouraged Palaeologan families to reinforce ties with lands on such a precarious frontier. Against this unstable political background, the increasingly common bequests of fields, orchards, vineyards, and fishponds to Athonite monasteries take on special poignance; the documents frequently mention gifts of already alienated properties and often reflect creative financial arrangements including joint purchase/donation packages.[73]

Conversely, the most active monastic patrons of secular rank were the Serbian rulers, whose donations are well-known at Athos as well as in Thessaloniki.[74] Their support of regional monasteries may be seen not only as expressions of personal religious devotion but as part of a concerted effort through gift exchange to reinforce cultural and political ties with the province.[75] Palaeologan officials like Kantakouzenos and Choumnos remained ac-

[72] For the historical background see Lemerle, *Philippes et la Macédoine orientale* (note 3 above), 198–213; A. E. Laiou, *Constantinople and the Latins: The Foreign Policy of Andronicus II, 1282–1328* (Cambridge, Mass., 1972), 220–26; Theocharides, Ἱστορία τῆς Μακεδονίας (note 8 above), 367–86; K. M. Setton, "The Catalans in Greece, 1311–1380," *A History of the Crusades*, eds. K. M. Setton and H. W. Hazard (Madison, 1975), 167–224; N. Oikonomidès, "Οἱ δύο σερβικὲς κατακτήσεις τῆς Χαλκιδικῆς τὸν ΙΔ' αἰ.," Δίπτυχα 2 (1980–1981), 294–99.

[73] Perhaps not coincidentally, many of these properties were sold or donated by women, e.g., Papachryssan-thou, *Actes de Xénophon* (note 53 above), 111–16 no. 10 (1315), 210–14 no. 30 (1364); W. Regel, E. Kurtz, and B. Korablev, *Actes de Zographou* (St. Petersburg, 1907), 64–68 no. 28 (1330); Petit and Korablev, *Actes de Chilandar* (note 17 above), 155–58 no. 69 (1321), 206–207 no. 98 (1324), 207–208 no. 99 (1324), 218–20 no. 106 (1326), 222–23 no. 108 (1326); N. Oikonomidès, *Actes de Dionysiou* (Paris, 1968), 110–14 no. 19 (1420); Lemerle, et al., *Actes de Saint-Pantéléèmôn* (note 24 above), 100–105 no. 12 (1358); Lemerle, et al., *Actes de Lavra* III (note 26 above), 108–12 no. 148 (1377), 206–209 Appendix XII (1341); Guillou, ed., *Les archives de Saint-Jean-Prodrome* (note 27 above) 110–13 no. 34; Lefort, *La Chalcidique occidentale* (note 3 above), passim. This conforms to a pattern noted elsewhere in the fragmented late empire; see, e.g., Charanis, "On the Social Structure" (note 16 above), 111–12.

[74] E.g., Lemerle, et al., *Actes de Lavra* III (note 26 above), 35–39 no. 128 (1347), 82–85 no. 140 (1361), IV, 177–200 Serbian acts nos. 1–12, cf. 124–32; *idem, Actes de Saint-Pantéléèmôn* (note 24 above), 157–90 Serbian acts nos. 1–15. Cf. G. C. Soulis, "Tzar Stephen Dušan and Mount Athos," in *Essays Dedicated to Francis Dvornik* (Cambridge, Mass., 1954), 125–39; Magdalino, "Some Additions and Corrections" (note 29 above), 283–84.

[75] G. C. Soulis, *The Serbs and Byzantium during the Reign of Tsar Stephen Dušan (1331–1355) and his Successors* (Washington, D.C., 1984). Cf. M. Mauss, *The Gift* (Paris, 1950, London, 1967); Rosenthal, *The Purchase of Paradise* (note 15 above), 123–33.

tive participants in court affairs in Constantinople; Macedonia could hardly offer comparable settings for conspicuous socio-spiritual display or for reinforcing ties of kinship with place. The larger settlements of Serres and Philippi, for example, had never fully recovered from their destruction by John I Asan after 1204. Despite the aggrandizing language of contemporary authors, few other settlements of any substantial size are known.

This disinterest of local landowners distinguishes Macedonia from other provinces of the late empire. To the south in δευτέρα Θετταλία powerful local families continued to endow important establishments in the late thirteenth and early fourteenth centuries. Among the largest monasteries were the well-documented foundations of Hilarion, Prodromos, and Makrinitissa at Nea Petra, which were built around 1271 by Nikolaos Komnenos Doukas Maliasenos with his wife Anna Palaeologina, who owned extensive lands at Dryanoubaene.[76] The great monastery of the Panagia τῶν Μεγάλων Πηλῶν was founded in 1283 by the sebastokrator John I Angelos.[77] Even Veroia enjoyed greater secular support of its churches and monasteries.

A contributing factor may have been the condition in which the monastic infrastructure was left in the wake of the Latin Empire. Eustathios and others speak of the destruction of villages and the despoliation of churches and monasteries in Byzantine lands beginning in the late twelfth century and continuing through the early years of Latin occupation. After twenty years of Frankish rule there was surely ample need for the repair and reconstruction of monasteries throughout the province. In Thessaloniki, the center of Latin authority in the province from 1204 to 1224, this need would have seemed especially acute.[78] On the other hand, the long-term impact of this foreign presence may have been mitigated by fourteenth-century restorations. A comparison of documents from before and after the Latin interlude suggests that most foundations survived in some form the years of Frankish rule. Table 3 summarizes the known testimonia for the city's Middle Byzantine monasteries. Just four foundations are known only before the thirteenth century, and of these only one, the Mastunes Theotokos, is attested in the eleventh or twelfth century but not later; all others, comprising two-thirds of the total, continue to appear in Palaeologan sources. The likely extent of damage to local monasteries in the early 1200s is reflected by a further characteristic of the city: after mid-century monastic patronage in Thessaloniki was directed not just to new foundations but mostly toward the renewal of earlier establishments

[76] *PLP* 7 (1985), 56–57 no. 16523; Koder and Hild, *Hellas und Thessalia* (note 4 above), 224–25; and recently A. Avraméa and D. Feissel, "Inventaires en vue d'un recueil des inscriptions historiques de Byzance. IV. Inscriptions de Thessalie (à l'exception des Météores)," *TM* 10 (1987), 357–98, at 377–79 nos. 19–20 (1274/76 and after 1280).

[77] *PLP* 1 (1976), 18 no. 208; A. K. Orlandos, "Ἡ Πόρτα Παναγιὰ τῆς Θεσσαλίας," Ἀρχεῖον τῶν βυζαντινῶν μνημείων τῆς Ἑλλάδος 1 (1935), 5–40; Koder and Hild, *Hellas und Thessalia* (note 4 above), 245–46; Avraméa and Feissel, "Inscriptions de Thessalie" (note 76 above), 380–81 no. 21 (1283).

[78] Eustathios, "De Thessalonica urbe a Latinis capta narratio," ed. T. L. F. Tafel, *Opuscula* (Frankfurt, 1832), 267–307; Charanis, "Monastic Properties" (note 1 above), 109. For conditions in Thessaloniki during the Latin occupation of the city see O. Tafrali, *Thessalonique, des origines au XIVe siècle* (Paris, 1919), 192–211; R. Janin, "L'église latine à Thessalonique de 1204 à la conquêt turque," *REB* 16 (1958), 206–16; A. E. Vacalopoulos, *A History of Thessaloniki* (Thessaloniki, 1963), 47–50; G. Fedalto, "La chiesa latina nel regno di Tessalonica 1204–1224, 1423–1430," Ἐπ. Ἑτ.Βυζ.Σπ. 41 (1974), 88–102.

7th	8th	9th	10th	11th	12th	13th	14th	15th	16th cent.

H. Matrona

       H. Loukas

       Latomos ————————————————————————————————————

       H. Theodora ————————————————————————————————————

           Akroullios

           Prodromos ——————————————————————————————

                Akapnios ——————————————————————————————

                      Mastunes Theotokos

                      H. Anysia ——————————

                      Vasilikon ——————————

                      Kyr Ioel ————————————

                      H. Vasileos ——————————

                      Theotokos Peribleptos ——————————

                      Philokales ——————————

Table 3. Thessaloniki, pre-Latin monasteries. Range of dated testimonia

(cf. Table 1). This process of reconstruction is clearly attested by documents at the Peribleptos and Dovrosontos, and by archaeology at the Vlatadon; it likely occurred elsewhere as well.[79]

The heightened interest of the Church in local monastic affairs should also be seen in the context of its institutional ascendance in local civic matters. Monastic supervision had always been one of the primary responsibilities of the Church, from the patriarch's office to the level of local bishops, and Athanasios in particular renewed this role.[80] Palaeologan sources record the heightened profile of prelates in adjudicating civil as well as ecclesiastical disputes, attesting donations and wills, and authenticating various documents. While noted throughout the late empire, the growth of metropolitan power is especially clear in Thessaloniki.[81]

The Church's entry into this local monastic renewal appears linked with a convergence of monastic and episcopal concerns that took place at the turn of the fourteenth century. The

[79] Refounding a complex as its second donor could carry full status of patronage; see Zhishman, *Das Stifterrecht* (note 14 above), 11–13, 24; E. Herman, "Ricerche sulle istituzioni monastiche bizantine. Typika ktetorika, caristicari e monasteri 'liberi'," *OCP* 6 (1940), 293–375, at 346–47; Thomas, *Private Religious Foundations* (note 2 above), 252–53. The buildings with their sources are discussed in Rautman, "Patrons and Buildings" (note 44 above).

[80] A.-M. Talbot, *The Correspondence of Athanasius I, Patriarch of Constantinople (1289–1293; 1303–1309)* (Washington, D.C., 1975), 152–59 no. 66, 216–21 no. 83; M. L. Rautman, "Notes on the Metropolitan Succession of Thessaloniki, c. 1300," *REB* 46 (1988), 147–59, at 156–58.

[81] Tafrali, *Thessalonique au quatorzième siècle* (note 3 above), 85–90; Vacalopoulos, *A History* (note 78 above), 53–55; and in general J. M. Hussey, *The Orthodox Church in the Byzantine Empire* (Oxford, 1986), 325–35.

administrative foundations for this synthesis had been laid much earlier by the restructuring of local ecclesiastical affairs under the Latin bishops, who by the Ravennika agreement of 1210 brought all monasteries under episcopal control.[82] This may also reflect larger reform policies of the emperor and especially the patriarch in Constantinople. Patriarchal interest in Thessaloniki operated on two levels in the early fourteenth century. The see was of personal interest to Athanasios, who appointed successively two of his associates, Iakovos and Malachias, to its metropolitan cathedra. Niphon was attracted by this wealthy see more deeply and perhaps for different reasons, as his deposition of Malachias and the appointment of his factotum Kallinikos in 1310 suggest.[83] A larger institutional connection is seen in the close ties that had long linked the city with Mount Athos, including the monastic domination of its episcopal succession in the Palaeologan period. The growth of the Athonite monasteries into the largest landholders of late fourteenth-century Macedonia is clearly chronicled by contemporary sources.

The buildings themselves suggest one final dimension to this synthesis of Church and monastery. Of the nineteen or more Macedonian foundations known from all sources, eight are preserved in some tangible form. More commonly surviving are buildings that have outlived their textual documentation and original patricinia. Of course, as the available architectural sample narrows, the dangers of generalization become especially hazardous. Even of this select group of eight documented katholika, however, no fewer than seven can be identified with clerical patrons.

Again, it is in Thessaloniki that the sources are most complete. Six late Byzantine churches survive in the city, ranging from small, rubble-built, timber-roofed basilicas to imposing polydomed structures of elaborate design and decoration. Despite considerable variations of scale, proportion, vaulting, and quality of construction, all of these buildings employ a similar plan that arranges paired chapels with a continuous ambulatory, often colonnaded, around the central naos with its eastern sanctuary. It hardly seems coincidental that these structures, which were built over a span of two or three generations, share an equally consistent pattern of clerical patronage. The Peribleptos (H. Panteleimon), HH. Apostoloi, and Vlatadon katholika preserve direct links between their ecclesiastical patronage and their symmetrically balanced ambulatory plans. While lacking textual documentation, the other extant buildings, the H. Aikaterini, Taxiarchai, and H. Nikolaos Orphanos, present similar plans that appear to have been influenced by these and other churches known only from the written sources.[84]

---

[82] R. L. Wolff, "Politics in the Latin Patriarchate of Constantinople, 1204–1261," *DOP* 8 (1954), 225–303, at 259–61, repr. in *Studies in the Latin Empire of Constantinople* (London, 1976); Thomas, *Private Religious Foundations* (note 2 above), 244–48.

[83] V. Laurent, "Notes de chronologie et d'histoire byzantine de la fin du XIIIe siècle. Le patriarche Niphon et les dépositions d'évêques pour délit de simonie," *REB* 27 (1969), 219–28.

[84] The standing churches are surveyed by Diehl, le Tourneau, and Saladin, *Les monuments chrétiens* (note 44 above); and Vokotopoulos, "Οἱ μεσαιωνικοὶ ναοὶ" (note 44 above). The latest of the group, the Vlatadon katholikon was rebuilt on late thirteenth- or early fourteenth-century foundations; see note 66 above. The small H. Nikolaos Orphanos may have been only a chapel within a larger monastery, which Xyngopoulos sought to identify with Milutin's building program (note 57 above). In any event the building's plan would have reflected local architectural and especially liturgical practice.

The compositional uniformity of these monastic churches is as striking as their documented support by the Church. This consistency of both sponsorship and planning is unique in the late Byzantine empire, as a review of the monuments in other cities would reveal.[85] Since buildings take shape only within a social framework, it seems plausible that the local correspondence of patronage with product reflects a standard building arrangement that was preferred by the city's prelates. The active participation of such sponsors in the design process also raises the possibility of a functional model known to members of this group. The city's metropolitan church, the eighth-century H. Sophia, would certainly have been familiar to these patrons; in fact, many would have regularly participated in its distinctive liturgy.[86] The building's monumental ambulatory plan may have formed at least a generic and possibly a liturgical inspiration for the later churches, which reflect similar spatial arrangements. These basic resemblances are found across the architectural spectrum, in both small monastic basilicas (H. Nikolaos Orphanos and Taxiarchai) and larger katholika (Peribleptos, H. Aikaterini, HH. Apostoloi, and the Vlatadon). While not excluding other factors of design, finance, and construction, these shared features testify to the persistence of a local tradition that can be credibly attributed to the wishes of a dominant local group of patrons.

When returned to its larger regional setting, this architectural phenonenon takes on the appearance of a short-lived merging of episcopal and monastic affairs that was centered in early fourteenth-century Thessaloniki. The limits of this building activity are suggested by the chronological and geographic distribution of such balanced, peripherally organized buildings. With few exceptions, these structures date from 1280 to 1320 and still stand in or near Thessaloniki itself. Apart from that city, two of the most closely related structures are found in nearby Veroia. The HH. Kyriakos kai Ioulitte church, apparently built in the late thirteenth century by the metropolitan Makarios, consists of a small basilica surrounded by a simple timber-roofed envelope. The similarly arranged and slightly later Anastasis church, while not clearly an episcopal foundation, early enjoyed patriarchal sanction. Further south at Elasson the Olympiotissa Monastery was also patriarchal within a few years of its founding by an unknown patron around 1306. The well-preserved domed katholikon is surrounded by a U-shaped ambulatory with paired chapels. The Olympiotissa's plan and details of construction closely resemble the contemporary monuments of Thessaloniki.[87]

The surviving buildings both reinforce and refine this hypothetical picture of a regional building tradition supported by episcopal interest. In the absence of textual explanation one

---

[85] Rautman, "Patrons and Buildings" (note 44 above), 306–309.

[86] The outlines of Thessaloniki's metropolitan liturgy are known from early fifteenth-century sources; see in general J. M. Phountoules, Συμεὼν ἀρχιεπισκόπου Θεσσαλονίκης τὰ λειτουργικὰ συγγράμματα I. Εὐχαὶ καὶ ὕμνοι (Thessaloniki, 1968); and for its reconstruction J. Darrouzès, "Sainte-Sophie de Thessalonique d'après un rituel," *REB* 34 (1976), 45–78.

[87] G. A. Soteriou, "Βυζαντινὰ μνημεῖα τῆς Θεσσαλίας ΙΓ΄ καὶ ΙΔ΄ αἰῶνος. 1. Μονὴ Ὀλυμπιωτίσσης," Ἐπ.Ἑτ.Βυζ.Σπ. 4 (1927), 315–31; E. A. Skouvaras, Ὀλυμπιώτισσα. Περιγραφὴ καὶ ἱστορία τῆς μονῆς (Athens, 1967). The Olympiotissa may have been constructed by a traveling workshop from Thessaloniki; in this case the builders themselves may have brought with them a type of plan with which they were familiar from work in that city.

can only speculate about the ultimate origins of and reasons for employing the ambulatory plan in these monastic contexts. Whatever the contemporary motives may have been, the surviving monuments suggest that this plan was the invariable choice of a dominant group of monastic patrons at the turn of the fourteenth century. The popularity of this architectural concept appeared across central Macedonia in the early Palaeologan period but may have faded as quickly as it arose. The plan was overlooked twenty to thirty years later near Serres, when the metropolitan Ioakeim built the Prodromos katholikon on a domed, single-aisled plan. Similarly, the small church of H. Nikolaos in the Serres acropolis was erected on a triconch plan before 1345.[88] In Thessaloniki itself shortly after mid-century Makarios Choumnos departed from local practice when he began his Nea Mone in the tradition of the Athonite triconch.[89] Apparently the ambulatory katholikon was favored by clerical patrons for only a few years around the turn of the century. In fact, the prominence of this group disappeared altogether amidst the political upheaval of the mid-1300s; apart from Mount Athos the Nea Mone is the latest documented new foundation in the Palaeologan province.[90]

The combined testimony of literary and architectural sources suggests that the Church played a special role in the history of monasticism in Macedonia. To be sure, no contemporary document expressly mentions such an undertaking or even hints at an organized program of episcopal initiative. The outlines of this phenomenon emerge not from individual texts but from a broadly-based analysis of sources pertaining to monastic foundation in the province. Evolving over the long term of centuries, such patterns of religious behavior reflect deeper social concerns than static archival sources allow: matters of need and response whose historical significance escaped the notice of contemporary observers. The sponsors themselves likely remained unaware that their collective activity briefly redirected the course of regional architecture. Illustrated by texts and buildings, their efforts preserve one local response to an increasingly uncertain Byzantine world, where monastic patronage receded from aristocratic support to ecclesiastical sponsorship, before finally retreating to the spiritual remoteness of Mount Athos.

---

[88] Hallensleben, "Das Katholikon" (note 40 above), pl. I; A. Xyngopoulos, Ἔρευναι εἰς τὰ βυζαντινὰ μνημεῖα τῶν Σερρῶν (Thessaloniki, 1965), 22–45.

[89] Diehl, le Tourneau, and Saladin, *Les monuments chrétiens* (note 44 above), 203–11; A. K. Orlandos, "Ἡ κάτοψις τοῦ Προφήτου Ἠλία τῆς Θεσσαλονίκης," Ἀρχεῖον τῶν βυζαντινῶν μνημείων τῆς Ἑλλάδος 1 (1935), 178–80. For the triconch tradition see P. M. Mylonas, "Le plan initial du catholicon de la Grande-Lavra, au Mount Athos et la genèse du type du catholicon athonite," *CahArch* 32 (1984), 89–112.

[90] Both the monydrion of H. Ioannes Theologos and the Vlatadon katholikon were rebuilt on the foundations of earlier churches; see above nn. 55 and 66. Makarios Choumnos reportedly erected the Nea atop the ruins of a palace; see Laurent, "Le métropolite Gabriel" (note 67 above), 253–54.

Constantinople, Bithynia, and Regional Developments in Later Palaeologan Architecture*

ROBERT OUSTERHOUT

FOLLOWING the restoration of Byzantine rule in Constantinople in 1261, that city—and, indeed, much of the Empire—witnessed a remarkable period of artistic and intellectual activity that has come to be known as the Palaeologan revival.[1] In addition to advancements in literature, the sciences, painting, and sculpture, this period also experienced a building boom. In Constantinople, this lasted for less than half a century, corresponding roughly with the reign of Andronikos II (1282–1328).[2] It may be recalled that Andronikos II was an intellectual and aesthete, and although there is little surviving evidence for his patronage, much of the building activity and the new developments in the architecture of the period can be directly associated with members of his court and family.

The age of Andronikos II accounts for some of the best preserved Byzantine monuments in modern Istanbul as well: a glimpse at the additions to the monasteries of the Pammakaristos (Figs. 2, 3), Lips, and particularly the Chora (Fig. 1) suggests the richness that this architecture could achieve, and these buildings reflect the lavish patronage and intellectual sophistication of the age.[3] More importantly, our understanding of Palaeologan architectural style has been defined by this brief, productive period. Indeed, the examination of architecture in the Byzantine capital rarely goes beyond this critical phase.

* Much of the research for this paper was supported by a Regional Research Grant to Greece and Turkey (1986–87) from the Fulbright Foundation, whom I gratefully acknowledge. I also benefitted from fruitful discussions and occasional adventures with my colleagues, Ch. Bakirtzis, G. Velenis, Y. Ötüken, A. Greenwood, A. Kuran, R. Lindner, and S. Ćurčić.

[1] See I. Ševčenko, "Society and Intellectual Life in the Fourteenth Century," in *Actes du XIVᵉ Congrès International d'Études Byzantines, Bucharest 1971*, I (Bucharest, 1974), 69–92; D. M. Nicol, *The Last Centuries of Byzantium 1261–1453* (London, 1972), among others.

[2] Neither the period before nor the period after Andronikos II were particularly conducive to the monumental arts: the reign of his father, Michael VIII (1261–82), was plagued by religious conflict, and the disputes with Andronikos' grandson, Andronikos III, led to civil war in the 1320s; for the personality of Andronikos II, see A. Laiou, *Constantinople and the Latins: The Foreign Policy of Andronicus II, 1282–1328* (Cambridge, Mass., 1972), esp. 1–5, and 24–25 for Andronikos' somewhat visionary reconstruction of the ancient city of Tralles in 1280, to be renamed Andronikopolis or Palaiologopolis.

[3] For an attempt to characterize the style of this architecture, see R. Ousterhout, *The Architecture of the Kariye Camii in Istanbul* (Washington, D.C., 1987), esp. 142–44. See also W. Müller-Wiener, *Bildlexikon zur Topographie Istanbuls* (Tübingen, 1977), 72–215 passim, for the major monuments of the period and pertinent bibliography; also S. Eyice, *Son Devir Bizans Mimarisi* (Istanbul, rev. ed. 1980). Ch. Bouras, "Byzantine Architecture in the Middle of the 14th Century," in *Dečani i vizantijska umetnost sredinom XIV veka* (Belgrade, 1989), 49–54 appeared too late to be considered here.

By the third decade of the fourteenth century, architectural productivity seems all but spent in Constantinople, and the legacy of this last great flourishing in Byzantine architecture remains to be determined. Certainly the political and economic situation had changed for the worse, and the favorable conditions of the reign of Andronikos II were not to be experienced again. Nevertheless, the picture of architectural development stands in stark contrast to that of the *art* of the period: the influence of the masterly style developed in the mosaics and frescoes of the Chora is evident until the fall of Constantinople and beyond.[4] The question remains: what happened to the builders of Constantinople and vicinity after around 1325–30? In this paper I shall address this question by examining the somewhat limited surviving evidence in Constantinople, as well as in neighboring regions, particularly Thrace and Bithynia, with an excursus into the Byzantine contribution to the formation of Ottoman architecture.

In the study of the built environment, it must be kept in mind that—despite frequent protests to the contrary—architecture is a conservative profession. Masons learn by doing: by participating in the production of a workshop they acquire knowledge of construction methods that have been tested over time. Thus, the identification of workshop practices—as opposed to stylistic similarities—may help to establish a more realistic relationship between works of architecture.[5] This is particularly important in understanding Byzantine architecture of the fourteenth century, a time in which planning was eclectic and the same workshop could have created a great variety of plans, types of vaults, and systems of spatial organization, often derived from the rich architectural heritage of Byzantium. (I suspect, for example, that the parekklesia of the Chora and of the Pammakaristos [Figs. 1, 2] were the product of the same workshop: whereas plans and vaulting forms have little in common, the wall construction is identical in both buildings, and numerous decorative motifs are similar as well.)[6] Therefore, my discussion will be based primarily on the study of construction techniques and related decorative details as a means of identifying builders or workshops of masons. By doing this, it should become possible to comment upon the continuity of workshop practices and the influence exerted by the masons of Constantinople in the orbit of the Byzantine capital.[7]

---

[4] See O. Demus, "The Style of the Kariye Djami and Its Place in the Development of Palaeologan Art," *The Kariye Djami*, IV, ed. P. Underwood (Princeton, 1975), 107–61.

[5] This approach has been encouraged by the recent study of G. Velenis, Ἑρμηνεία τοῦ ἐξωτερικοῦ διάκοσμου στη βυζαντινή ἀρχιτεκτονική (Thessaloniki, 1984), esp. ch. I passim.

[6] As I have discussed elsewhere; Ousterhout, *Architecture* (note 3 above), esp. 119–20; also 91ff., for compositional considerations in late Byzantine architectural planning.

[7] With a few exceptions, I have not included examples of defensive architecture in this discussion, because these are usually lacking the sort of technical detail that lends itself to visual analysis and the identification of workshop practices. Moreover, few have been properly surveyed. C. Foss and D. Winfield, *Byzantine Fortifications: An Introduction* (Pretoria, 1986), suggest the difficulties in the study of fortifications, with numerous examples from Bithynia; see also Y. Ötüken and R. Ousterhout, "Notes on the Monuments of Turkish Thrace," *AnatSt* 39 (1989), 121–49, for bibliography on Thracian fortifications and some unpublished examples.

CONSTANTINOPLE

I should begin by stating that there are no surviving securely dated buildings in Constantinople from the last two-thirds of the fourteenth century. This is not to say that building activity ceased, although the period of civil wars and economic decline certainly did not encourage new projects. A number of architectural undertakings are documented, but those that survive represent additions or repairs to existing buildings. For example, at the Pammakaristos, the monastic church complex continued to expand. The early fourteenth-century parekklesion was apparently succeeded by the construction of an exonarthex to the west (Figs. 2, 3), which Prof. Hallensleben has dated to the second quarter of the century: mosaics recorded in the sixteenth century seem to have portrayed the emperor Andronikos III and his wife Anna.[8] Whereas the junctures with the earlier building are awkward, the alternating brick and stone construction, the banded voussoirs of the arches, and the stepped responds indicate the continuation of earlier practices.

Perhaps the greatest architectural achievement of the period was the repair of the dome of Hag. Sophia (Fig. 4). In May 1346 the eastern portion of the dome, including parts of the arch and semi-dome, collapsed following an earthquake. The repair of the arch and semi-dome seems to have been carried out by Anne of Savoy shortly thereafter. But it was several years before the missing section of the dome could be replaced. This was either undertaken or at least completed by John Kantakouzenos in 1353.[9] Whereas this was technically a repair, it was certainly an achievement of great magnitude, considering the scale of Hag. Sophia: the area spanned by the *repair* alone—about one-third of the dome—was considerably greater than the span of any vaulted building constructed in this period. But it is perhaps not without significance that an Italian master builder, Giovanni Peralta, helped to direct the reconstruction, and that much of the financing was foreign, provided by the Grand Duke of Moscow.

The major concern in Constantinople during this period was not religious architecture, but the security of the city. The Land Wall, first constructed in the early fifth century, seems to have been in a continual state of repair through the Palaeologan period.[10] In 1343/4 Alexios Apokaukos ordered a thorough restoration of both the inner wall and the outer

[8] H. Hallensleben, "Untersuchungen zur Baugeschichte der ehemaligen Pammakaristoskirche, der heutigen Fethiye Camii in Istanbul," *IstMitt* 13–14 (1963–64), 128–93, esp. 137–39, 174ff., fig. 4 and pl. 68; also C. Mango and E. Hawkins, "Report on Field Work in Istanbul and Cyprus, 1962–1963," *DOP* 18 (1964), 319–333, esp. 331.

[9] Most recently, R. Mainstone, *Hagia Sophia: Architecture, Structure and Liturgy of Justinian's Great Church* (New York, 1988), 92 and figs. 106–109; also I. Ševčenko, "Notes on Stephen, the Novgorodian Pilgrim to Constantinople in the Fourteenth Century," *SOforsch* 12 (1953), 165–75, esp. 169–72, for historical considerations.

[10] Müller-Wiener, *Bildlexikon* (note 3 above), 286–319, for an overview and pertinent bibliography; note also fig. 337, showing Palaeologan repair. Also A. Van Millingen, *Byzantine Constantinople: The Walls of the City and Adjoining Historical Sites* (London, 1889); B. Meyer-Plath and A. M. Schneider, *Die Landmauer von Konstantinopel*, II (Berlin, 1943). C. Foss in Foss and Winfield, *Byzantine Fortifications* (note 7 above), 44–77, attempts to clarify the chronology of construction.

curtain, the most thorough undertaking since their initial construction.[11] Later repairs are documented by John V, John VI, John, VII, and John VIII—although not necessarily in that order—with inscriptions surviving from the last two.[12] Repairs are primarily in stone, although banded voussoirs of brick and stone continue to be used in the arches, as may be observed on the inner surface of the Blachernae wall (Fig. 5).[13]

Additions were also made to the Golden Gate in this period. It was strengthened by John VI Kantakouzenos at mid-century, and he referred to it as a *frourion*, or fortress. Work was continued by John V toward the end of the century, using building materials taken from destroyed churches in the vicinity. This seems to have included the outer gate. The additions of John V were apparently dismantled in 1391 at the insistence of the Ottoman sultan Bāyazīd, so the chronology of the surviving portions is not entirely clear.[14] I suspect that the blocking of the north arch of the main gate should also be placed in the mid- or late fourteenth century (Fig. 6). Construction is similar to the outer wall: of re-used materials, with broken brick as filler in the mortar joints. The decorative niche is also notable.

Often overlooked in the discussion of Palaeologan architecture is the church of St.-Benoît in the suburb of Pera, founded by Benedictine monks in 1427.[15] Much of its middle portion has been reconstructed, but the belfry and the domed chapel date from the fifteenth century (Figs. 7, 8). The corbel table frieze of the belfry is unique in Constantinople and perhaps shows Western medieval influence; the arches are trilobed and slightly pointed. Both these and the arches of the large bifora below the corbel table were outlined with ceramic decoration, of which only fragments survive. These details were more characteristic of Byzantine architecture, although they were rare in the capital. The brick dome of the chapel is also purely Byzantine. St.-Benoît indicates that church building continued into the fifteenth century, and it will provide a convenient point of reference in our later discussion.

On the other hand, one of the best known Palaeologan monuments, the Tekfur Saray is something of an enigma (Figs. 9, 10).[16] Sandwiched between sections of the Land Wall, the three-storied building may have imitated the form of an Italian palazzo. Its facades are lavishly decorated with ceramic and stone inlays. Apparently it was attached to the Blachernae Palace, which lay further down the hill to the north. The standing wall of another wing of the palace remains atop a portion of the Land Wall, further to the north. The marble

[11] Van Millingen, *Byzantine Constantinople* (note 10 above), 103–104.

[12] *Ibid.*, 104–108.

[13] Foss in Foss and Winfield, *Byzantine Fortifications* (note 7 above), 59ff. notes the plain stone construction of the later Palaeologoi, but not the banded voussoirs.

[14] Müller-Wiener, *Bildlexikon* (note 3 above), 297–300 and figs. 341–42. See also J. Barker, *Manuel II Palaeologus (1391–1425): A Study in Late Byzantine Statesmanship* (New Brunswick, 1969), 467–68.

[15] Müller-Wiener, *Bildlexikon* (note 3 above), 100–101; R. Janin, *Les églises e monasteres* (Paris, 1969), 586.

[16] Van Millingen, *Byzantine Constantinople* (note 10 above), 109–14; Meyer-Plath and Schneider, *Landmauer* (note 10 above), II, 95ff.; C. Mango, "Constantinopolitana," *JdI* 80 (1965), 330–36. W. Allen, *Tekfur Saray in Istanbul: An Architectural Study* (diss.: Johns Hopkins Univ., 1981), adds little to the discussion.

frames of doors and windows, which may have opened to a balcony, are topped by relieving arches with banded voussoirs.[17]

Van Millingen associated the Tekfur Saray with the House of the Porphyrogenitos first mentioned in 1328.[18] Schneider and Mango have identified the Porphyrogenitos in question as Constantine, the unhappy third son of Michael VIII, rendering a date of between 1261 and 1291.[19] Although the evidence is flimsy, this interpretation has been generally accepted. Recently, however, Velenis has re-evaluated the construction and suggested a date *after* 1350.[20] He notes certain features of construction and decoration on the building that are unique among the surviving monuments of the capital. A larger proportion of stone is used in the banded brick and stone wall construction, mortar joints are thin, and putlog holes appear prominently in the stone courses. Although it is *similar* to other Palaeologan buildings, the Tekfur Saray is the product of a different workshop and a very different sensibility. Velenis notes that the brick and stone elements of the banded voussoirs do not line up in concentric arches: such a treatment is illogical in Constantinopolitan architecture and appears elsewhere only in buildings dated after the mid-fourteenth century. The ceramic decoration may also suggest a late date: rather than patterned brick integral with the wall construction, as was common in Constantinopolitan architecture, we find a veneer of ceramic and stone tiles. In addition, rows of glazed ceramic rosettes outline the arches: in Constantinople similar ceramic decoration is found only at St.-Benoît. Intriguingly, the Tekfur Saray is represented on the fifteenth-century plans of Buondelmonti and identified as *palatium imperatoris*, and it may have served as the final residence of the Byzantine emperors.[21]

For the later fourteenth century, the picture of architectural activity within Constantinople is sketchy at best. Could Constantinopolitan masons have worked elsewhere in this period? Controlled by a guild system, workshops were normally tied to a specific location and did not travel.[22] But the political and economic turmoil of the later fourteenth century may have induced workshops of masons to seek greener pastures. The *influence* of Constantinople is seen in a number of other centers, but it remains to be determined if this is the result of stylistic similarities or workshop connections. Turning to the hinterland of

---

[17] The construction of this wing reveals brick-filled mortar joints, a technique that also appears in other buildings in the capital, such as İsa Kapı Mescidi, the Bogdan Saray, and the blocked arch of the Golden Gate, discussed above; see also below, n.35.

[18] Van Millingen, *Byzantine Constantinople* (note 10 above), 109.

[19] Schneider in Meyer-Plath and Schneider, *Landmauer* (note 10 above), 95ff.; Mango, "Constantinopolitana" (note 16 above), 335–36. In 1291 Constantine was imprisoned for the remainder of his life.

[20] Velenis, Ἑρμηνεία (note 5 above), esp. 102–103, 163–65.

[21] Schneider in Meyer-Plath and Schneider, *Landmauer* (note 10 above), 96; and Mango, "Constantinopolitana" (note 16 above), 336. For plan and views, see also, Müller-Wiener, *Bildlexikon* (note 3 above), 244–47.

[22] Velenis, Ἑρμηνεία (note 5 above), 13, discusses restrictions on workshops, at least as recorded in the time of Leo the Wise (886–912); see also A. Christophilopoulos, Τὸ Ἐπαρχικόν βιβλίον Λέοντος τοῦ Σοφοῦ καὶ αἱ συντεχνίαι ἐν Βυζαντίῳ (Athens, 1935), 92; E. H. Freshfield, trans., *Roman Law in the Later Roman Empire* (Cambridge, 1938).

the capital we can look for evidence of technical continuity and stylistic reflections in the architecture.

THRACE

European Thrace became increasingly important in the Palaeologan era. As the empire shrank, Thrace became the heartland of Byzantium and a frequent battleground. Unfortunately, much evidence has vanished in Eastern Thrace since the population exchange of 1922–23, and Western Thrace is only beginning to be explored.[23] At Ainos (Turkish Enez), for example, Lampakis recorded some twenty-two churches at the turn of the century; of these only two can be positively identified today—and both were in Muslim use in Lampakis' time.[24] Of the recently excavated remains of Byzantine churches and chapels, none can be matched with certainty to the names of buildings recorded by Lampakis.[25] Certainly Ainos continued to be an important center in the later fourteenth century, having come into the hands of the Gattelusi in 1355, from whom numerous inscriptions have been recorded.[26] But we can say virtually nothing about Palaeologan architecture in Ainos.

The nobleman Alexios Apokaukos built a church at Selymvria, about 80 kilometers from Constantinople, around 1325 (Fig. 11).[27] What remains of the church today serves as a planter, and the meager surviving fragment of a niched apse has been plastered and painted. From older photographs it would appear that the construction and decorative features conform with standard practice: alternating bands of brick and stone, decorative arcading, niched apses, and so on, all elements clearly associated with the capital. Hence the building was presumably the product of a Constantinopolitan workshop.[28]

The most important centers in Thrace in this period were Adrianople and Didymoteichon, and these cities figured prominently in the civil wars and territorial disputes of

[23] For the state of research in eastern Thrace, see Ötüken and Ousterhout, "Notes on the Monuments" (note 7 above), 121–49. For Western Thrace, see the useful guidebook by Ch. Bakirtzis and D. Triantaphyllos, *Thrace* (Athens, 1988). Papers from the First International Symposium for Thracian Studies (*Byzantine Thrace: Image and Character*) (Komotini, 1987) have appeared in *ByzF* 14 (1989).

[24] G. Lampakis, "Περιεγήσεις," Δελτ.Χριστ.Ἀρχ.Ἑτ. 8 (1908), esp. 4–32. For a more recent survey, see S. Eyice, "Trakya'da Bizans Devrine ait Eserler," *Belleten* 33 (1969), esp. 348–354. The church called Fatih Camii, thought to be of Palaeologan date, is more likely twelfth-century; see R. Ousterhout, "The Byzantine Church at Enez: Problems in Twelfth-Century Architecture," *JÖB* 35 (1985), 261–80.

[25] Eyice, "Trakya'da" (note 24 above), passim; A. Erzen, "1986 Yılı Enez Kazısı Çalışmalari," *IX. Kazı Sonuçları Toplantısı* (Ankara, 1987), II, 279–98, for recent excavations.

[26] F. W. Hasluck, "Monuments of the Gattelusi," *BSA* 15 (1908–09), esp. 249–57.

[27] S. Eyice, "Alexis Apocauque et l'église byzantine de Sélymbria," *Byzantion* 34 (1964), 77–104; O. Feld, "Noch einmal Alexios Apokaukos und die byzantinische Kirche von Selymbria," *Byzantion* 37 (1967), 57–65; S. Eyice, "Encore une fois l'église d'Alexis Apocauque à Sélymbria," *Byzantion* 48 (1978), 406–16.

[28] For the characterization of Constantinopolitan facade decoration, see Ousterhout, *Architecture* (note 3 above), 116–26. See also Velenis, Ἑρμηνεία (note 5 above), 162–66, and passim. Another Palaeologan church from Selymvria vanished in the last century; see A. Stamoulis, "Ἀνέκδοτα βυζαντινὰ μνημεῖα ἐν Θράκη," Δελτ.Χριστ.Ἀρχ.Ἑτ. 3 (1926), 62–63, with photographs; M. Stamoulis, "Ὁ ἐν Σελύμβρια βυζαντίνος ναὸς τοῦ Ἁγίου Σπυριδόνος," Θρακικά 9 (1938), 37–44, with description and measurements; H. Hallensleben, "Die ehemaligen Spyridonkirche in Silivri (Selymvria)—Eine Achtstützenkirche im Gebiet Konstantinopels," *Studien zur spätantiken und byzantinischen Kunst F. W. Deichmann gewidmet* (Mainz, 1986), 35–46.

mid-century. Almost nothing remains of Byzantine Adrianople, although fragments of an inscription by either John VI or John V have recently come to light on one of the defensive towers (Fig. 12). The original, recorded in the nineteenth century, read: "Κ[ΥΡΙ]Η ΒΟΗΘΕΙ Τῼ ΕΥΣΕΒΑΣΤΑΤῼ Κ[ΑΙ] ΦΙΛΟΧΡΙΣΤῼ ΒΑΣΙΛΕΙ ΗΜῼΝ, ΙῼΑΝΝΗ." The surviving fragment reads " . . . ΧΡΙΣΤῼ ΒΑ . . . "[29]

The remains of Didymoteichon are more substantial. The city had been destroyed by Kaloyan in 1206 and apparently rebuilt by the Laskarids. It continued to enjoy imperial attention in the fourteenth century, and it was the site of the coronation of John Kantakouzenos in 1341.[30] Much of the fortification wall of the citadel survives, rising above the Erythropotamos River. Within the enclosure are the remains of dwellings, cellars, and cisterns cut into the soft stone of the citadel. A palace stood at the top of the hill, but its foundations remain to be explored. Two Palaeologan ecclesiastical buildings also survive, in poor states of repair, and neither can be dated securely.[31] The first, located on the north flank of the metropolitan church of Hag. Athanasios, was probably a trapeza, or monastic dining hall, judging from its attenuated, niched plan (Figs. 13, 14).[32] One wall remains, partially obscured on the exterior, with seven arched niches on the interior; a portion of the apse also survives, preserving some elements of decoration. Some features may be compared with the church at Selymvria, such as the lack of relationship between the apse and lateral facade. I therefore would hazard a date in the third decade of the century for the trapeza. Numerous Constantinopolitan characteristics are evident: banded construction in walls and arches, the arcaded exterior facade, and the apse preserving an engaged colonnette and niches on two levels. At the same time, numerous distinctive features appear in the construction, such as the stone conches to the niches, which find no comparison in the capital.

The second building in Didymoteichon is similar. The small cemetery chapel of Hag. Aikaterini was probably constructed toward the middle of the century (Figs. 15, 16). It similarly exhibits numerous Constantinopolitan stylistic features. As in the other example from Didymoteichon, there is a general lack of correspondence between interior forms and the external articulation, characteristic of Palaeologan architecture. The external arcading, stepped responds, shallow niches flanking the apse and entrance, brick decoration, and the banded wall construction compare with the capital. Ceramic rosettes were also used, and these are found in Constantinople on the Tekfur Saray and St.-Benoît, although they are

---

[29] S. Eyice, "Bizans Devrinde Edirne ve bu Devre ait Eserler," *Edirne. Edirne'nin 600. Fetih Yıldönümü Armağan Kitabi* (Ankara, 1965), esp. 65–66; *idem*, "Edirne Saat Kulesi ve Üzerinde Bizans Kitabesi," *Güney-Doğu Avrupa Araştirmaları Dergisi* 8–9 (1979–80), 1–22, with several illustrations.

[30] Bakirtzis and Triantaphyllos, *Thrace* (note 23 above), 70–75; for a survey of the sources, see K. Asdracha, *La région de Rhodopes aux XIIIe et XIVe siècles* (Athens, 1976), 130–37; also Ph. Giannopoulos, *Didymoteichon. Geschichte einer byzantinischen Festung* (diss. Univ. of Cologne, 1975).

[31] R. Ousterhout, "The Palaeologan Architecture of Didymoteicho," in *Acts of the First International Symposium for Thracian Studies (Byzantine Thrace: Image and Character), (Komotini, 1987)* = *ByzF* 14/1 (1989), 429–43, for a more detailed discussion and additional illustrations. The buildings were studied under the auspices of the Twelfth Ephoreia of Byzantine Antiquities, Kavala. Hag. Aikaterini was excavated under the direction of Ch. Bakirtzis; a fuller report of this work will appear in the Χρονικά of Ἀρχ.Δελτ.

[32] Compare A. K. Orlandos, Μοναστηριακὴ ἀρχιτεκτονικὴ (Athens, 1958), 43–60, and figs. 47 (Daphni), 57 (Nea Moni), 59 (Brontochion at Mistra). Similar buildings appear at Latmos but are not identified; see Th. Wiegand, *Der Latmos*, Milet III, i (Berlin, 1913), nos. 13, 14, 17, 23.

more common elsewhere. Like examples from Serbia, the rosettes are not glazed.[33] More-over, the construction finds no good comparison in the capital: unlike the solid wall construction characteristic of Constantinople, at Didymoteichon we find a facing on a rubble core, and the large putlog holes are also unparalleled.[34] The chapel seems to have been constructed entirely of spoils, and both buildings in Didymoteichon employ brick filling in the mortar beds, a technique found only occasionally in Constantinople.[35] Thus, for both buildings in Didymoteichon, Constantinopolitan *style* continued to exert influence, but the construction is the product of locally trained workshops.

Although defensive architecture is more difficult to assess, I think the same conclusion may be drawn from the fortress at Pythion, which John VI Kantakouzenos claimed to have constructed as his treasury (Figs. 17, 18).[36] The two towers are of different dates, and Kantakouzenos may have simply added to the larger tower. The machicolated design is one of the most sophisticated of the period. The vaulting forms may compare favorably with Constantinople—both domical vaults and ramping barrel vaults are employed, but the construction technique may be more similar to nearby Didymoteichon, with brick filling in the mortar beds.[37]

SERBIA

Constantinopolitan style also affected the architecture of Serbia during the reigns of Stefan Dušan and Stefan Uroš (1331–71), and this period of architectural activity has been illuminated in a recent study by S. Ćurčić.[38] In this period of dramatic changes in politics and patronage, Serbia experienced an era of prosperity while Byzantium was on the decline. Thus it would have been possible for masons from the Byzantine capital to have sought employment in the Serbian court. Nevertheless, it seems to me that in most of the Serbian buildings of this period, the Byzantine style is conservative, generic, and probably interpreted by local builders, rather than being the product of Byzantine workshops on

---

[33] For Serbian examples and extensive bibliography, see G. Subotić, "Keramoplastični Ukras," in *Istorija Primenjene Umetnosti kod Srba*, I, ed. B. Radojković (Belgrade, 1977), 43–70, with English summary, p. 380.

[34] Velenis, Έρμηνεία (note 5 above), 32, 88, and passim.

[35] The technique of "brick-filled mortar joints" employing *spolia* as fill material seems to have become popular in Laskarid Asia Minor during the thirteenth century, from which it apparently was learned in Constantinople and Thrace; see R. Ousterhout, "Observations on the 'Recessed Brick' Technique during the Palaeologan Period," Ἀρχ.Δελτ. (in press); and *idem*, "Παρατήρησεις στην τεχνική της κρυμμένης πλίνθου κατά την Παλαιολογεία περίοδο," Ἕβδομο Συμπόσιο Βυζαντινής και Μεταβυζαντινής Ἀρχαιολογείας και Τέχνης (Athens, 1987), 61–2.

[36] Asdracha, *Rhodopes* (note 30 above), 137ff.; Bakirtzis and Triantaphyllos, *Thrace* (note 23 above), 75; and M. Korres, "The Architecture of the Pythion Castle," in *Acts of the First International Symposium for Thracian Studies (Byzantine Thrace: Image and Character)*, *(Komotini, 1987)* = *ByzF* 14/1 (1989), 273–78.

[37] Ousterhout, "Observations" (note 35 above); also P. L. Vokotopoulos, "The Concealed Course Technique: Further Examples and a Few Remarks," *JÖB* 28 (1979), esp. 253 and fig. 9; for a discussion of Constantinopolitan vaulting techniques, see Ousterhout, *Architecture* (note 3 above), 131–33.

[38] S. Ćurčić, "Architecture in the Byzantine Sphere of Influence around the Middle of the Fourteenth Century," in *Dečani i vizantijska umetnost sredinom XIV veka* (Belgrade, 1989), 55–68. My thanks to Prof. Ćurčić for sharing his research with me prior to publication.

foreign soil. This may be witnessed at both Markov Manastir, begun ca. 1345 (Fig. 19), and Matejić, built after ca. 1355, where—unlike the architecture of Milutin earlier in the century—detailing may be closer to Middle Byzantine Constantinople than to Palaeologan developments. That is, we may detect a clear correspondence between the exterior articulation and the spatial divisions of the interior.[39] If Byzantine masons were present in Serbia at mid-century, they were more likely individual artisans than workshops. The standard methods of wall construction have not been affected, and similarities with Palaeologan Constantinople are most easily detected in the decorative details.

BULGARIA

The picture is rather different at Nesebar (Mesemvria), on the Black Sea coast of Bulgaria, another center which has been discussed by Ćurčić.[40] Here I suspect we can see the direct continuation of architectural practices from the Byzantine capital. Although the city was disputed, changing hands six times in the course of the century, this did not seem to affect architectural production.[41] Numerous churches have been attributed to the period of Ivan Alexander (1331–71), although there is no clear documentation of this. In general, Bulgarian architecture maintained close ties with Constantinople, so it is often difficult to distinguish distinctively Constantinopolitan input from the continuation of standard practices. Nevertheless, the solid wall construction of banded masonry is identical with that of the capital, and this is to be found in almost all the late churches in Nesebar.

Two buildings may be singled out because of their close resemblance to the architecture of Constantinople: the Pantokrator and St. John Aliturgetos (Figs. 20, 21). Both were laid out on cross-in-square plans, but because they were constructed *de novo* and with relatively simple plans, it is impossible to make comparisons with planning in Palaeologan Constantinople, where the surviving examples of ecclesiastical architecture consist of additions to earlier buildings. Nevertheless, numerous features of construction, structure, and decorative details encourage the association of these buildings with the Byzantine capital. For example, the use of domical vaults supported on brackets in the church of St. John Aliturgetos is noteworthy, and this is similar to the Chora in Constantinople.[42] The Pantokrator has a staircase covered by a ramping barrel vault, and this was a distinctive element of Palaeologan architecture in Constantinople: identically vaulted staircases are found at the Chora and the Pammakaristos.[43]

Stylistic similarities are also numerous. At the Pantokrator, the facade is treated as a series of three horizontal arcades which lack vertical relationship. This may be best compared with the facade of the Tekfur Saray. At St. John, the pilasters of the facade arcade are broken by small, setback niches similar to those at the Lips and Pammakaristos monasteries

[39] S. Ćurčić, "Articulation of Church Facades during the First Half of the Fourteenth Century," *L'art byzantin au début du XIVᵉ siècle* (Belgrade, 1978), 17–27.

[40] Ćurčić, "Architecture in the Byzantine Sphere" (note 38 above), 62–65.

[41] *Ibid.*; and A. Rachénov, *Églises de Mésemvria* (Sofia, 1932); Velenis, Ἑρμηνεία (note 5 above), passim, for numerous technical observations.

[42] Ousterhout, *Architecture* (note 3 above), 76–78, and pls. 119–20.

[43] For vaulted staircases in Constantinople, see Ousterhout, *Architecture* (note 3 above), 116.

in Constantinople.[44] In all three examples, the decorative niches detract visually from the solidity of the pilaster. The panels of tile patterns at St. John are similar to those at the Tekfur Saray, and the use of sculpted decoration is also comparable. For example, a sculpted fleur-de-lis decorates an arch at St. John; this motif also appeared at the Tekfur Saray, and it may have had some specific associations with the Palaeologos family.[45] The indented heart motif is characteristic of Constantinople as well: it may be seen at the Lips Monastery and at the Chora, where it is constructed with brick arches, while the motif appears nowhere else in Bulgaria.[46]

There are enough distinctively Constantinopolitan stylistic and constructional features at the Pantokrator and St. John Aliturgetos to recommend a direct workshop connection with the Byzantine capital. But neither is without local input. Both include extensive use of glazed ceramic decoration—unusual in Constantinople and found only at two of the latest Byzantine monuments, the Tekfur Saray and St.-Benoît.[47] Decorative corbel table friezes are common in Nesebar, but in the capital are seen only at St.-Benoît. These similarities suggest "foreign" influences in later Constantinopolitan architecture, as well as a dynamic interaction of architectural centers, effected by the movement of workshops. Thus, the churches of Nesebar may help to extend our picture of the building activity of Constantinopolitan workshops into the middle of the fourteenth century and to explain the anomalous features in the later architecture of the capital.

BITHYNIA

A final area of influence remains to be examined. Little survives of the Christian buildings from the Palaeologan period in Bithynia, and these reflect the strong local tradition of the region. With the arrival of the Ottomans in the early fourteenth century, the region was lost forever to the Byzantine Empire. Nevertheless, the area is of some significance to the understanding of later Byzantine architecture, and I shall thus examine it in some detail.

The city of Bursa, known to the Byzantines as Prousa or Brusa, had figured prominently in the earlier Byzantine history of the region.[48] In 1326 it was captured by the Osmanlı Turks and became the capital of the emerging Ottoman state. As such, the city witnessed a new burst of architectural activity during the course of the fourteenth century. Aside from some of the fortifications, most Christian structures have long since vanished;

---

[44] For illustrations, see, Müller-Wiener, *Bildlexikon* (note 3 above), figs. 112 and 122.

[45] See comments by Mango, "Constantinopolitana" (note 16 above), 335–36.

[46] See R. Ousterhout, "The Byzantine Heart," *Zograf* 17 (1986) [= Belgrade, 1989], 36–44, for the Constantinopolitan origin of the motif.

[47] For glazed ceramic decoration, see the survey by D. Sasalov, "Problèmes sur l'origine de la décoration de façade céramoplastique," *BIABulg* 35 (1979), 92–109, who favors a Bulgarian origin for such decoration; however, he overlooks numerous examples from Greece and Asia Minor; see H. Buchwald, "Lascarid Architecture," *JÖB* 28 (1979), 276–78, 287–89, for examples on Chios; and *idem*, "Sardis Church E—A Preliminary Report," *JÖB* 16 (1977), 268, for an example from Sardis; and S. Eyice, "Quatre édifices inédits ou malconnus," *CahArch* 10 (1959), 252–56, for a Muslim (?) example at Tokat.

[48] For what is known about the Byzantine monuments of the city, see R. Janin, *Les églises et les monastères des grands centres byzantins* (Paris, 1975), 174–75.

nevertheless, Bursa still seems remarkably Byzantine.[49] The Byzantine-ness of Bursa's architecture reflects the complex period of cultural overlap that occurred in northwest Asia Minor during the fourteenth century, as the Ottomans gradually settled and assumed control of Byzantine territories in Bithynia and Mysia.[50]

The origins of Ottoman architecture are problematic: although they lacked a tradition of architecture in permanent materials, by the third decade of the fourteenth century the recently settled nomads had begun building in earnest, and in a manner markedly different from that of the builders of the earlier Muslim monuments in other parts of Anatolia.[51] This architectural accession suggests that the Osmanlı Turks must have employed local Byzantine masons in the early projects. Nevertheless, the nature of the Byzantine involvement and the Byzantine contribution to early Ottoman architecture still remain to be assessed.

Rarely has a comparison of Byzantine and Ottoman buildings gone beyond the discussion of superficial similarities, such as the development of the portico facade or decorative brick patterning. The appearance of Byzantine forms in Ottoman architecture might thus be attributed simply to imitation: that is, it could be postulated that Ottoman builders looked and copied, borrowing Byzantine details, just as they borrowed columns, capitals, and other building materials. An examination of materials and construction practices helps to clarify the relationship. In the final section of this paper, I shall examine several early Ottoman buildings that reflect the strong local—that is, Byzantine—tradition in the architecture of the region.

The Orhan Camii in Bursa is one of the oldest Ottoman buildings to survive (Fig. 22).[52] Originally constructed in 1334, it was repaired in 1417 and heavily restored in the nineteenth century. Nevertheless, I believe most of the wall construction is original, although the rather intricate forms of the vaulting must be later. The plan—an inverted T, characteristic of the early mosques of Bursa—seems to have been derived ultimately from Anatolian

[49] At least one Byzantine building, identified by Texier as the church of St. Elijah, remained until the earthquake of 1855; it had served as the mausoleum of Sultan Orhan; see Ch. Texier and R. Pullan, *Byzantine Architecture* (London, 1864), 169 and fig. 56. See also E. H. Ayverdi, *Osmanlı Mimarisinin İlk Devri* (Istanbul, 1966), 105–107. The last contains documentation and extensive illustrations for early Ottoman buildings.

[50] For the history of the period, see particularly R. P. Lindner, *Nomads and Ottomans in Medieval Anatolia* (Bloomington, Ind., 1983), 1–50 passim ("The Tent of Osman, the House of Osman"). Also P. Wittek, *The Rise of the Ottoman Empire* (London, 1967); S. Vryonis, *The Decline of Medieval Hellenism in Asia Minor and the Process of Islamization from the Eleventh through the Fifteenth Century* (Berkeley, 1971); R. C. Jennings, "Some thoughts on the Gazi-Thesis," *WZKM* 76 (1986) [Festschrift A. Tietze], 151–61; H. Inalcık, "The Question of the Emergence of the Ottoman State," *International Journal of Turkish Studies* 2, no. 2 (1981–82), 71–80.

[51] For a brief survey of Anatolia, see J. D. Hoag, *Islamic Architecture* (New York, 1977), 222–49. For architectural developments throughout Turkey in the fourteenth century, see O. Aslanapa, ed., *Yüzyıllar Boyunca Türk Sanatı (14. yüzyıl)* (Istanbul, 1977), with numerous illustrations. For early Ottoman architecture, see Ayverdi, *Osmanlı* (note 49 above); for the Ottoman monuments of Bursa, see also A. Gabriel, *Une capitale turque: Brousse, Bursa* (Paris, 1958).

[52] Ayverdi, *Osmanlı* (note 49 above), 61–89; A. Kuran, *The Mosque in Early Ottoman Architecture* (Chicago, 1968), 98–101.

Seljuk architecture.[53] On the other hand, the rough brick and stone masonry is unlike anything produced by the Seljuks, who rarely used brick in mosque construction, although it was commonly employed in the construction of minarets.[54] But the construction technique of Orhan Camii is remarkably close to the traditional Byzantine architecture of Bithynia, as for example the thirteenth-century additions to Hag. Sophia in Nicaea, Turkish İznik (Fig. 23), as well as the ruins of the church identified as Hag. Tryphon in the same city.[55] In all three, the walls are constructed of alternating bands of brick and stone, normally alternating one roughly-cut stone course to two of brick; occasionally vertical bricks appear in the stone courses. The somewhat distracting pointing of the mortar beds at the Orhan Camii is apparently modern, and does not appear in photographs of the nineteenth century.

Numerous Byzantine details appear at the Orhan Camii: the facade is articulated with blind arcades; banded voussoirs of alternating brick and stone are employed in the arches; many of the arches are semicircular and outlined with dogtooth—bricks set at a 45-degree angle. These elements are seen in numerous Byzantine buildings in western Asia Minor from the thirteenth century, such as the island monastery churches of Bafa Gölü, below Mt. Latmos.[56] Also common to both is the decorative roundel; a better comparison is at the Pammakaristos in which radiating elements of brick and stone are used.[57] An area of herringbone patterning survives in a spandrel, a motif common in the Byzantine architecture of Constantinople.[58] The use of curved roofing tiles to decorate the field of an arched niche is somewhat less common, but such decoration is seen occasionally in late Byzantine architecture, as at St. John of Lips in Constantinople; a similar detail is also to be found in the church on Kahve Asar Ada at Latmos.[59] Based on the numerous technical similarities, we may postulate that Byzantine masons participated in the construction of the Orhan Camii.

The combination of Seljuk forms and Byzantine construction techniques reflects the cultural associations of the early Ottomans: they were connected religiously and politically

---

[53] See Kuran, *Mosque* (note 52 above), 71–77, for hints that the "axial eyvan mosque" and the "cross-axial eyvan mosque"—the latter term is applied to the Orhan Camii—were developed out of the Seljuk architectural tradition. S. Eyice, "Zaviyeler ve Zaviyeli-Camiler," *İstanbul Üniversitesi İktisat Fakültesi Mecmuası* 23 (1963), 1–80, makes some significant observations about the functional origins of "inverted T-plan" mosques, which he thus terms "convent-mosques" (*zaviyeli-camiler*).

[54] See introductory comments by F. Yenisehirlioğlu, "L'emploi de la brique sur les façades des édifices byzantins et ottomans aux XIVᵉ et XVᵉ siècles," *JÖB* 32/5 (1982), 327–37. See also G. Öney, *Anadolu Selçuklu Mimarisinde Süsleme ve El Sanatları* (Ankara, 1978), 12–104 passim, for Seljuk architectural decoration in various materials, esp. 59–69, for brick decoration.

[55] S. Y. Ötüken, et al., *Türkiye'de Vakıf Abideler ve Eski Eserler*, IV (Ankara, 1986), 206–12; 228–29; S. Eyice, "Die byzantinische Kirche in der Nähe des Yenisehir-Tores zu Iznik," *Materialia Turcica* 7–8 (1981–82), 152–67.

[56] Buchwald, "Lascarid Architecture" (note 47 above), 261–96, esp. 268–74; figs. 10–14, 25–27; also Th. Wiegand, *Der Latmos*, Milet, III, i (Berlin, 1913).

[57] Buchwald, "Lascarid Architecture" (note 47 above), figs. 12 and 14. A useful, but not complete, compendium of brick details from Constantinopolitan buildings is provided by A. Pasadaios, Ὁ κεραμοπλαστικός διάκοσμος τῶν βυζαντινῶν κτηρίων τῆς Κωνσταντινουπόλεως (Athens, 1973); see pls. 23, 24, and 33 for roundels.

[58] Pasadaios, Κεραμοπλαστικός (note 57 above), pls. 11–17.

[59] Buchwald, "Lascarid Architecture" (note 47 above), fig. 26; Pasadaios, Κεραμοπλαστικός (note 57 above), pls. 15, 16, and 19.

with the Seljuks, or at least with the vestiges of Seljuk culture, but they occupied a formerly Byzantine territory with a strong building tradition. Lacking an architectural heritage of their own, it is not surprising that the once-nomadic Osmanlı Turks would have looked to both cultures for inspiration. The design of the mosque may have been created by a Muslim master who came from the interior of Anatolia in the 1320s and 1330s along with other schoolmen and bureaucrats fleeing the disorder of the Mongol rule.[60] On the other hand, the construction was apparently carried out by locals—that is, by former Byzantines—who followed the dictated designs but constructed the walls according to their traditional workshop practices.

The picture of architecture in this region becomes richer if we consider the church of the Pantobasilissa (Kemerli Kilise) in Trilye, on the Sea of Marmara, some forty or fifty kilometers from Bursa (Fig. 24).[61] Its construction is a rough mixture of brick and stone, comparable to the Orhan Camii, and many of its details are also similar, including the banded voussoirs and the dogtooth outlining. Although the church had been previously dated to the thirteenth century, recent dendrochronological studies suggest a date sometime *after* 1336 for the church—that is, at least ten years after the conquest of Bursa.[62] Thus, Byzantine masons continued to produce Christian architecture in the region well after the fall of the major centers. The Ottoman conquest of Bithynia proceeded only gradually, and we know that Trilye was still in Byzantine hands in 1337, although the date of its ultimate capitulation is unknown.[63]

The Hüdâvendigâr Camii at Behramkale, ancient Assos, is somewhat removed from the heartland of Bithynia; nevertheless, it provides another instructive example of early Ottoman architecture (Fig. 25).[64] Dated to the third quarter of fourteenth century, the mosque is often said to have originally been a Byzantine church, a claim dating to the first excavation report from Assos by the Archaeological Institute of America in 1881, but retracted in the *errata* of the same report.[65] The plan is standard for a single-space Anatolian mosque, and the confusion seems to have resulted from the numerous *spolia* used in the construction, including an inscribed door frame. There are also ancient *spolia* used here; in fact, *all* of the construction materials are reused.[66] Again, decorative details such as the

---

[60] Lindner, *Nomads and Ottomans* (note 50 above), esp. 6–7.

[61] C. Mango and I. Ševčenko, "Some Churches and Monasteries on the South Shore of the Sea of Marmara," *DOP* 18 (1964), 235–40, figs. 20–39. Also Ötüken, et al., *Türkiye'de* (note 55 above), 484–86.

[62] P. I. Kuniholm and C. L. Striker, "Dendrochronological Investigations in the Aegean and Neighboring Regions, 1983–1986," *Journal of Field Archaeology* 14 (1987), 385–98, esp. 396, table 2.

[63] Mango and Ševčenko, "Churches and Monasteries" (note 61 above), 236.

[64] Ayverdi, *Osmanlı* (note 49 above), 224–29; Kuran, *Mosque* (note 52 above), 38–39.

[65] A close examination of the building was not possible during the first season of excavations at Assos; see J. T. Clarke, "Report on the Investigations at Assos, 1881," *Papers of the Archaeological Institute of America*, Classical Series, I (Boston, 1882), 122–23, noting, incidently, that earlier the traveler Poujoulat had mistaken the building for a Greek temple. However, in the errata, p. x (correcting p. 123), Clarke states clearly, "The edifice is referable to the earliest ages of Turkish architecture—probably to the fourteenth century."

[66] Kuran, *Mosque* (note 52 above) 38, sees two phases in the wall construction, indicated by a change of materials, which he speculates to have occurred when the large dome was introduced with the conversion of the building to a mosque. However, the small stone construction in the upper portion indicates the springing of the vaulting, and as the walls supported the vaults, it was impossible to continue the large stone construction beyond this point.

round arches with banded voussoirs and dogtooth outlining suggest Byzantine workmanship, as does the use of brick in the wall construction, laid with wide mortar joints.

I must sound a note of caution here: when I first examined the Hüdâvendigâr Camii I was thrilled to discover smaller roofing tiles inserted into the mortar joints between the bricks. Such construction, known as the "recessed brick" technique or "brick-filled mortar joints", was common in Byzantine architecture, and was frequently employed when building materials were reused.[67] Its appearance would certainly strengthen the postulated workshop connection. However, this detail appears to be the result of recent restoration—conforming to the modern "folk style" buildings of the town, and it doesn't appear in older photographs.

The technique of "brick-filled mortar joints" *is* found occasionally in early Ottoman architecture, as in the mosque at Tophisar, Byzantine Lentiana, built around 1400 (Fig. 26).[68] Such a construction detail would have been invisible when the building was completed—the recessed courses would have been covered with mortar, and thus it could not have resulted from imitation. The same technique appears in the upper level of the Kırgızlar Türbesi at İznik, from the mid-fourteenth century (Fig. 27).[69] The repeated use of "brick-filled mortar joints" suggests the continuity in the workshop tradition of northwest Asia Minor.

The Türbe of Lala Şahin Paşa at Mustafa Kemalpaşa (formerly Kirmasti) is one of the most curious buildings of the period, said to have been constructed around 1348 (Figs. 28–30).[70] The reconstruction is problematic: Ayverdi suggested that the building was an *ayvan* tomb: according to this interpretation, the square interior space, topped by a conical roof, would have been preceded by a barrel-vaulted entrance. As to the construction, Ayverdi regarded it as "Byzantinizing" in style, and this seems to be the commonly held opinion.[71]

On the other hand, Hasluck noted in passing that the building was said to have been a church.[72] Indeed, the neat, alternating brick and stone construction, the banded voussoirs in rounded arches, the decorative use of blind arcades with stepped pilasters, the decorative roundel, and the quantities of sculpture all find close Byzantine comparisons.[73] The form and construction of the arcading resembles the exonarthex of the Pammakaristos in the

[67] As above, note 35.

[68] Ötüken, et al., *Türkiye'de* (note 55 above), 388–92, figs. 226–29, pls. 56, 57.

[69] Ayverdi, *Osmanlı* (note 49 above), 197–82; Ötüken, et al., *Türkiye'de* (note 55 above), 224–27, esp. pl. 26.

[70] Ayverdi, *Osmanlı* (note 49 above), 190–97; Ötüken, et al., *Türkiye'de* (note 55 above), 525–30.

[71] Ayverdi, *Osmanlı* (note 49 above), 192–94.

[72] F. W. Hasluck, *Cyzicus* (Cambridge, 1910), 74–75; the illustration shows a typically Ottoman marble grille in the window; also A. Ersen, *Erken Osmanlı Mimarisinde Cephe Biçim Düzenleri ve Bizans Etkilerinin Niteliği* (diss.: Istanbul Technical University, 1986), 33.

[73] At the Lala Şahin Paşa Türbesi, the setbacks of the arches are frequently carved into a single stone or brick; in the right-hand arch—partly broken away and repaired—the innermost arches of the portal have a quarter-circular concavity between arches rather than a squared-off setback; the latter is also seen at the Pantobasilissa in Trilye; as above, n. 61. It is also worth noting that the voussoirs are not aligned between the facade arch and the arch of the portal; according to Velenis, this should suggest a later date for the türbe; see Ἑρμηνεία (note 5 above), esp. 102–103, 163–65,

capital. The sculpted arch from the window has a curled leaf motif, common in late Byzantine sculpture, and is similar to examples at the Chora, although it is executed in a softer stone and relationship of leaf face and curled tip is misunderstood.[74] The marble string courses are decorated with a common Byzantine palmette motif, and they follow the setback profile of the pilasters—they must have been carved specifically for this building.[75] The frieze of X's may be unique, but a thirteenth-century church in Philadelphia (Alaşehir) had something similar.[76] The corbel table frieze is also unique, but finds several comparisons in the mid-fourteenth-century churches of Nesebar, Bulgaria, as well as in the church of St.-Benoît in Galata, already discussed. For the most part, these features are common in Byzantine architecture and rare in Ottoman.

A look at the other side of the building provides something of a contrast: rough construction of mortared rubble, added to but not bonded with the brick and stone walls. Several Byzantine fragments appear here as well, including the door frame and lintel, and the sculpted arch above—its two pieces turned on end to form a pointed arch. I suspect that the building was in fact originally a Byzantine church of the early fourteenth century—Kirmasti fell to the Ottomans in 1342. It was probably a single-aisled basilica. Built on the unstable river bank, it suffered partial collapse shortly after construction and was later incorporated into the türbe. Most of the features, including the wall construction technique, are unique in Bithynia and find their best comparisons in Constantinople, and this building may have originally been the product of a workshop from the Byzantine capital.

The Convent or *Zaviye* of Mehmet Dede at Yenişehir, probably built sometime around 1360–89, is equally problematic (Fig. 31).[77] The facades are articulated by blind arcades topped by round arches with banded voussoirs. A number of common Byzantine decorative motifs also appear. Eyice saw the facades as revealing handiwork more Byzantine than Ottoman.[78] Indeed, earlier scholars such as Hartmann suggested that the convent was a Byzantine building.[79] But the plan and vaulting forms are clearly Ottoman. Although there are numerous superficial similarities with Byzantine architecture at Yenişehir, the differences are worth noting. Unlike the last example, the surface is reduced to two planes, and there is a precision uncommon in Byzantine architecture of the period. Moreover, construction materials are all new, with bricks thinner than standard for Byzantine architecture.[80] It is noteworthy that, unlike the other sites discussed, Yenişehir was *not* an older Byzantine foundation, but a new town begun by Osman. In addition, no marble detailing appears; string courses are of the same rough stone as the wall construction. The larger rounded

[74] Compare Ø. Hjort, "The Sculpture of the Kariye Camii," *DOP* 33 (1979), 27, 61, and 66.

[75] Compare to examples from Constantinople: *ibid.*, figs. 38–41.

[76] Buchwald, "Lascarid Architecture" (note 47 above), 279–80, and fig. 30.

[77] Ayverdi, *Osmanlı* (note 49 above), 208–16; Ötüken, et al., *Türkiye'de* (note 55 above), 603–607.

[78] S. Eyice, "La mosquée-zaviyah de Seyyid Mehmed Dede à Yenişehir. Recherches sur l'architecture turque du XIVe siècle," in *Beitrage zur Kunstgeschichte Asiens. In memoriam Ernst Diez* (Istanbul, 1963), 49–66.

[79] R. Hartmann, *Im neuen Anatolien, Reisedrücke* (Leipzig, 1928), 42–43, and Eyice, "Mosquée-zaviyah" (note 78 above), passim.

[80] M. I. Tunay, "Masonry of the Late Byzantine and Early Ottoman Periods," *Zograf* 12 (1981), 76–79.

arches are not always semicircular, and the voussoirs sometimes diverge from radial, with some awkwardness evident at the crowns.

Among the decorative details, both the roundel and the indented heart motif have been noted above. The heart motif was popular in Constantinople and in areas under its influence, and its appearance in a Muslim building deserves further comment.[81] In wall decoration, the heart was either treated independently, as at St. John of Lips; or nestled into the spandrel of an arcade, as at the Chora. The motif at Yenişehir appears as something of a compromise between the two variations. Although positioned in a spandrel, the motif is given independent definition with clearly articulated, sloping sides. These were necessary because of the dogtooth outlining of the arcades, unique in this example. The dogtooth would have formed an awkward border for the indented design. As executed at Yenişehir it looks almost as if the dogtooth has pushed the heart out of its proper position. These numerous details suggest that the Mehmet Dede Zaviyesi should be regarded as Byzantinizing, reflecting the transformations in the workshop tradition of western Asia Minor as the Ottoman masons became more firmly established and direct ties with Byzantine practices weakened.

The architectural picture of Bithynia that emerges conforms to the historical one. The Ottoman conquest in northwest Asia Minor proceeded gradually, and the indigenous population and its institutions were assumed into the nascent empire. Among those institutions were workshops of builders who maintained their established construction practices through the changes in patronage and the consequent changes in architectural forms. It was a period of transformation, both for the Ottomans and for the Byzantines. Clearly, Byzantine architecture in the region did not cease in 1326; nor did Ottoman architecture begin as abruptly.

To conclude, by separating *design* and *construction*, we can more easily distinguish the various influences that affected the architectural developments of the later Palaeologan period. Still, the picture that emerges from the above discussion is not a positive one, at least for the Byzantine Empire. We have a few scattered buildings in Thrace and the Balkans that may be associated with Constantinople in the latter part of the Palaeologan period—far too many of them undocumented and undated. There is little to suggest a coherent line of development following the great undertakings of the first decades of the century. Nevertheless, the architectural achievements of the capital continued to exert an influence in Serbia and Bulgaria, where Constantinopolitan features were mixed with regional developments. In Bulgaria, at least, this may have been due to the presence of artisans from the Byzantine capital.

Bithynia provides a significant point of contrast with Constantinople and its hinterland in Thrace. Curiously, whereas it was the first area to fall to the Ottomans, Bithynia presents the clearest picture of continuity in workshop practices—in spite of the changes in religion

---

[81] *Ibid.*, 76–79; also Ousterhout, "Byzantine Heart" (note 46 above), 36–44.

and patronage. We are reminded that the early Ottoman state was based as much on coöperation as on coercion, and it was for mutual benefit that the disaffected Byzantines of Bithynia—presumably including workshops of masons—were assumed into the tribe of Osman.[82] Although some of the decorative details in these buildings may reflect the architecture of Constantinople, by and large the wall construction does not; instead we find a continuation of the local workshop practices of northwestern Asia Minor.

As Constantinople declined politically, so did its cultural influence. The architecture of the city continued to inspire production in neighboring regions. But often, as in Serbia, it was past greatness, not current developments—and probably not Constantinopolitan workshops—that were looked to for guidance and inspiration. These later developments either revert to an earlier style or lack the intellectual rigor of the early Palaeologan monuments. Facades often become busy, merely decorative, and construction standards also decline. Moreover, without the authoritative presence of Constantinople in the later period, provincial architecture takes on greater significance. In the workshop interchanges between Nesebar and Constantinople, for example, "foreign" elements find their way into the architecture of the capital.

The developments in Bithynia may be seen as the beginning of something new, and there one can see the importance of regional workshops in the creation of a new architecture for a new patron and a different religion. However, the new architecture of Bithynia seems to have had little direct connection with Constantinople. In the final analysis, the architecture of the later Palaeologan period stands as a mute testimony to the waning power of the Byzantine capital.

[82] Lindner, *Nomads and Ottomans* (note 50 above), 5 and passim.

1. Constantinople, Chora Monastery, from the southeast; parekklesion ca. 1316–21 (photo: author)

2. Constantinople, Pammakaristos Monastery, from the southwest; parekklesion ca. 1310, exonarthex, second quarter fourteenth century (photo: author)

3. Constantinople, Pammakaristos Monastery. Exonarthex, detail, from west (photo: author)

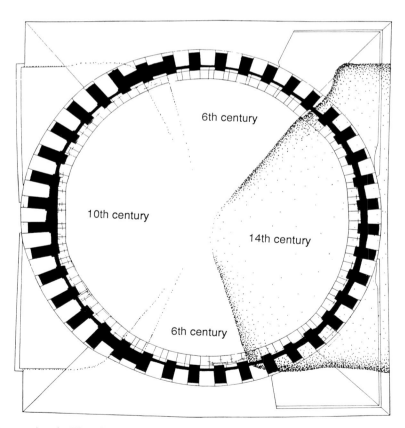

4. Constantinople, Hag. Sophia. Diagram of dome showing repairs (redrawn after Van Nice)

9. Constantinople, Tekfur Saray. North facade of main block, ca. mid-fourteenth century (photo: S. Ćurčić)

3. Constantinople, Pammakaristos Monastery. Exonarthex, detail, from west (photo: author)

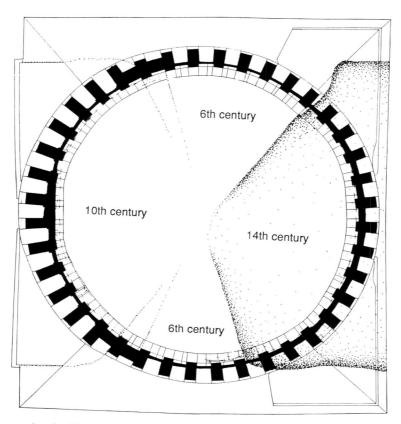

4. Constantinople, Hag. Sophia. Diagram of dome showing repairs (redrawn after Van Nice)

5. Constantinople, Blachernae
Wall (photo: author)

6. Constantinople, Golden Gate, from west.
Blocked arch (left), late fourteenth century
(photo: S. Ćurčić)

7. Constantinople, St.-Benoît, from south. Tower and domed chapel, ca. 1427 (photo: author)

8. Constantinople, St.-Benoît, from south. Detail of tower (photo: author)

9. Constantinople, Tekfur Saray. North facade of main block, ca. mid-fourteenth century (photo: S. Ćurčić)

10. Constantinople, Tekfur Saray. West facade of north wing, ca. mid-fourteenth century (photo: author)

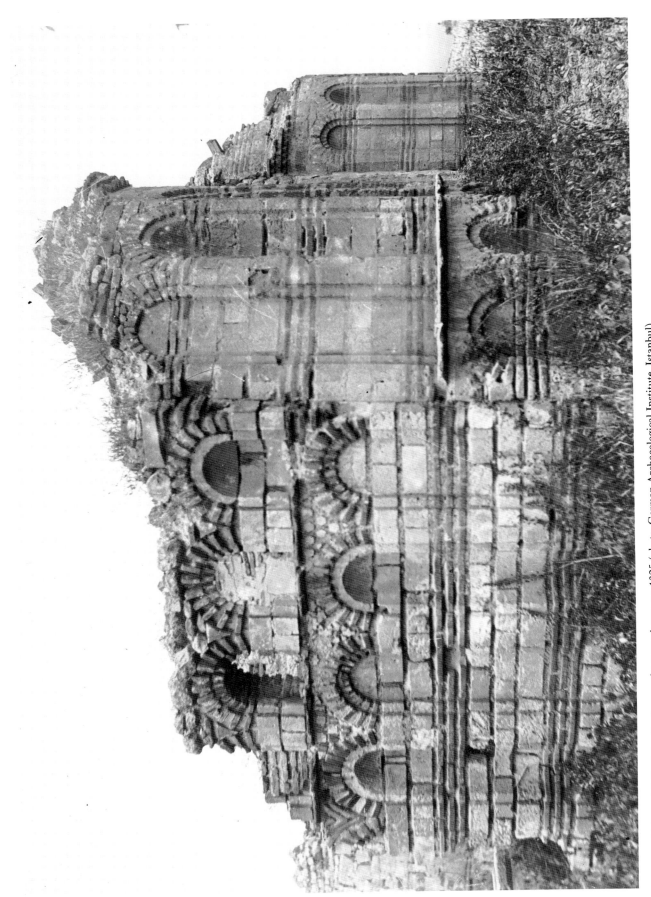

11. Silivri (Selymvria), St. John Prodromos, from southeast, ca. 1325 (photo: German Archaeological Institute, Istanbul)

12. Edirne (Adrianople), Saat Kulesi. Remains of an inscription of John VI or V, mid-fourteenth century (photo: Y. Ötüken)

13. Didymoteichon, ruined building next to Hag. Athanasios, from southeast, showing interior arcading, ca. second quarter fourteenth century (photo: Ephoreia of Byzantine Antiquities, Kavala)

14. Didymoteichon, ruined building next to Hag. Athanasios, from northeast (photo: Ephoreia of Byzantine Antiquities, Kavala)

15. Didymoteichon, Hag. Aikaterini. North facade, ca. mid-fourteenth century (photo: Ephoreia of Byzantine Antiquities, Kavala)

16. Didymoteichon, Hag. Aikaterini. East facade (photo: Ephoreia of Byzantine Antiquities, Kavala)

17. Pythion, castle, mid-fourteenth century. General view (photo: Ephoreia of Byzantine Antiquities, Kavala)

18. Pythion, castle. Interior of large tower (photo: Ephoreia of Byzantine Antiquities, Kavala)

19. Markov Manastir, church. North facade, ca. 1345 (photo: S. Ćurčić)

20. Nesebar (Mesemvria), Pantokrator. South facade, mid-fourteenth century (photo: author)

21. Nesebar (Mesemvria), St. John Aliturgetos. North facade, mid-fourteenth century (photo: author)

22. Bursa, Orhan Camii. Lateral facade, ca. 1334 (photo: author)

23. İznik (Nicaea), Hag. Sophia. Domed chapel, from southeast, thirteenth century (photo: author)

24. Trilye, Pantobasilissa (Kemerli Kilise). North facade, detail, after 1336 (photo: author)

25. Behramkale (Assos), Hüdâvendigâr Camii. Lateral facade, third quarter fourteenth century (photo: author)

26. Tophisar, mosque. Facade, ca. 1400 (photo: author)

27. İznik, Kırgızlar Türbesi. Detail showing recessed brick construction, mid-fourteenth century (photo: author)

28. Mustafa Kemalpaşa, Lala Şahin Paşa
Türbesi. South facade, first half fourteenth
century (photo: author)

29. Mustafa Kemalpaşa, Lala Şahin Paşa Türbesi.
South facade, detail (photo: author)

30. Mustafa Kemalpaşa, Lala Şahin Paşa Türbesi, from northeast (photo: author)

31. Yenişehir, Mehmet Dede Zaviyesi. Lateral facade, ca. 1360–89 (photo: author)

The Frescoes of the Parekklesion of St. Euthymios in Thessaloniki: Patrons, Workshops and Style*

THALIA GOUMA-PETERSON

IN 1302–1303 the protostrator Michael Doukas Glabas Tarchaneiotes and his wife Maria Doukaina Komnene Branaina Palaeologina renovated the parekklesion of St. Euthymios in Thessaloniki (Figs. 1–3), as the dedicatory inscription in the north aisle indicates.[1] The ensemble of frescoes which were part of this undertaking have been treated rather summarily in discussions of Palaeologan style, in large part because of their poor state of preservation. However, as I have shown elsewhere in an analysis of the iconographic program of the parekklesion and its meaning in the context of the broader political and cultural milieu of the first two decades of the reign of Andronikos II, the small parekklesion was a very prestigious monument and should figure prominently in any consideration of Palaeologan art.[2]

St. Euthymios is part of the most significant and highly revered shrine of Thessaloniki, the Basilica of St. Demetrios, and is dedicated to an outstanding monastic saint, St. Euthymios the Great of Melitine (377–473), the founder of Palestinian Cenobite monasticism. It

* I am indebted to a grant from the College of Wooster's Henry Luce III Fund for Distinguished Scholarship that enabled me to complete the research for this article. Professor Carl A. Peterson of Oberlin College I thank for his editorial advice and critical insight.

[1] On the inscription and dedication of the parekklesion see T. Gouma-Peterson, "The Parecclesion of St. Euthymios in Thessalonica: Art and Monastic Policy under Andronicos II," *ArtB* 59 (1976), 168–83, with bibliography. The frescoes of the parekklesion were first published by George and Maria Soteriou, Ἡ βασιλικὴ τοῦ Ἁγίου Δημητρίου Θεσσαλονίκης, (Athens, 1952), 213–30.

There is no general consensus as to whether the renovation was confined to providing an already extant structure with a new ensemble of paintings or whether the chapel itself was built at that time. The Soterious, Ἡ βασιλικὴ, 138, 213–30, 244–25, consider the parekklesion to be a Palaeologan foundation, as does A. Xyngopoulos, Ἡ βασιλικὴ τοῦ Ἁγίου Δημητρίου Θεσσαλονίκης (Thessaloniki, 1980), 13. More recently P. L. Vokotopoulos, and G. M. Velenis identify the parekklesion as a Middle Byzantine structure, predating the church of the Panagia ton Chalkeon in Thessaloniki, that is, before ca. 1028. See P. L. Vokotopoulos, "Οἱ μεσαιωνικοὶ ναοὶ τῆς Θεσσαλονίκης καὶ ἡ θέση τους στὰ πλαίσια τῆς Βυζαντινῆς ναοδομίας," Θεσσαλονίκη μεταξὺ Ἀνατολῆς καὶ Δύσεως. Πρακτικὰ Συμποσίου Τεσσαρακονταετηρίδος τῆς Ἑταιρείας Μακεδονικῶν Σπουδῶν, 1980 (Thessaloniki, 1982), 100–101, and G. M. Velenis, Ἑρμηνεία τοῦ ἐξωτερικοῦ διακόσμου στὴ Βυζαντινὴ ἀρχιτεκτονική, I (Thessaloniki, 1984), 131–33, 243–81. I thank Mrs. Eutychia Kourkoutidou-Nikolaidou, Ephor of Byzantine Antiquities of Thessaloniki, for making the Velenis monograph available to me.

On Michael Glabas and Maria Palaeologina see C. Mango, "The Monument and its History," in H. Belting, C. Mango, D. Mouriki, *The Mosaics and Frescoes of St. Mary Pammakaristos (Fethiye Camii) at Istanbul*, DOS 15 (Washington, D.C., 1978), 11–22.

[2] Gouma-Peterson, "The Parecclesion" (note 1 above), and *eadem*, "Christ as Ministrant and the Priest as Ministrant of Christ in a Palaeologan Cycle of 1303," *DOP* 32 (1978), 199–216.

was renovated by powerful and influential donors: Michael Glabas was the highest ranking general of Andronikos II, and his wife, Maria Palaeologina, was connected by birth to the imperial family. The renovation of the parekklesion was undertaken when Michael and Maria's religious adviser, Kosmas II, was patriarch of Constantinople. Kosmas, until his elevation to the patriarchal throne, had been abbot of the monastery of the Virgin Pammakaristos (now Fethiye Camii) in Constantinople, of which Michael and Maria were the owners and renovators.

The parekklesion, a miniature three-aisled basilica attached to the south aisle of the Basilica of St. Demetrios (Figs. 1, 2), contains the complete iconographic program of an independent church. This program is carefully worked out and adjusted to the small size of the chapel. It includes the Enthroned Virgin Hodegetria in the apse (Fig. 5) and a bust of St. John the Baptist (Fig. 4) in the diakonikon (the equivalent image in the prothesis is destroyed); a cycle of twelve major events from Christ's life, commonly referred to as the Twelve Feasts, in the upper register of the nave walls (Figs. 9–11); a cycle devoted to Christ's Ministry, consisting of scenes from his teaching and miracles, in the spandrels of the two nave arcades (Figs. 2, 12–15); a complex eucharistic cycle in the sanctuary, including the scenes of the Communion of the Apostles (Figs. 6, 7), the *Melismos*, and Old Testament prototypes of the Eucharist; and, in the south aisle, an abbreviated cycle of the Passion, now almost completely destroyed. The parekklesion also contains a full complement of figures of saints representing all major categories. The grouping begins with the images of St. Demetrios and St. Euthymios, who, as patron saints of the large basilica and its chapel, hold the most prestigious positions on the north and south piers of the sanctuary respectively (Figs. 2, 16). They serve as monumental icons flanking the templon screen in positions normally occupied by images of Christ and the Virgin. These two figures become focal points of the iconographic program at ground level and establish a parallelism between the monastic and military elements continued in the placement of figures throughout the chapel. Busts of monastic saints occupy the soffits of the nave arcades (Figs. 17, 18), and the lower register of the north wall of the north aisle (the single largest wall surface in the chapel) is devoted almost exclusively to life-size figures of standing military saints (Figs. 3, 19, 20). The equivalent position on the west wall of the north aisle is occupied by three doctor saints—the Anargyroi (Fig. 21). In the uppermost register of the west wall are busts of martyrs. The tripartite sanctuary has a full complement of bishop and deacon saints (Figs. 22, 23).

In the middle register of the north aisle is a splendid cycle of the life of St. Euthymios (Figs. 3, 25–30), specially created for the parekklesion and closely following the almost identical textual accounts of the saint's life by Kyrillos of Skythopolis (mid-sixth century) and Symeon Metaphrastes (second half of the tenth century). This cycle, which to our present knowledge is unique, is carefully worked out in its narrative sequence and has a complex symbolic meaning linked with the cycle of Christ's Ministry in the nave.[3] The

---

[3] For a discussion of the life of St. Euthymios in the parekklesion and its correspondence with the textual sources see Gouma-Peterson, "The Parecclesion" (note 1 above), *passim*. For a detailed discussion of the

multivalence of its content is equalled by the imaginativeness and liveliness of its form, much of which now has to be reconstructed because of the damage the cycle has sustained.

The carefully thought-out symbolic structure which underlies the iconographic program of the parekklesion suggests that the protostrator and his wife, Maria Palaeologina, had expert advice originating in the highest ecclesiastical circles of the period, the circles that advised the emperor himself. The imaginative adjustment of the iconographic program to the small dimensions and to the architectural design of the building also suggests that Michael and Maria hired one of the best workshops available to decorate the parekklesion. This is borne out by the quality of the frescoes; they are an outstanding example of Palaeologan painting of ca. 1300. Stylistically they are close to three other important ensembles of the same period: the frescoes added by Michael and Maria to the south facade of their monastery of the Pammakaristos, sometime between 1290 and 1304 (Figs. 44–46); the paintings of the Protaton at Mt. Athos for which there are no documented dates, but which, scholars generally agree, should be placed ca. 1300 (Figs. 40–43); and the frescoes of the Virgin Peribleptos (now St. Clement) in Ohrid, Yugoslavia, dated by an inscription to 1294–95 and signed by the painters Michael Astrapas and Eutychios (Figs. 31–39).[4]

These four ensembles form a group crucial for an understanding of the character and style of Palaeologan painting during the period from ca. 1290 to 1310. All are recognizably Palaeologan in their classicism and their repertory of human types (derived from ninth- and tenth-century prototypes, especially manuscripts) and their narrative intent, but the expressive rendering of the content, the massive and intense figures, and the dramatic presentation

---

symbolic and spatial correspondences in the cycles of Christ's Ministry and of the Life of St. Euthymios in the parekklesion see Gouma-Peterson, "Christ as Ministrant" (note 2 above) 199–216.

[4] On the frescoes of the Pammakaristos see C. Mango and E. J. Hawkins, "Report on Field Work in Istanbul and Cyprus, 1962–1963," *DOP* 18 (1964), 323–30. On the Virgin Peribleptos see O. Demus, "Die Entstehung des Paläologenstils in der Malerei," in *Berichte zum XI. Internationalen Byzantinisten-Kongress, München 1958* (Munich, 1958), 30–31, and P. Miljković-Pepek, *Deloto na zografite Mihailo i Eutihij* (Skopje, 1967), *passim*.

On the Protaton see A. Xyngopoulos, *Thessalonique et la peinture macedonienne* (Athens, 1955), *passim*; M. Soteriou, "Ἡ Μακεδονικὴ σχολὴ καὶ ἡ λεγόμενη Σχολὴ Μιλούτην," Δελτ.Χριστ.Ἀρχ.Ἑτ., ser. 4, 5 (1966–69), 11–30; Miljković-Pepek, *Deloto*, 203–12. The most recent study is by B. Todić, "Le Protaton et la peinture Serbe des premières décennies du XIVe siècle," in *L'art de Thessalonique et des pays Balkaniques et les courants spirituels au XIVe siècle. Recueil des Rapports du IVe Colloque Serbo-Grec, Belgrade 1985* (Belgrade, 1987), 21–31, with bibliography.

The Protaton frescoes could not possibly have been painted between 1305 and 1309, during which time Thrace and Macedonia were terrorized by the Catalans who settled in the peninsula of Cassandra and repeatedly raided and vandalized the monasteries of Mt. Athos. See A. E. Laiou, *Constantinople and the Latins, the Foreign Policy of Andronicus II, 1282–1382* (Cambridge, Mass., 1972), 190–91. In view of the stylistic relationships between the frescoes of the Protaton and those of the Peribleptos (1294–95) and St. Euthymios (1302–1303), as I argue in this article, the Protaton paintings should be placed between 1295 and 1302. Opinions on the dating of the Protaton frescoes vary. For example Miljković-Pepek, *Deloto* (note 4 above), 259 has proposed a date between 1296 (the Peribleptos) and 1308–1313 (the church of the Virgin Ljeviška in Prizren, Yugoslavia). O. Demus, "The Style of the Kariye Djami and its Place in the Development of Palaeologan Art," *The Kariye Djami* IV. *Studies in the Art of the Kariye Djami*, ed. P. A. Underwood (Princeton, 1975), 85, considers the Protaton frescoes inferior to those of the Peribleptos and later than both the Peribleptos and St. Euthymios. Soteriou, "Ἡ Μακεδονικὴ σχολή", 22, believes that the Protaton frescoes were completed before 1295.

of events are characteristic of the art of 1290–1310. This very dynamic and clearly articulated style, which has been variously called the "Ohrid manner," "the heroic style," "the heavy style," "the cubist style," and "the end-phase of the thirteenth century" has generally been seen as a transition between the classical style of the third quarter of the thirteenth century, exemplified at its best by the frescoes of the naos of the church of the Trinity at Sopoćani (ca. 1260–70), and the fully evolved Palaeologan style of the second decade of the fourteenth century of which the mosaics and frescoes of the church of Christ in Chora (now Kariye Camii) in Constantinople (ca. 1316–21) are the most famous example. Actually, however, these works done between 1290 and 1310 have a distinct style of their own. It is, as Otto Demus has observed, one of the most human and overtly dramatic styles created in Byzantine monumental painting.[5] It is very original and creative and is, I believe, the product of a particular workshop. It should not be minimized as a stage of transition between two other more clearly defined styles.

The stylistic connections between the Peribleptos, the Pammakaristos, and the Protaton have been recognized by scholars, as have those between St. Euthymios and the Protaton. But the connections between the frescoes of St. Euthymios and the Peribleptos have escaped attention, partly, no doubt, because the scratched, abraded, and faded paintings of the parekklesion look in their present state strikingly different from the almost intact images of the Peribleptos, and partly because of the substantial difference in scale (the parekklesion is roughly one fourth of the size of the Peribleptos). It is, however, surprising that the similarities between the frescoes of St. Euthymios and the Pammakaristos, sponsored by the same donors, also have escaped general attention. My own studies of the paintings of the parekklesion, based on a close and careful examination of the chapel in 1957, 1963, 1982, and 1989, and on photographs taken before 1950, have convinced me that they hold a key position in the formulation of the style of ca. 1300.

In this study I will first analyze the style of the frescoes of St. Euthymios; I will then show their connections with the paintings of the three other monuments through a comparative discussion of specific examples; I will then examine the significance of these connections for the possible existence of a common workshop in which the painters of all four

---

[5] Demus's 1958 and 1975 articles remain central to an understanding and identification of the major characteristics of Palaeologan painting in general and of the style of ca. 1290–1310 in particular; in both "Die Entstehung" (note 4 above), 30 and "The Style" (note 4 above), 145 he characterizes the style of ca. 1290–1310 as the concluding phase of the thirteenth century. See also: S. Radojčić, "Die Entstehung der Malerei der Paläologischen Renaissance," *JÖBG* 7 (1958), 105–23, and *idem, Geschichte der Serbischen Kunst von den Anfängen bis zum Ende des Mittelalters* (Berlin, 1969), 49–67; V. J. Djurić, *Byzantinische Fresken in Jugoslawien* (Munich, 1976), and *idem,* "La peinture murale serbe au XIIᵉ siècle," in *L'art byzantin du XIIᵉ siècle. Symposium de Sopoćani 1965* (Belgrade, 1967), 146–66; D. Mouriki, "Stylistic Trends in Monumental Painting of Greece at the Beginning of the Fourteenth Century," in *L'art byzantin au début du XIVᵉ siècle, Symposium de Gračanica 1973* (Belgrade, 1978), 55–83; H. Belting, "The Style of the Mosaics," in Belting, Mango, and Mouriki, *Pammakaristos* (note 1 above), 77–111, and especially 95 and n. 35 where he discusses the various designations used to describe the style of ca. 1290–1310; M. Chatzidakis, "Classicisme et tendances populaires au XIVᵉ siècle: Les recherches sur l'évolution du style," in *Actes du XIVᵉ Congrès International d'Études Byzantines, Bucharest 1971,* I (Bucharest, 1974), 153–88; W. Grape, "Zum Stil der Mosaiken in der Kilise Camii in Istanbul," *Pantheon* 32/1 (1974), 3–13; and Todić, "Protaton" (note 4 above), *passim.*

monuments were trained; and, finally, I will consider the possible influence of patrons on the popularity of new workshops and, therefore, new styles.

The frescoes of St. Euthymios are a perfect illustration of the style first defined by Demus, primarily on the basis of such examples as the Peribleptos and the Protaton, as characteristic of Palaeologan painting of ca. 1290–1310.[6] Their most striking feature is the human, dramatic, and emotional interpretation of the narrative. This is achieved through the use of posture and gesture and the placement of the figures on a well-furnished stage, on which they act out a drama intended to touch the spectator directly. Massive figures are crowded together and fully occupy their niches, thrones, or benches. The corporeality of the figures is further emphasized through the complex layering of garments which often creates pyramidal or exceedingly broad shapes (Figs. 6, 7, 13, 26, 29, 30). The material of the garments varies: in some instances, it hangs loosely around the figures and drapes in curved folds, while in other cases it is heavy and stiff. At other times it is rather light, fusing with the body (Figs. 7, 8, 11, 15) and emphasizing the mobility of the figures. Loose ends of mantles frequently fly upward or curl into mobile shapes that, denoting action, intensify the dynamism of the figures. They also become visual manifestations of emotional agitation (Figs. 6, 7, 15, 26), most notably in stationary figures engaged in animated conversation. All of these formal devices remain within the range of classicizing medieval conventions. For example, the clinging folds of garments which emphasize the plasticity of certain parts of the body often become so exaggerated as to deny the organic cohesion of the body (Figs. 6–8, 13, 29), which is further undermined by sharp angular folds that interrupt the smooth flow of outlines. This variety in the structure of garments and the seemingly unmotivated interruptions of body contours do create an effect of agitation and inner tension. The figures themselves, both active and mobile, are frequently shown in strangely twisted angles. In the Communion of the Wine, for example, the central apostle is almost twisted into a spiral (Fig. 6). Such "combination views" result in unnaturally compressed or broad and bulky figures (Figs. 7, 13, 29), which through exaggeration intensify the drama of the narrative.[7]

This drama is further enhanced through a wide range of gestures, expressing a variety of emotions. Figures reach out toward each other in open and expansive gestures or withdraw from each other in fear and agitation (Figs. 8, 13). Inner states of mind are also suggested through the intense and piercing gazes that protagonists direct at each other. The emotional involvement of secondary figures is similarly rendered (Figs. 8, 11, 25, 27). The depth and meaningfulness of the glances and the dynamic tension in gestures, postures, and actions both convey the nature of dramatic relationships and clarify the action. The impact of such scenes upon the spectator is direct and powerful and is intensified through the individualization of the figures. A wide range of facial types is employed, ranging from the very

[6] The following discussion of the general stylistic traits of the frescoes of St. Euthymios is indebted to Demus's "Die Entstehung" (note 4 above) and "The Style" (note 4 above).
[7] Demus, "Die Entstehung" (note 4 above), 13.

young to the very old. Stern, elderly figures with hooked noses, bushy eyebrows, and un-
kempt hair and beards are especially popular, both in narrative scenes and in single figures,
because of the potential for individualization and exaggeration (Figs. 11, 22, 23). The contrast between such figures and the classicizing handsome youthful types, used for both
young men and for women, is particularly effective.

The stories are acted out within architectural settings that are voluminous and solid,
but do not function primarily as spatial enclosures (Figs. 6–8, 14, 26, 30). They are scenic
props which identify events and emphasize the most important figures. They do not enclose
the figures, which are too large to fit within the structures, but create a spatial ambience
through their emphatic curved and angular forms. Frequently placed in oblique and oppos-
ing directions, these structures enhance the complexity and intensity of the compositions.
They often function illogically and irrationally, if judged from the point of perspectival
organization, but they do create, in Demus's words, "a vacuum filled with spatial energy,"
in which all component parts are held dynamically together.[8]

The figures of the Peribleptos (Figs. 31–39) and the Protaton (Figs. 40–43), to which
the paintings of St. Euthymios are closely related, have often been described as heroic because of the combination of volume, large scale, and emotional intensity. The paintings of
the parekklesion, because of the reduced scale in the narrative scenes necessitated by the
small dimensions of the building, do not appear as heroic. But in the single figures, such as
the Enthroned Hodegetria (Fig. 5), the Baptist (Fig. 4), the busts of monastic saints in the
nave arcades (Figs. 17, 18), and the full-length images of saints (Figs. 3, 19–21), where the
painters had larger wall surfaces to work with, the figures certainly do become heroic. This
is most vividly illustrated by the large image of the Hodegetria (Fig. 5) which fully occupies
her equally large, high-backed, cylindrical throne. The heroic effect of this central image in
the apse is enhanced through the contrast with the relatively short flanking archangels. This
large scale is also evident in a number of the narrative scenes, in spite of their small size, as,
for example, in the Virgin in the Nativity (Fig. 9), the Virgin and Symeon in the Presentation in the Temple, Christ in the Expulsion of the Merchants from the Temple (Fig. 13)
and in Christ Teaching in the Temple (Fig. 12), and St. Euthymios in the Descent of the
Heavenly Fire (Fig. 30). It is especially characteristic of the work of one of the main painters working in the parekklesion, as will be shown below.

Some scholars have maintained that the frescoes of St. Euthymios have a painterly
quality which distinguishes them from the paintings of the Peribleptos and the Protaton.[9]
But they are mistaken: it is because they have deteriorated so badly that the frescoes seem to
be painterly. Close inspection of the wall surfaces reveals that in hardly any part of the
chapel is the final layer of paint preserved intact and that in some parts, especially in the
nave, the color surface has been severely damaged by fire, in all likelihood by the fire of 1917
that destroyed most of the Basilica of St. Demetrios. This explains why in the cycles in the
upper nave walls (Festivals and Ministry of Christ) and in some of the busts of monastic

---

[8] Demus, "Die Entstehung" (note 4 above), 14.

[9] Demus, "The Style" (note 4 above), 85, especially stresses the impasto technique of the frescoes of St.
Euthymios, which he believes may be "the most painterly method to be found in the frescoes of the period."

saints in the nave arcades, parts normally painted yellow (e.g., haloes, the Virgin's throne in the Annunciation) or parts where yellow ocher would have been used as a constituent part of the color scheme (e.g., faces, hands, hair) are red, and other colors have acquired a dull reddish or grey cast. The red in these sections looks burnt and faded and differs from the reds in garments and ornamental cloths draped over buildings in other parts of the chapel. It would seem, then, that the fire, which affected primarily the higher parts of the nave, caused a chemical reaction which turned yellow-ocher and perhaps other pigments into burnt sienna.[10] In view of this and of the extensive abrading, the discussion of the color scheme of the frescoes can be, at best, partial and tentative. The following discussion is offered as an attempt to reconstruct, as far as possible on the basis of the evidence available, the original color effect in parts of the fresco decoration.

In general, the painters seem to have used bright and contrasting colors which stood out against the dark blue background. Gabriel in the Annunciation (Fig. 8) wears a white chiton and a light green himation. The dark blue tunic and purple maphorion of the Virgin, on the other side of the triumphal arch, contrast both with Gabriel's garments and with the greyish-purple architectural setting that is draped with an ornamental red cloth. Red accents occur frequently in garments and lesser accessories both in the narrative scenes and in the single images (e.g., the garments of the first magus and the young shepherd in the Nativity, the tunic of the Paralytic, the maphorion of Dionysia and of the Woman with the Curved Back). Throughout the Ministry cycle and in the scenes of the Communion (Figs. 6, 7, 12–15), Christ wears a light purple—almost orchid—chiton with a dark purple clavus, and a dark blue himation. In the Expulsion of the Merchants from the Temple (Fig. 13) he is framed by a light purple ciborium hung with a red curtain and flanked by a merchant dressed in brown. In Christ's encounter with the Samaritan at the well (Fig. 15), the woman wears a long lilac tunic, a shorter green tunic, and a red cape. In the scenes of the Communion (Figs. 6, 7) the apostles are dressed in violet, light green, dark blue, blue-grey,

---

[10] The burnt red is most evident in the scenes and single images on the triumphal arch, the Festival cycle on the upper nave walls, including the Dormition of the Virgin on the west wall, and to a lesser degree in the Ministry cycle in the register below the Festivals. It occurs to a lesser degree in the scenes of the Communion, the busts of bishops in the apse, and the standing bishops on the north and south piers in the sanctuary, but is very pronounced in the busts of monastic saints in the south arcade of the nave. In some instances the redness in the affected areas is not uniform. For example, in the Nativity (Fig. 9) the Virgin's halo, the mattress on which she sits, the cave opening, and the Christ Child in the manger have acquired various tones of red. The same has happened to Joseph's face, halo, and part of his garments (which originally seem to have been green), and to the wings and bodies of the two adoring angels. The garments of the midwife and Salome are mainly green, but this is the underpaint rather than the original finished surface. The background in the lower part of the scene is a faded green and the rest of the setting is a nondescript brownish grey with occasional traces of green. The Virgin's dark blue tunic and her purple maphorion, the red mantle of the first magus, and the young shepherd's red tunic are the only sections which retain their original color. It is clear that in these instances the red is the original hue because the color surface is much richer.

The late Richard Buck, Chief Conservator of the Intermuseum Laboratory in Oberlin, Ohio, conducted for me laboratory tests that demonstrated that both yellow ocher and raw sienna, the pigments used by medieval painters to obtain yellow, turned red when exposed to heat, the value of the red depending on the length of time the pigments were kept over the flame. He also subjected terra verde (used in the modelling of faces and hands) to this test and that pigment also acquired a reddish cast. This would seem to confirm my hypothesis that the burnt reds in certain sections of the frescoes of St. Euthymios were caused by the fire of 1917.

and yellow; the ciboria are light purple and are hung with wine-red curtains; the altar cloths are wine-red with a yellow border. In the Pentecost, in the soffit of the triumphal arch, where the color surface is less damaged than in most scenes, the apostles are dressed in lilac, blue-grey, light green, brick red, and yellow. The traditional dark blue and purple garments of the Virgin in the apse (Fig. 5) contrast with the yellow garments of the Christ Child and the yellow throne (both intended to represent gold). The flanking archangels are clad in imperial garments of purple (right) and medium-green and under the Virgin's feet is a crimson cushion. In the first two scenes from the Life of St. Euthymios (Fig. 26), on the west wall of the north aisle, the rather bright green structures with many red accents (the roof of the church, the columns of the semicircular structure, the cloth draped over the roof) create a varied and lively composition in conjunction with the medium blue tunic and red maphorion of Dionysia, the yellow tunics of Paul and Euthymios, and the blue-grey tunic of the seated Eudoxios. In the Healing of the Paralytic Child of the Saracene (Fig. 28), on the north wall, we find a combination of light green, yellow, purple, light blue, white, dark ocher, and greenish brown.

The love of polychromy and varied combinations is also evident in the single figures of saints. The colors of the costume of Saint George (Fig. 19), for instance, range from blue-grey, yellow, and green, to purple, dark blue, and red, contrasting with the more restrained dark blue, purple, white, and yellow of the garments of Saint Nicholas. Similarly, the light blue, blue-grey, and yellow of the garments of St. Cosmas (Fig. 21) contrast with the dark green, medium green, dark red, and yellow of the costume of St. Panteleimon.

Demus describes the color scale in early Palaeologan painting as ranging from the overly delicate to the overly garish. He cites new "poisonous" colors as characteristic of this period: sulphur-yellow, hard red, cold blue grey, and green in interchanging tones, as well as gold and white in separate strokes in the midst of darker tones. He finds that the extreme tensions in contrasting values often have an atmospheric effect and a "storm-like" character, which enhances the dramatic intensity of the narrative.[11] This certainly is true of the paintings of the Peribleptos and to a lesser degree of those of the Protaton. Most of the colors Demus cites also occur in St. Euthymios and, if the frescoes were better preserved, they would have appeared more extreme and "storm-like." Even in their present condition, when so much of the original effect is lost, the dominant qualities appear to be contrasting variety and dynamic activity.

Some scholars, partly on the basis of coloristic differences (a criterion which, as I have shown above, is not reliable) have attributed the frescoes of St. Euthymios to two painters. To one they attribute the Christological cycles and to the other the life of St. Euthymios. The work of one of these painters they consider to be especially close to portions of the frescoes of the Protaton.[12] My own examination of the frescoes confirms that two painters

---

[11] Demus, "Die Entstehung" (note 4 above), 14–15.

[12] For example the Soterious, Ἡ βασιλική (note 1 above), 218, find in the Christological cycles the most striking similarities with the Protaton and attribute these to one painter. The cycle of the life of St. Euthymios they find more schematic and attribute to another painter who, they believe, was influenced by the model which he used as a prototype. Xyngopoulos, *Thessalonique* (note 4 above), 30, disagreeing, maintains that the most striking analogies are to be found in the work of the artist who painted the life of St. Euthymios. To this

did indeed work in St. Euthymios, but that there is definitely no clear division of labor among cycles. Furthermore, given the present condition of the frescoes, one cannot safely use color as a basis of authorship, as I have already noted. Finally in attempting to identify hands, one must not overlook the possible participation of workshop assistants.

Careful study of the basic structure of scenes indicates that both of the two main painters of St. Euthymios worked on parts of the same cycles. For example, the scenes of the Communion of the Apostles (Figs. 6, 7), though iconographically identical, exhibit significant formal differences, most noticeably in the architectural setting, which in the Communion of the Wine (Fig. 6) is less complex and voluminous. Even taking into account that the pronounced flatness of the structures is accentuated by the faded colors (this is especially clear in the semicircular shape in the center which was originally the front plane of an open apsidal structure), it is obvious that in this scene the structures are not as clearly defined and complex, nor do they create as much of a sense of volume as in the Communion of The Bread (Fig. 7). In the latter scene, in addition to the elaborate ciborium and the prominent rectangular building on the left, a number of architectural elements (now barely visible) also project behind the wall in the center of the composition. Especially revealing are the differences in the treatment of the ciboria: in the Communion of the Bread the painter has placed a rectangular platform and a turret on top of the domical ciborium. In general, his stuctures occupy space more convincingly than those in the Communion of the Wine. The figures, too, are different. In the Communion of the Bread they are more balanced, less agitated, and occupy their alotted space with greater ease. They are organized into two groups: three figures in the front moving toward Christ and three in a second plane looking in the opposite direction. In the Communion of the Wine (Fig. 6), the figures, restless and excited, are not divided into groups but crowded together. The rhythm of the scene is irregular and agitated.

On the basis of such differences in the two Communion scenes, it is possible to identify the work of each of the two painters in other scenes. The differences in their work are not the result of training and the handling of sources, but rather of personal habits in treating the conventions of pictorial composition. The difference reflects, one might say, two distinct temperaments. The work of artist A, as I shall henceforth identify him, is, as evidenced in the Communion of the Wine, more passionate and intense than that of artist B (Communion of the Bread). His compositions are crowded and less balanced. Not as spatially developed, they are unstable and explosive. In his compositions figures appear to push each other, and all component parts are close to the picture plane. Jarring spatial incongruities occur often, as in the right column of the ciborium in the Communion of the Wine (Fig. 6), which abruptly ends on top of John's head, and in the figure of the dead Euthymios in the scene of his Dormition (Fig. 29), which floats in front of the crowded semicircular cluster of agitated monks. Frequently A devotes a large part of the total space to one or two figures, which he frames with a dominant architectural element, subordinating all other parts to this primary unit, as, for example, Christ and John in the Communion of the Wine (Fig. 6),

---

artist he also attributes some of the single figures of saints, but does not specify which. See also Demus, "The Style" (note 4 above), 85, and Miljković-Pepek, *Deloto* (note 4 above), 260.

Christ and the merchant in the Expulsion of the Merchants from the Temple (Fig. 13), Christ in Christ Teaching in the Temple (Fig. 12), the Virgin and Child in the Nativity (Fig. 9), St. Euthymios and the ciborium in the Descent of the Heavenly Fire (Fig. 30), and the Enthroned Hodegetria in the apse (Fig. 5). This frequently results in a lack of balance, which however adds to the expressive tension. The elements that are out of balance vary. Figures and structures are too massive, groups are too schematic, and compositions are overly crowded, but the result is always the same: an effect of antithesis and intensity. His figures are often agitated, as in the Communion of the Wine (Fig. 6) and the Enthroned Hodegetria in the apse (Fig. 5), where one least expects it. Occasionally they become bulky and awkward (Figs. 13, 29, 30). Garments cling to figures or are arranged in hard, linear folds which cross the body. On the basis of such features, I believe that artist A painted the following, in addition to the Communion of the Wine: the Nativity (Fig. 9), the Presentation in the Temple, and most of the other festival scenes on the south wall of the nave; Christ Teaching in the Temple (Fig. 12) and the Expulsion of the Merchants (Fig. 13), from the Ministry cycle; the scenes of the Life of St. Euthymios on the north wall (Figs. 25, 27–30); St. John the Baptist (Fig. 4) and the Hodegetria (Fig. 5) in the sanctuary, and St. Demetrios and St. Euthymios on the sanctuary piers (Figs. 2, 16). His work is both stylistically and temperamentally close to the frescoes of the Peribleptos in Ohrid.

Artist B, who painted the Communion of the Bread (Fig. 7), centralizes his compositions and balances them carefully. In his narratives figures move with ease, and complex architectural settings and voluminous figures are combined without overcrowding. The buildings are in harmony with the figures and become accents or frames for them. Though intense, the figures are never awkward and usually have a dignified nobility. Artist B also has a developed sense of pictorial depth, within the parameters of medieval conventions. He is able to create spatially harmonious units, often in very restricted wall spaces (Figs. 14, 15, 26). Hardly ever in his work is there a sense of pushing and crowding or any awkwardness of transition between scenes. Generally garments are softer and more loosely draped. In my view, artist B painted the following, in addition to the Communion of the Bread: the Annunciation on the east wall (Fig. 8), the Anastasis (Fig. 11) and the Crucifixion (Fig. 10) on the north wall of the nave; the Healing of the Paralytic (Fig. 14) and Christ and the Samaritan (Fig. 15) on the same wall; the two first scenes of the Life of St. Euthymios (Fig. 26) on the west wall of the north aisle; and most of the full-length figures of saints in the north aisle (Figs. 19–21). His work is closely related to that of the best painter of the Protaton.

The attribution of scenes and single images in the parekklesion to two painters on the basis of personal habits in the handling of pictorial conventions yields a rather sensible division of labour. Artist A painted primarily on the south wall of the nave and sanctuary (Communion of the Wine, Nativity, Presentation, Christ Teaching in the Temple, Expulsion of the Merchants) and in the sanctuary (Baptist, Hodegetria, St. Demetrios, St. Euthymios). B painted primarily on the north wall of the nave and sanctuary (Communion of the Bread, Anastasis, Crucifixion, Healing of the Paralytic at Bethesda, Christ and the Samaritan) and the triumphal arch (Annunciation) and also did most of the full-length images of saints in the north aisle. The two divided the life of St. Euthymios, with B painting the scenes on the west wall and A those on the north.

It is tempting to pursue the differences in the work of these two painters further through a consideration of their use of color and their modelling technique. But, as I pointed out above, the deterioration of the frescoes makes this extremely difficult and at best tentative. Generally, it seems that painter B prefers lighter and more varied color schemes and tends to use light greens, blues, reds and yellows abundantly (cf. the first two scenes of the Life of St. Euthymios, Christ and the Samaritan Woman, the Communion of the Bread, the Anastasis, St. George). Also in the modelling of faces and exposed parts of the body he does not use dark green (ocher) as much as artist A does. Generally painter A uses a darker color scheme and contrasts light and dark tonalities both in the compositions as a whole (e.g., dark brown versus light violet, dark blues and purples contrasted with white) and in the modelling of individual parts where highlights strongly contrast with darker flesh tones. These differences correspond with differences that have been identified in the work of two of the main painters active in the Protaton.[13]

In spite of the presence of two distinct artistic personalities, the St. Euthymios frescoes as a whole do belong stylistically to the heroic, dramatic, and volumetric style of ca. 1290–1310. For example, the large figure of the Hodegetria in the apse (Fig. 5) is seated in a large and projecting throne, which further enhances her presence. She turns to the right to motion toward the Christ Child whom she holds on her left arm. This surely is one of the most active and dramatic, as well as heroic, representations of the Virgin to be found in the apse of a Byzantine church. The same overemphasis is evident in the rather short and broad figures of the bending Archangels flanking the Virgin and in the large and heavy figures of the full-length military saints, of which St. George is the best preserved (Fig. 19). These saints belong to the same family as the military saints in the Protaton and the Peribleptos. It is on the weapons and garments of these saints in the Peribleptos that Michael Astrapas and Eutychios inscribed their names, for example, ΧΕΙΡ ΜΙΧΑΗΛ ΤΟΥ ΑΣΤΡΑΠΑ, which we read on the sword of St. Merkourios (Fig. 36). The similarities in the figures of Sts. George and Theodore Stratilates in St. Euthymios and the Protaton (Figs. 19, 43), St. Merkourios in the Peribleptos and the Protaton (Figs. 36, 42), and Sts. Theodore Teron and Demetrios in St. Euthymios (Figs. 2, 20) and the Peribleptos (Fig. 37) indicate that they are products of the same workshop, if not of the same artists.

One of the most striking examples of the close connections between the Peribleptos and St. Euthymios are the almost identical images of the Baptist in the diakonikon (Figs. 4, 31). These broad and weighty figures stand out because of their overemphatic presence. Both the emotional intensity and the planar and segmented articulation are striking in the well preserved Peribleptos image. It is impossible to determine whether the scratched and abraded image in St. Euthymios was originally as emotionally intense. Nevertheless, the similarities in the two figures are so striking (the physical type, the structure of the garments and their color scheme, the hairy patterning on the exposed area of the Baptist's throat and on his hands) that it is difficult to imagine that the faces would not also have been very similar.

[13] Todić, "Protaton" (note 4 above), 24.

Other closely related figures in the Peribleptos and the parekklesion are Christ and John in the Communion of the Wine (Figs. 6, 32) and Christ in the Expulsion of the Merchants from the Temple (Figs. 13, 33). Painter A of St. Euthymios, to whom I have attributed these scenes and the figure of the Baptist, retained, in his representation of the Communion of the Wine, the intense relationship between Christ and John, even repeating the disciple's profile and flattened mop of hair and the awkward ciborium column which in St. Euthymios, where there is no room to include haloes, abruptly ends over John's head. In the Expulsion of the Merchants (Fig. 13) Christ and the first merchant are fairly well preserved and provide evidence not only for specific similarities with the Peribleptos scene, but also for the existence in St. Euthymios of the planar and segmented (or "cubist") garment structure. In both the Communion and the Expulsion, painter A had to adjust the scenes to a very restricted wall surface, but was still able to retain the sense of both physical volume and dramatic intensity. The work of painter A, which gains in dramatic expressiveness what it lacks in harmony and refinement, is clearly evident in the seven scenes from the life of St. Euthymios on the north wall of the north aisle (Figs. 25, 27–30). Massive buildings and obliquely placed objects such as beds, baptismal fonts, and ciboria push the figures forward and crowd them together. Because the space is more limited, the crowding is more extreme than in the related cycle of the life of the Virgin in the Peribleptos (Fig. 38). But the overall effect in both cycles is one of extreme physical and emotional presence.

However, not all artists working in these churches painted in the extreme version of this style, as the differences in the work of artists A and B of St. Euthymios have shown, and as comparisons of scenes in the other churches further demonstrate. The figures in the Presentation of Christ in the Temple in the Peribleptos, for example, are more slender and restrained and less dramatically intense than those of the Nativity of the Virgin (Fig. 38) or the Communion of the Wine (Fig. 32). Also, the planar, angular layering of garments is less pronounced. Similar differences exist in the work of painter A and B in St. Euthymios, as pointed out above.

The work of artist B, who painted the Annunciation and most of the scenes of the Festival cycle on the north wall of the nave (Figs. 8, 10, 11), is most closely related to the Protaton. The scenes of the Anastasis (Figs. 11, 41) in the two churches are almost identical, except that in St. Euthymios the relative position of the figures has been reversed so that Christ strides out of the East to raise Adam. Both compositions also are similar to the Peribleptos Anastasis (Fig. 35). In all three the intense relationship of Christ and Adam, who look into each other's eyes, is emphasized, as is Adam's inert physicality and windswept white leonine mane. The scenes of the Crucifixion (Figs. 10, 34, 40) are even more closely related. In all three churches they include the sorrowful John and agitated centurion, framed by a semicircular structure, the tightly packed group of Maries, the lamenting Virgin with left hand against her cheek, and the weeping angels. In all three renderings the substantial loincloth of Christ hangs diagonally, as if pulled down by the force of gravity.

The fragments on the south facade of the Pammakaristos in Constantinople (now south ambulatory) exhibit both the physicality and the emotional reality characteristic of the style of ca. 1290–1310.[14] In the scene of the Virgin Praying in her House (a scene that was part of a Dormition cycle) the Virgin looks up intently toward Christ with arms raised and palms extended (Fig. 44), and is framed by a voluminous building. She is almost identical with the figure of Dionysia praying in church (Fig. 26), in the opening scene of the life of St. Euthymios, and both are closely related to the praying Virgin in the Protaton Ascension. The similarites extend to such specific details as the shape of the face, the draping of the substantial maphorion, and the articulation of the tense hands. The fragment of St. Peter (Fig. 45) from the same Dormition cycle in the Pammakaristos resembles, both in facial type and garment structure, many of the figures in St. Euthymios (e.g., Paul praying in church, Fig. 26, St. Peter in the Pentecost, a prophet on the triumphal arch, Fig. 24) and the Protaton (e.g., St. Peter in the Ascension). It also has the weightiness and physicality characteristic of the style of this period. The third and best preserved fragment in the Pammakaristos, a representation of the Closed Door (Fig. 46) with Aaron and his sons before the altar, exemplifies the less extreme variant of this style. The more slender figures have smaller heads, are less emotionally intense, and are stylistically close to the Communion of the Bread in St. Euthymios (Fig. 7) and the Peribleptos Presentation of Christ in the Temple. Even the structure of the faces and their more refined features are similar (cf. Symeon in the Peribleptos and the central Apostle in St. Euthymios with the two figures on the right in the Pammakaristos). These stylistic variants within each monument indicate that, while working within the parameters of the same general style, individual painters retained their personal idiosyncrasies. These, however, did not alter the dominant characteristics of the style.

There is enough overlap between the frescoes of St. Euthymios, the Protaton, the Peribleptos, and the Pammakaristos to suggest that some of the same painters worked in all four churches and that all painters were trained in the same workshop. The workshop must have been fairly large, well-established, and popular to have been employed by such prestigious patrons. The workshop may have included, besides Michael Astrapas and Euthychios, another Astrapas (perhaps the father of Michael) who is mentioned in the dedicatory inscription of the church of the Virgin (Bogorodica Ljeviška) in Prizren, Yugoslavia, and perhaps the legendary Panselinos associated by oral tradition and eighteenth-century documents with the Protaton frescoes.[15] It also may have included Kalliergis, who in 1315 painted the

[14] Neither Mango and Hawkins, "Report on Field Work" (note 4 above), 329–30, nor Belting, "The Style" (note 4 above), 110–11 consider the Pammakaristos frescoes to have been done by the same workshop as those of St. Euthymios.

[15] The churches painted by Michael Astrapas and Eutychios for King Milutin of Serbia have been discussed by, among others: Xyngopoulos, *Thessalonique* (note 4 above), 34–44; S. Radojčić, *Majstori starog srpskog slikarstva* (Belgrade, 1955), 19–30, and *idem*, "Die Entstehung der Malerei" (note 5 above) 105–123; Demus, "The Style" (note 4 above), 147–50; Miljković-Pepek, *Deloto* (note 4 above), 245–62; H. Hallensleben, *Die Malerschule des Königs Milutin. Untersuchungen zum Werk einer byzantinischen Malerwerkstatt zu Beginn des 14. Jahrhunderts*, Osteuropastudien der Hochschule des Landes Hessen, Reihe II, Bd. 5: Die Monumentalmalerei in Serbien und Makedonien 3–5 (Giessen, 1963), 22–34; Todić, "Protaton" (note 4 above), *passim*.

Whether Manuel Panselinos of Thessaloniki, to whom the Protaton frescoes were attributed by Dionysios of Fourna in his *Hermeneia*, completed between 1729 and 1733, was a real person or a fictitious character

church of the Ascension of Christ (now church of Christ) in Veroia, and who is described in the dedicatory inscription as the best painter of Thessaly (i.e., Macedonia).[16] The echoes of the frescoes of St. Euthymios, especially of artist B, in Kalliergis' work are so strong, though done some thirteen years later, that they can only be explained through an origin in the same workshop. But the differences are significant enough that I do not believe that artist B, whose work is almost identical with that of the best painter in the Protaton, should be identified with Kalliergis.[17] The art of this workshop, which put its stamp on the decades between ca. 1290 and 1310, is not a provincial phenomenon. Its clients included, in addition to the protostrator Michael and his wife Maria Palaeologina, the Great Hetaeriarch Progonos Sgouros and his wife Eudokia, the donors of the Peribleptos (who assert in the dedicatory inscription that they are related to the imperial family), and the Protos of Mount Athos who sponsored the renovation of the Protaton, the main church of Karyes, the capital of the most significant and powerful monastic community in the Empire.[18]

---

remains an open question. Xyngopoulos, *Thessalonique* (note 4 above), 29–33, and *idem, Manuel Panselinos* (Athens, 1956), was convinced of his authorship of the Protaton frescoes. The tendency in more recent scholarship has been to doubt that such a person did exist and to attribute the Protaton frescoes to the workshop of Michael Astrapas, who, in the opinion of a number of scholars, was from Thessaloniki. See, for example, C. Kissas, "Solunska umetnička porodica Astrapa," *Zograf* 5 (1974), 35–37; P. Miljković-Pepek, "L'atelier artistique proéminent de la famille thessalonicienne d'Astrapas de la fin du XIIIe et des premières décennnies du XIVe siècle," *JÖB* 32/5 (1982), 491–94; Todić, "Protaton" (note 4 above).

The possibility that Michael Astrapas and his workshop painted the frescoes of St. Euthymios needs to be at least considered, since, in addition to the stylistic similarities between the frescoes of St. Euthymios and the Peribleptos discussed above, in the border of Paul's tunic in the opening scene of the Life of St. Euthymios (Fig. 26) one can clearly see the letter M followed by what appear to be fragments of an I and X. These three letters can be an abbreviated version of Michael's signature (MIX). In fact there is room in the border for two more letters and Michael's full name could fit, with perhaps one letter partly obscured by a fold in the tunic. Both Michael and Eutychios did sign on garments, especially in the Peribleptos where there are multiple signatures, and both used various abbreviated forms of their names, as for example MXH, MX, M, and E. In one instance, in the narthex of the Peribleptos, Michael signs M M on the border of the tunic of St. Damian (north of the entrance and next to the dedicatory inscription). This suggests that the M in Paul's tunic could be a signature (or could have been part of a fuller version of Michael's signature). Its placement in the border of the garment of a praying figure immediately above the dedicatory inscription is well chosen. But, since so much of the border design is missing, the context of what now reads as an M is unclear and its identification as a signature will have to remain a tempting and likely possibility.

On the signatures of Michael and Eutychios see: G. Millet and A. Frolow, *La peinture du moyen âge en Yougoslavie*, III (Paris, 1962), xii; Miljković-Pepek, *Deloto* (note 4 above), 19–22; Xyngopoulos, *Thessalonique* (note 4 above), 37; Radojčić, "Die Entstehung der Malerei" (note 5 above), 105–23, and *idem, Majstori* (note 15 above), 22–27, where he also reproduces accurate drawings of some of the signatures; Hallensleben, *Die Malerschule* (note 15 above), 22–30.

[16] S. Pelekanidis, Καλλιέργης ὅλης Θετταλίας ἄριστος ζωγράφος (Athens, 1973), 7–12.

[17] Most telling is a comparison of the iconographic scheme of the triumphal arch, which in both churches combines the Annunciation and Mandylion (cf. Fig. 8 and Pelekanidis, Καλλιέργης, figs. B, 11, 15). Both the overall composition and the treatment of individual figures are very similar. But the Veroia figures do not have either the vitality or the intensity of the work of painter B. Gabriel at Veroia is earthbound and rather heavy as opposed to the light and dynamic figure in the parekklesion which, in his windblown garments, appears to be propelled by a supernatural force. It is possible, however, that Kalliergis was a younger member of the workshop that painted St. Euthymios.

[18] For the Peribleptos dedicatory inscription see Millet and Frolow, *La peinture* (note 15 above), xv and C. Mango, Review of Millet and Frolow, *La Peinture*, in *ArtB* 45 (1963), 153. Hallensleben, *Die Maler-*

The workshop, which would seem, from the surviving evidence, to have specialized in fresco painting, could have originated in either Thessaloniki or Constantinople. Regardless of where it originated, it seems to have had a number of members from Thessaloniki; and, based on the evidence of surviving monuments, its activities appear to have been concentrated in Thessaloniki and Macedonia.[19] But, as the frescoes of the Pammakaristos indicate, the workshop was also active in Constantinople. The extensive loss of monuments in the Capital makes it impossible to determine the extent of its activity there. It would seem, however, that during this period of constant movement of officials and members of the court between the two cities, it is unnecessary and perhaps even counterproductive to think in terms of localized schools. Rather, as the departure of Michael Astrapas and Eutychios from Byzantine Macedonia to work for King Milutin in Serbia suggests, workshops apparently moved along with the patrons who hired them.

By ca. 1310 a different workshop was becoming popular, as evidenced by the mosaic decorations of the Pammakaristos parekklesion in Constantinople, built sometime between 1306 and 1310 by Maria Palaeologina as a burial chapel for her husband, the protostrator Michael. Her decision to decorate the small, elegant building with mosaics showed that she was determined that no expense would be spared and that her deceased husband would rest in a building worthy of those devoted to his most illustrious predecessors in the capital of the Empire.[20] There are elements of both traditionalism and extravagance in her decision and it may have set a precedent for other patrons of high rank, for both Patriarch Niphon I, in restoring the church of the Holy Apostles in Thessaloniki in ca. 1310–14 (at that time a monastery dedicated to the Virgin), and Theodore Metochites in his restoration of the Chora Monastery (now Kariye Camii) in Constantinople, in ca. 1316–21, opted to use primarily mosaic.[21] The traditionalism and the conservatism of the preferred medium and

---

schule (note 15 above), 23, has published the Greek text of the inscription and a German translation. However, his reading of the date is incorrect.

[19] Both Xyngopoulos, *Thessalonique* (note 4 above), *passim*, and Radojčić, "Die Entstehung der Malerei" (note 5 above), 111–13, explain the stylistic changes from ca. 1290 to 1320 in terms of an opposition between Thessaloniki and Constantinople. Demus, "Die Entstehung" (note 4 above), 30 and n. 31, and *idem*, "The Style" (note 4 above), 141, 146–47, also entertains the possibility of the existence of local schools. All of these scholars see the work of Michael Astrapas and Eutychios as being characteristic of Thessaloniki. V. J. Djurić, "La peinture murale serbe du XIIIᵉ siècle," in *L'art byzantin du XIIIᵉ siècle. Symposium de Sopoćani 1965* (Belgrade, 1967), 150–67, cites evidence that painters from both Constantinople and Thessaloniki were brought to Serbia by royal and clerical patrons. For more recent opinions see Mouriki, "Stylistic Trends" (note 5 above), 58–66, and Todić, "Protaton" (note 4 above), 30–31.

[20] Belting, Mango, and Mouriki, *Pammakaristos* (note 1 above), *passim*. For the dating of the Pammakaristos parekklesion see especially pp. 15, 96–98.

[21] For the Holy Apostles see A. Xyngopoulos, Ἡ ψηφιδωτὴ διακόσμησις τοῦ ναοῦ τῶν Ἁγίων Ἀποστόλων Θεσσαλονίκης, Μακεδονικὴ Βιβλιοθήκη, 16 (Thessaloniki, 1953), and *idem*, "Les fresques de l'église des Saints-Apôtres à Thessalonique," in *Art et société à Byzance sous les Paléologues, Actes du Colloque organisé par l'Association Internationale d'Études Byzantines à Venise en Septembre 1968*, Bibliothèque de l'Institut Hellénique d'Études Byzantines et Post-byzantines de Venise 4 (Venice, 1971), 83–89. See also Christine Stephan, *Ein byzantinisches Bildensemble: die Mosaiken und Fresken der Apostelkirche zu Thessaloniki*,

of the new style seem to go hand in hand. This workshop, which worked extensively, though not exclusively, in mosaic, created a different style. The differences become clear in comparing the Baptism in St. Euthymios, the Protaton, and the Peribleptos with the mosaic of the Pammakaristos (Fig. 48), or the Anastasis in the same three churches (Figs. 11, 35, 41) with the mosaic of the Holy Apostles (Fig. 47). This more restrained and elegant phase of Palaeologan art lacks the dynamism, the physicality, and the emotional intensity of the earlier style. Most striking is the melancholy and inward-looking expression of the figures and the restraint of their actions.

The new style quickly became popular as the workshop came to be employed by a succession of important patrons. Regardless of the particular reasons that prompted the choice of workshop and medium by these patrons, the stylistic changes which occurred ca. 1308–1310 were widespread. In the case of the Pammakaristos, the differences between the frescoes of the south ambulatory and the mosaics of the parekklesion, sponsored by the same donor, can be attributed both to the presence of a different workshop and to the difference in medium. But the frescoes of the Peribleptos in Ohrid (1294–95) and those of St. Nikita near Čučer (ca. 1316) were painted by the same artists, Michael and Eutychios, who by ca. 1310 were employed on a regular basis by King Milutin of Serbia, the son-in-law of Andronikos II. Milutin, who between ca. 1307 and 1321 founded and renovated a succession of churches in his flourishing kingdom, spent a good part of his time with his mother-in-law, the Empress Irene, in Thessaloniki and also renovated churches in that city as well as on Mt. Athos.[22] The significant change in Michael and Eutychios' style can only be attributed to a conscious decision. This decision may have been prompted in part by King Milutin, who wanted his foundations to be decorated in the latest and most fashionable style, in order to compare with the most prestigious churches in Constantinople and Thessaloniki. In other words, the stylistic change may reflect as much a change in taste among important patrons as it does one of independent decisions by the artists.[23]

Manuskripte zur Kunstwissenschaft, Bd. 7 (Worms, 1986). Recently, a much later date for the Holy Apostles (after 1329) has been proposed by P. I. Kuniholm and C. L. Striker, "Dendrochronology and the Architectural History of the Church of the Holy Apostles in Thessaloniki," *Architectura* 20 (1990), 1–26. The authors' conclusions bring into question the meaning of the dedicatory inscriptions in the Holy Apostles, which clearly identify Patriarch Niphon I (1310–1314) as *ktētor*. Their conclusions will have to be subjected to further scrutiny.

For the mosaics and frescoes of the monastery of Christ in Chora see P. A. Underwood, *The Kariye Djami* I–III (New York, 1966), and *The Kariye Djami* IV (note 4 above).

[22] For Milutin's foundations in Serbia see note 15 above. See also: V. J. Djurić, "L'art des Paléologues et l'état serbe. Rôle de la cour et de l'église serbe dans la première moitié du XIVe siècle," in *Art et société à Byzance sous les Paléologues. Actes du Colloque organisé par l'Association Internationale des Études Byzantines à Venise en Septembre 1968* (Venice, 1971), 179–91; B. Todić, *Gračanica. Slikarstvo* (Belgrade, 1988); G. Babić, *Kraljeva crkva u Studenici* (Belgrade, 1987); D. Panić and G. Babić, *Bogorodica Ljeviška* (Belgrade, 1975). For Milutin's patronage of churches on Mt. Athos see V. J. Djurić, "La peinture de Chilandar à l'époque du roi Milutin," *Hilandarski zbornik (Recueil de Chilandar)* (1978), 31–62.

[23] The role of the patron as a contributing factor not only to the content but also to the form of Byzantine paintings has been discussed by, among others: Radojčić, "Die Entstehung der Malerei" (note 5 above), 122; Djurić, "La peinture murale" (note 19 above), 161–67, and *idem, Sopoćani* (Leipzig, 1967), 204–207; H. Belting, "Zum Palatina-Psalter des 13. Jahrhunderts," *JÖB* 21 (1972), 32–33; *idem, Das Illuminierte Buch*

The frescoes in King Milutin's foundations are not as elegant and refined as the mosaics of the Pammakaristos, the Holy Apostles, or the Chora, but they do show the same reduced scale and elaboration of narrative detail as well as a predilection for classicizing motifs. In comparing the Dormition of the Virgin in the Peribleptos (Fig. 39) and St. Nikita, for example, the shrinking of physical mass and the loss of dramatic intensity are striking. Equally significant is the addition of descriptive detail. In St. Nikita, candles and candlesticks have been added, St. Peter holds a censer and pyxis, and the bishops hold open books. All of these details fill out the story. The same holds true for the Expulsion of the Merchants (Figs. 33, 50), where the sparse and intense scene of the Peribleptos has been elaborated with multiple individualized figures, including a group of women holding babies, a motif of Classical origin which also adds to the story-telling interest. The differences between the frescoes of the Peribleptos and St. Nikita are such that, had the artists not signed (or had the inscriptions been lost), the two ensembles would never have been attributed to the same painters.

Both narrative complexity and elegant refinement reach a more advanced stage in the Chora mosaics (Fig. 49). Again, it would seem that these qualities reflect to a large degree the taste of the learned patron, Theodore Metochites. A man of culture who loved books and was well-versed in ancient Greek literature, Metochites took a passionate interest in the restoration of his monastery.[24] He even engaged the services of a younger and equally learned man, Nikephoros Gregoras, to supervise the restoration. Furthermore, it is clear from his writings that Metochites was very aware of the visual arts. His admiration of antiquity extended beyond literature to include such outstanding artists as Polykleitos, Zeuxis, and Phidias. And in his pantheon of great artists he also included the famous Byzantine painter and mosaicist Eulalios.[25]

The specific influence of Metochites on the mosaics and frescoes of his monastery has been questioned, for during a time of religious controversy Metochites prudently avoided discussion of theological issues.[26] However, even if he deferred to clerical advice on the theological content of the program, the mosaics and frescoes of the Chora do reflect his personal taste, not only in the classicizing visual elaborations but also in the traditionalism of the theological program and its uncontroversial straightforwardness. Banal religious conformity is one of the main characteristics of the mosaic program, a trait that has been attributed to Metochites himself.[27] The mosaics are a detailed, almost exhaustive, account of the

---

in der spätbyzantinischen Gesellschaft, Abhandlungen der Heidelberger Akademie der Wissenschaften, Phil.-hist.-Klasse, 1970, 1 (Heidelberg, 1970); H. Buchthal and H. Belting, *Patronage in Thirteenth-Century Constantinople. An Atelier of Late Byzantine Book Illumination and Calligraphy*, DOS 16 (Washington, D.C., 1978); and R. Cormack, "Painting after Iconoclasm," in *Iconoclasm. Papers Given at the Ninth Spring Symposium of Byzantine Studies, University of Birmingham, March 1975*, A. Bryer and J. Herrin, eds. (Birmingham, 1977), 147–64.

[24] I. Ševčenko, "Theodore Metochites, the Chora, and the Intellectual Trends of his Time," *The Kariye Djami* IV (note 4 above), 30–35.

[25] *Ibid.*, 50–51.

[26] *Ibid.*, 52.

[27] *Ibid.*, 53. The theological program of the Chora parekklesion, though a bit more complex, is as much of a straightforward affirmation of Chalcedonian dogma as is the program of the mosaics.

life of the Virgin and Christ, presented in a straightforward narrative sequence and filled
with such incidental elaborations and flourishes as flora and fauna, garden and landscape
elements, richly draped buildings, maidens with windblown garments, and playing children. It is these repeated charming, elegant, and classicizing details that give the Chora
mosaics their special character.

It is a pity that none of the four churches founded in Constantinople by Patriarch Athanasios I survive, since his two patriarchates (1289–1293, 1303–1309) span the period here
under consideration. It would have been instructive to see what effect the austere monk and
religious reformer who, on principle, condemned rich ornamentation in churches had on the
decoration of his own foundations, especially that of his favorite monastery of Christ near
Xerolophos where he retired after 1309 and where he was buried.[28] One wonders whether
he would have chosen fresco, a less ostentatious and expensive medium, and whether the
workshop he employed would have adopted the style that became popular ca. 1310.

This style, which reads like a book of illustrations intended to inform and soothe and in
which anecdotal story telling is devoid of intense and dramatic effects, is characteristic of the
brief period of stability and peacefulness of the reign of Andronikos II, from ca. 1310 to
1321. This decade opened with a series of successful diplomatic actions: the conclusion of a
peace treaty with Venice (1310); the establishment of peaceful relations, through matrimo-
nial alliances, with the kings of Serbia and Bulgaria; the settling in the Duchy of Athens
(1311) of the Catalans, who had devastated Macedonia and Thrace between 1305 and
1309. It was also the decade of reconciliation in the church, when, after the deposition of the
controversial Patriarch Athanasios (1309), the Arsenites were finally reconciled with the
church under his successor, Patriarch Niphon (1310–1314).[29] The relative stability that all
this produced ended in 1321, the year of the outbreak of civil war between the emperor and
his grandson Andronikos III.

It was during this decade also that Andronikos II came increasingly under the influence
of Theodore Metochites, whom he appointed Prime Minister of the Byzantine Empire in
1305–1306.[30] Metochites, because of his political power, cultural prestige, and great
wealth, must also have exercised considerable influence on contemporary taste. The splendid decoration of his monastery of Christ in Chora, which he began restoring ca. 1315, was
no doubt well-known in aristocratic circles. This decade (1311–21), which has been called
the most productive of the reign of Andronikos II, in spite of disasters in Asia Minor,[31] is
also the period richest in monuments in Constantinople, Thessaloniki, Mt. Athos, and Serbia, and the period during which the more restrained, elaborately detailed and often more

---

[28] J. Meyendorff, "Spiritual Trends in the Late Thirteenth and Early Fourteenth Centuries," *The Kariye
Djami* IV (note 4 above), 98–99. A.-M. Talbot, *The Correspondence of Athanasius I, Patriarch of Constanti-
nople: Letters to the Emperor Andronicus II, Members of the Imperial Family, and Officials* (Washington,
D.C., 1975).

[29] Laiou, *Constantinople and the Latins* (note 4 above), 242–48, 281.

[30] Ševčenko, "Theodore Metochites" (note 24 above), 27–29.

[31] Laiou, *Constantinople and the Latins* (note 4 above), 283.

elegant pictorial *koinē*, which transcended political boundaries, was clearly formulated. This pictorial *koinē* presented an easily graspable version of traditional religious beliefs and therefore was safe and acceptable to a society that increasingly looked toward the past. It differs fundamentally from the forceful, intense, and dynamic style of ca. 1290–1310, which coincides with the most agitated period of Andronikos' reign and of which the frescoes of St. Euthymios are a prime example.

1. Thessaloniki, St. Euthymios, parekklesion. Exterior, southeast (photo: L. Bouras)

2. Thessaloniki, St. Euthymios, parekklesion. Interior, nave (photo: Lykides, Thessaloniki)

4. Thessaloniki, St. Euthymios, parekklesion. St. John the Baptist, diakonikon (photo: Benaki Museum)

3. Thessaloniki, St. Euthymios, parekklesion. Interior, north aisle (photo: Lykides, Thessaloniki)

5. Thessaloniki, St. Euthymios, parekklesion. Enthroned Virgin Hodegetria, apse (photo: Benaki Museum)

6. Thessaloniki, St. Euthymios, parekklesion. Communion of the Wine (photo: Benaki Museum)

7. Thessaloniki, St. Euthymios, parekklesion. Communion of the Bread (photo: Benaki Museum)

8. Thessaloniki, St. Euthymios, parekklesion. Annunciation and Mandylion, triumphal arch (photo: Benaki Museum)

9. Thessaloniki, St. Euthymios, parekklesion. Nativity (photo: Benaki Museum)

10. Thessaloniki, St. Euthymios, parekklesion. Crucifixion (photo: Benaki Museum)

11. Thessaloniki, St. Euthymios, parekklesion. Anastasis (photo: Benaki Museum)

12. Thessaloniki, St. Euthymios, parekklesion. Christ Teaching in the Temple (photo: Benaki Museum)

13. Thessaloniki, St. Euthymios, parekklesion. Expulsion of the Merchants from the Temple (photo: Benaki Museum)

14. Thessaloniki, St. Euthymios, parekklesion. Healing of the Paralytic at Bethesda (photo: Benaki Museum)

15. Thessaloniki, St. Euthymios, parekklesion. Christ and the Samaritan Woman (photo: Benaki Museum)

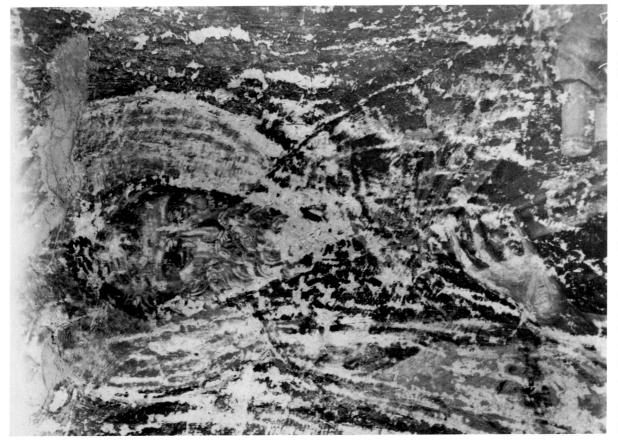

17. Thessaloniki, St. Euthymios, parekklesion. Monastic Saint (photo: Benaki Museum)

16. Thessaloniki, St. Euthymios, parekklesion. St. Euthymios (photo: Benaki Museum)

19. Thessaloniki, St. Euthymios, parekklesion. Sts. George and Nicholas (left to right) (photo: Benaki Museum)

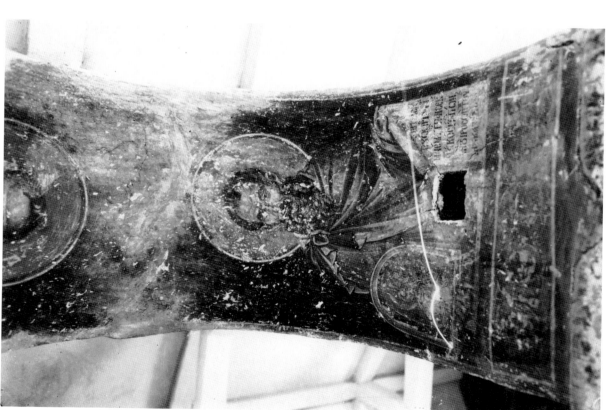

18. Thessaloniki, St. Euthymios, parekklesion. St. Stephen the Younger (photo: Benaki Museum)

21. Thessaloniki, St. Euthymios, parekklesion. Sts. Cosmas, Panteleimon, and Damian (left to right) (photo: Benaki Museum)

20. Thessaloniki, St. Euthymios, parekklesion. Sts. Prokopios, Theodore Teron, and Theodore Stratelates (left to right) (photo: Benaki Museum)

23. Thessaloniki, St. Euthymios, parekklesion. Bishop, apse (photo: Benaki Museum)

22. Thessaloniki, St. Euthymios, parekklesion. Bishops, apse (photo: Benaki Museum)

25. Thessaloniki, St. Euthymios, parekklesion. St. Euthymios Ordained Presbyter, detail (photo: Benaki Museum)

24. Thessaloniki, St. Euthymios, parekklesion. Prophet, triumphal arch (photo: Benaki Museum)

26. Thessaloniki, St. Euthymios, parekklesion. Paul and Dionysia Praying in the Church of St. Polyeuktos, Dionysia Entrusting her Child to her Brother Eudoxios (photo: Benaki Museum)

27. Thessaloniki, St. Euthymios, parekklesion. St. Euthymios Ordained Deacon, St. Euthymios Ordained Presbyter (photo: Benaki Museum)

28. Thessaloniki, St. Euthymios, parekklesion. St. Euthymios Heals the Paralytic Child of the Saracene
(photo: Benaki Museum)

29. Thessaloniki, St. Euthymios, parekklesion. St. Euthymios Heals a Demoniac, Dormition of St. Euthymios
(photo: Benaki Museum)

30. Thessaloniki, St. Euthymios, parekklesion. St. Euthymios Officiating in Church and the Descent of the Heavenly Fire (photo: Benaki Museum)

31. Ohrid, Peribleptos (St. Clement). St. John the Baptist, diakonikon (photo: Archaeological Service, Skopje)

32. Ohrid, Peribleptos (St. Clement). Communion of the Wine (photo: Archaeological Service, Skopje)

33. Ohrid, Peribleptos (St. Clement). Expulsion of the Merchants from the Temple (photo: Archaeological Service, Skopje)

35. Ohrid, Peribleptos (St. Clement). Anastasis (photo: Archaeological Service, Skopje)

34. Ohrid, Peribleptos (St. Clement). Crucifixion (photo: Archaeological Service, Skopje)

37. Ohrid, Peribleptos (St. Clement). St. Demetrios
(photo: Archaeological Service, Skopje)

36. Ohrid, Peribleptos (St. Clement). St. Merkourios
(photo: Archaeological Service, Skopje)

38. Ohrid, Peribleptos (St. Clement). Meeting of Joachim and Anna at the Golden Gate, Nativity of the Virgin (photo: Archaeological Service, Skopje)

39. Ohrid, Peribleptos (St. Clement). Dormition of the Virgin (photo: Archaeological Service, Skopje)

40. Mt. Athos, Karyes, the Protaton. Crucifixion (photo: Benaki Museum)

41. Mt. Athos, Karyes, the Protaton. Anastasis (photo: N. Tombazi)

43. Mt. Athos, Karyes, the Protaton. St. George (photo: Benaki Museum)

42. Mt. Athos, Karyes, the Protaton. Sts. Merkourios and Artemios (photo: Benaki Museum)

45. Constantinople, Pammakaristos (Fethiye Camii). St. Peter (photo: Dumbarton Oaks)

44. Constantinople, Pammakaristos (Fethiye Camii). Virgin Praying (photo: Dumbarton Oaks)

47. Thessaloniki, Holy Apostles. Anastasis (mosaic) (photo: Benaki Museum)

46. Constantinople, Pammakaristos (Fethiye Camii). Closed Door (photo: Dumbarton Oaks)

48. Constantinople, Pammakaristos (Fethiye Camii), parekklesion. Baptism (mosaic) (photo: Dumbarton Oaks)

49. Constantinople, Christ in Chora (Kariye Camii). Virgin Taken to Joseph's House (mosaic) (photo: Dumbarton Oaks)

50. Čučer, St. Nikita. Expulsion of the Merchants from the Temple (photo: Archaeological Service, Skopje)

The Palaeologan Refectory
Program at Apollonia

JOHN J. YIANNIAS

AT ONE TIME in the Orthodox world there must have been hundreds of monastic refectories with wall paintings; yet, leaving aside the uncounted examples in Russia, only a small number of these buildings retain so much as fragments of their decoration, which in most cases is post-Byzantine. A refectory preserving any wall paintings from the Palaeologan period is a rarity. In the monastery at Apollonia in central Albania, known variously as the monastery of the Panagia or of the Dormition of the Theotokos, we have the greater part of a whole program from that period. I shall discuss briefly the choice of subjects in this refectory and touch on the corollary problem of the meaning of Eastern refectory programs in general. Apollonia has one of the earliest preserved Byzantine refectory programs of sufficient complexity to permit analysis of this kind.

The refectory, or trapeza, at Apollonia has the only wall paintings to be seen in the monastery, aside from a few fragments and a Palaeologan imperial family portrait in the katholikon. Cleaned after World War II, the refectory paintings were described in 1961 by Viktoria Puzanova, and more fully in 1976 by Helmut and Heide Buschhausen, in a book that is likely to remain for some time the basic study of this monument.[1] I have relied on it for most of the data concerning the trapeza program, although an examination of photographs from another source has led me to question some of the Buschhausens' identifications.[2]

The refectory is built into the west side of the courtyard, perpendicular to the katholikon (Fig. 1), a fairly common location for a refectory.[3] It is an oblong space with three apses, one on each side but the north (Fig. 2). Paintings remain on the three walls containing the apses; those on the north wall have been destroyed.[4]

Following Lazarev's assignment of the paintings to the fourteenth century, there has been general agreement that they are Palaeologan, and tacit agreement that they were

---

[1] V. Puzanova, "Manastiri 'Shën-Mëria e Apollonisë në Pojan," *Buletin i Universitetit Shtetëror të Tiranës, Seria Shkencat Shoqërore* 15 (1961), 147–54 (English summary 153–54); H. and H. Buschhausen, *Die Marienkirche von Apollonia in Albanien: Byzantiner, Normannen und Serben im Kampf um die Via Egnatia* (Vienna, 1976) esp. chap. 5, with further references. I am not aware of any other detailed treatments of the refectory paintings. The description in A. Ducellier, "Observations sur quelques monuments de l'Albanie," *RA* (1965, II), 182, is cursory.

[2] Photographs available through the Conway Library of the Courtauld Institute of Art.

[3] A. Orlandos, Μοναστηριακὴ ἀρχιτεκτονική, 2nd ed. (Athens, 1958), 45.

[4] On the structural histories of the refectory and church, see now the review of Buschhausen by A. Meksi, in *Monumentet* 23 (1982), 141–68 (French resumé 158–68). To Meksi's references should be added the review of Buschhausen by S. Ćurčić in *Speculum* 54 (1979), 353–58. On the monastery's restoration, see R. Gega, "Restaurimi i manastirit të Apollonisë dhe vizitueshmëria e tij," *Monumentet* 32 (1986), 161–63 (French resumé 163).

executed by a single workshop. But attempts to narrow the chronology have not produced a consensus. The Buschhausens propose 1315 to 1320, citing what they see as the debt of the master artist to the style of the "school of Milutin." This chronology has been challenged, C. Walter suggesting a date in the latter part of the reign of Stefan Dušan (1331–55), and V. Djurić a date around 1275.[5]

The walls are divided by painted bands into horizontal registers (Fig. 3), forming an arrangement like that commonly seen in churches, with narrative scenes at the top, in this case unbroken by vertical borders; medallion portraits or smaller narrative scenes in the next register; below these, standing figures of saints; and near the bottom of the wall a zone of painted imitation marble panels (now extensively effaced). The higher south wall also has a triangular zone just under the pitched ceiling. The apses are divided into three registers: the conch, below this a row of standing saints in line with those on the adjoining surfaces, and along the bottom a continuation of the ornamental zone.

The Buschhausens describe the subjects as follows. On the south wall (Figs. 3B and 4), before which the abbot's table stood, a Hospitality of Abraham occupies the center of the top zone. In the left angle of the gable are remnants of a seascape, possibly a First Miraculous Draught of Fishes. The deteriorated scene in the right angle of the gable is not identifiable. Directly over the apse, in three medallions, are Christ Emmanuel and, flanking him, two Archangels (Figs. 4 and 5). To the viewer's left of these is a Washing of the Feet, and to the right, Christ Instructing the Apostles, with an inscription from John 13:14: "If I then, your Lord and Master, have washed your feet, ye also ought to wash one another's feet."[6] In the next lower zone, on the left, appears a Communion of St. Mary of Egypt (Fig. 7), and opposite this, Prophet Elijah Fed by the Raven. In the conch of the apse is a fragmentary Last Supper, with three seated disciples and the edge of the table visible at the far left, and Christ (sic) standing at the far right, holding a scroll (Fig. 6). Below the narrative scenes, all the way across, were standing saints, of whom some are now missing. The one bordering the apse on the left (*B11*; Fig. 7) wears a monk's cowl. The names of the last two on the right (*B17* and *18*) are legible: they are Gregory the Theologian and John of Damascus.

On the east wall (Fig. 3A) (again, according to the Buschhausens), we find, from left to right in the top zone, Christ Raising the Widow's Son, then two unidentifiable scenes, followed by Christ Healing the Possessed Man, and finally a Christ Child among the Doctors (Fig. 8). The five medallions in the next zone contain bust-length portraits of saints, with no legible inscriptions—two men to the viewer's left of the apse and three women (sic) to the right of it (Fig. 10). The painting in the conch of the apse, now largely destroyed, may

---

[5] V. Lazarev, *Storia della pittura bizantina*, rev. and enl. ed. (Turin, 1967), 431 n. 172; Buschhausen, *Marienkirche* (note 1 above), 225–29; C. Walter's review of Buschhausen in *REB* 35 (1977), 314; V. Djurić, "La peinture de Chilandar à l'époque de roi Milutin," *Recueil de Chilandar* 4 (1978), 43–44 n. 10. See also the review by M. Tatić-Djurić in *Zograf* 9 (1978), 76–77. A. Ducellier's claim that the style of the paintings points to the early twelfth century, a view once held by Puzanova and Dhamo (see Ducellier's review of Buschhausen in *CahCM* 22 [1979], 376, and Meksi [note 4 above], 168), is, in my opinion, simply not substantiated by the paintings themselves.

[6] Εἰ οὖν ἐγὼ ἔνιψα τοὺς πόδας ὁ κύριος καὶ ὁ διδάσκαλος, καὶ ὑμεῖς ὀφείλετε ἀλλήλων νίπτειν τοὺς πόδας.

have depicted the Myrrh-Bearers at the Tomb. Below were standing saints, ending at the extreme right with St. Symeon Stylite. One of the saints in the apse (*A17*) is shown by his clothing to be a monk. Figures of saints, now unidentifiable, were also painted on the jambs of the window to the right of the apse.[7]

On the west wall (Fig. 3C), the top zone displays, from left to right, the Annointing of Christ's Feet, the Miracle at Cana, an unidentifiable scene, then either the Healing of a Blind Man or the Blessing of the Child, and the Purging of the Temple. The four medallions contain portraits of male saints. Of these the two on the viewer's left are beardless; those on the right, bearded, are possibly patriarchs, and the one nearer the apse may be Abraham. In the apsidal conch is the Prayer in the Garden. The zone below has the stylite St. Symeon the Younger (directly opposite the stylite on the east wall), followed by standing saints. Of these the first, next to the stylite, is dressed as a monk (*C12*).

I would amend the Buschhausens' identifications as follows, as a preliminary to any further discussion of the program. The figure at the far right in the Last Supper (Fig. 6) is surely not Christ. He has a long beard and white hair, his halo bears no evidence of an inscribed cross, and the words on his scroll were not spoken by Christ but are a slight variation on the text of Isaiah 55:1: K[αὶ] φάγεστε / κ[αὶ] πείεσθε / ἄνευ ἀργυ/ρίου κ[αὶ] τ[ιμῆς οἶνον καὶ στέαρ], ("And eat and drink [wine and fat] without money [or price],").[8] This passage comes at the beginning of the second Prophetic reading for the day before Mid-Pentecost.[9] The figure must represent Isaiah.

It seems questionable that the seascape on the south wall (*B2*), provisionally identified by the Buschhausens as a First Miraculous Draught of Fishes (Lk. 5:1–11), depicts any event in Christ's life, given its small size and subordinate position relative to the Hospitality of Abraham. The Buschhausens make out marine creatures and a boat. Even if we assume that the scene is from Christ's life, there seems no reason to rule out as possible subjects other events that took place on the water, such as Christ Stilling the Tempest or Christ Walking on the Water.[10] The scene is probably better left unidentified until reexamined at close range.

---

[7] Buschhausen, *Marienkirche* (note 1 above), 197; one on each jamb, I assume. A halo can be seen on the south jamb in Courtauld 815/54 (12A).

[8] The critical edition of the Septuagint has: Καὶ πίετε ἄνευ ἀργυρίου καὶ τιμῆς οἶνον καὶ στέαρ, (*Septuaginta*, XIV: *Isaias*, ed. J. Ziegler, 3rd ed. [Göttingen, 1983], 327). The Buschhausens transcribe the inscription as: Οὖ φαγεστε / καὶ πείεσθε / ανευ ἀγ.. / ρίου τ (*Marienkirche* [note 1 above], 197). I have altered their transcription to make it conform more closely to what can be seen in the photograph reproduced in our Fig. 6. The Buschhausens' failure to identify the text probably stems from their having overlooked the rho between the alpha and gamma in the third line, faintly visible in Fig. 6 as a loop attached to the vertical stroke of the alpha.

[9] *Monumenta Musicae Byzantinae*, I: *Prophetologium*, pt. 1: *Lectiones anni mobilis*, ed. C. Høeg and G. Zuntz (Copenhagen, 1939–70), 85–86. The text as given here reads: Καὶ φάγεσθε καὶ πίεσθε, καὶ πορεύεσθε καὶ ἀγοράσατε ἄνευ ἀργυρίου καὶ τιμῆς οἶνον καὶ στέαρ.

[10] Tempest: Mt. 8:23–27; Mk. 4:35–41; Lk. 8:22–25. Walking: Mt. 14:22–33; Mk. 6:45–52; Jn. 6:16–21. I am ruling out the Second Miraculous Draught of Fishes (Jn. 21:1–14), which usually shows Peter attempting to swim toward Christ, because the Buschhausens report seeing no human form in the water (*Marienkirche* [note 1 above], 196).

The painting on the east wall interpreted as a Christ Child among the Doctors (*A5*) may be, rather, Christ (as an adult) Teaching in the Synagogue at Nazareth, although the composition, showing Christ seated between flanking figures, is admittedly appropriate to the former subject (Fig. 8). Christ's age cannot be determined, since his face is no longer visible. But in the open book held by him (Fig. 9), as the Buschhausens observe, are the first four words of the passage from Isaiah that, according to Luke (4:16–22), Christ chose to expound in the synagogue at Nazareth: Πνεῦμα κυρίου ἐπ' ἐμέ, [οὗ εἵνεκεν ἔχρισέν με], ("The spirit of the Lord is upon me, [because he has anointed me,]") (Isaiah 61:1).[11] Unless the text represents a conscious anachronism, the painting seems to depict the event in Nazareth.

The saints in the three medallions on the right half of the east wall (*A9–A11*) are not women but the Three (Hebrew) Youths, the τρεῖς παῖδες—Ananias, Misael, and Azarias. This identification is borne out by the youthful features and the miter and courtly costume of the one who can be seen clearly (Fig. 10).

The standing saints in the west apse are depicted in one of the Buschhausens' drawings as fully clothed.[12] But it can be seen in photographs that the two in the left half of the apse (*C13* and *14*) are wearing almost nothing (Figs. 11, 12). They are undraped anchorites, perhaps Onuphrios and Peter the Athonite, typically shown with naked torsoes and pencil-thin arms. Their contours are distinguishable in spite of the deteriorated condition of the painting.

The garments of six additional standing saints—*B10* (Fig. 7), *B12*, *B17*, *B18*, *C17*, and *C18*—can be discerned to consist of a monk's habit. In addition, the cape worn by the first saint on the left in the south apse (*B12*) has traces of three horizontal stripes near the bottom edge. This feature, which denotes the habit of a hierarch, establishes that the figures in the main apse, three of which are completely destroyed, were not depicted wearing liturgical vestments.

How are we to explain the choice of subjects at Apollonia?

The Buschhausens characterize the program—or what is left of it—as one centered on the events and ideas celebrated in the Lenten liturgies.[13] The new identifications only confirm this characterization, as will some additional observations. Virtually all of the identifiable paintings have in common the fact that their subjects are either described or implied in the texts that are read or chanted during Lent, and many of them can be further narrowed down to Holy Week. The Buschhausens have made several of these textual connections.[14] What follows is an attempt to present a somewhat fuller account of them.

As shown in Fig. 13, the paintings depicting subjects that are narrated explicitly in the lections of Holy Week are, on the south wall, the Last Supper, the Washing of the Feet, and

[11] Buschhausen, *Marienkirche* (note 1 above), 199. This is not the place to attempt a history of the iconography of Christ Teaching in the Synagogue, but it should be remarked that he is often shown standing at a lectern: e.g., Berlin Staatsbibliothek Cod. Gr. 66, fol. 62v and Chicago University Library Ms. 965, fol. 180r (A. Weyl Carr, *Byzantine Illumination 1150–1250* [Chicago and London, 1987], microfiches 3E9 and 8E9), and a wall painting in the Metropolis at Mistra (G. Millet, *Monuments byzantins de Mistra* [Paris, 1910], pl. 76:2). In the last instance, the opened book contains our inscription from Isaiah.

[12] Buschhausen, *Marienkirche* (note 1 above), fig. 24.

[13] *Ibid.*, esp. 232.

[14] *Ibid.*, 231–32.

Christ Instructing the Apostles (all based on readings for Holy Thursday);[15] on the west wall, the Annointing of Christ's Feet (the Gospel account is read on Palm Sunday and recalled in the hymns of Holy Wednesday and Holy Thursday) and the Prayer in the Garden (commemorated on Holy Thursday);[16] and on the east wall, the hypothetical Myrrh-Bearers in the apse (corresponding to the Gospel reading for the Liturgy of St. Basil on Holy Saturday).[17] The story of the Prophet Elijah's prediction of a drought and his subsequent sojourn, first in the wilderness and then at Sarepta (Zarephath), summarized in Elijah Fed by the Raven, is recalled on Holy Saturday, as well as earlier, on the first Sunday of Lent.[18] The Miracle at Cana is mentioned, albeit briefly, in the canon of Good Friday.[19]

The Three Youths are mentioned frequently during Holy Week, as well as earlier in Lent; and the part of the Book of Daniel that tells of their being thrown into the fiery furnace is read on Holy Saturday.[20] Interestingly their abstention from the king's table, a point not likely to arrest the attention of the casual modern reader of Daniel, is underscored both by commentators (Clement of Alexandria, John Chrysostom) and by hymnographers.[21] The doxastikon for orthros of the first Sunday of Lent reads: "And the three Abrahamic youths triumphed over the lawbreaking tyrant through fasting."[22]

The Communion of St. Mary of Egypt conjures up an important Lenten figure. This saint's vita is read on the fifth Wednesday, and her feast is celebrated on the fifth Sunday.[23]

---

[15] E. Colwell and D. Riddle, *Prolegomena to the Study of the Lectionary Text of the Gospels* (Chicago, 1933), 121–22, based on a collation of four Lectionaries of the tenth through the twelfth or thirteenth century; and A. Dmitrievsky (ed.), *Opisanie liturgicheskikh rukopisei*, vol. I: *Typika*, pt. 1: *Pamiatniki patriarshikh ustavov i ktitorskie monastyrskie tipikony* (Kiev, 1895), 546–50 (twelfth-century typikon of the Evergetidos Monastery in Constantinople). For a convenient collection of the prescribed readings and hymns for the major feasts following current usage, see the Μέγας καὶ ἱερὸς συνέκδημος ὀρθοδόξου χριστιανοῦ, rev. and enl. ed. (Athens, 1966).

[16] Annointing (Jn. 12:1–18): Colwell and Riddle, *Prolegomena* (note 15 above), 118; Dmitrievsky, *Pamiatniki* (note 15 above), 542; Συνέκδημος (note 15 above), 976ff., 1049ff. Prayer (Mt. 26:21–46): Colwell and Riddle, 122; Συνέκδημος, 1065–66.

[17] Holy Saturday (Mt. 28:1–20): Colwell and Riddle, *Prolegomena* (note 15 above), 126; Συνέκδημος (note 15 above), 1208–1209. Mark's account of the episode (Mk. 15:43–16:8) is read on the Sunday of the Myrrh-Bearers, the second Sunday after Easter: Colwell and Riddle, *Prolegomena*, 86; Συνέκδημος, 1236–37.

[18] The episodes at Sarepta involving the widow and her son (III Kings 17:8–24) form one of the Prophetic readings for Holy Saturday: see Høeg and Zuntz, *Lectiones* (note 9 above), 462–65. First Sunday of Lent: Dmitrievsky, *Pamiatniki* (note 15 above), 521 and Συνέκδημος (note 15 above), 842 ('Ηλίας νηστεύσας οὐρανοὺς ἀπέκλεισε: "By fasting, Elijah closed up the heavens").

[19] Συνέκδημος (note 15 above), 1103.

[20] Συνέκδημος (note 15 above), 840, 852, 917, 941, 964, etc. Holy Saturday reading: Høeg and Zuntz, *Lectiones* (note 9 above), 479–88; J. Mateos, *Le Typicon de la Grande Eglise*, II (Rome, 1963), 223; Dmitrievsky, *Pamiatniki* (note 15 above), 133; Συνέκδημος, 1200–1204.

[21] Clement, *Stromateis*, III.4 (PG 8:1137B; *Library of Christian Classics*, II: *Alexandrian Christianity*, ed. and trans. J. Oulton and H. Chadwick [Philadelphia, 1954], 55); St. John Chrysostom's commentary on Daniel, in PG 56:193ff.

[22] Dmitrievsky, *Pamiatniki* (note 15 above), 521. Text in Συνέκδημος (note 15 above), 842: Τρεῖς δὲ παῖδες 'Αβραμιαῖοι τύραννον παρανομοῦντα διὰ νηστείας ἐνίκησαν. This passage immediately follows the one about Elijah that is quoted above, n. 18.

[23] Wednesday: Dmitrievsky, *Pamiatniki* (note 15 above), 536; Συνέκδημος (note 15 above), 875 (Great Canon of St. Andrew of Crete). Sunday: Dmitrievsky, *Pamiatniki*, 538; Συνέκδημος, 902.

Some of the other paintings, as further indicated in Fig. 13, are of subjects which are not specified by name in the Lenten texts but are implied in the general references to Christ's miracles of healing and resurrection that occur in prayers read during Holy Week.[24] Included in this category is the Healing of the Possessed Man, on the east wall: although one of four such healings is related in a Lenten reading (Mk. 9:17–31, fourth Sunday), the bearded demoniac in the painting looks too old to be the afflicted youth of Mark's description.[25] Then there are the Raising of the Widow's Son, on the east wall, and the Healing of the Blind Man, on the west wall.[26] If the latter actually depicts the Blessing of the Child, which the Buschhausens suggest as an alternative identification, it is still relevant to Lent, since this "acted parable," in which Christ holds up a child (figuratively) as an example to the disciples (Mt. 18:1–6; Mk. 9:33–37; Lk. 9:46–48), addresses the persistent Lenten theme of acceptance into Heaven.[27]

Christ Teaching in the Synagogue (A5, assuming this identification to be correct) is based on a Gospel text read in September,[28] but the subject is also directly related to Matthew's account of the arrest in the Garden, read on Holy Thursday. Matthew quotes Christ as reproaching his captors with the words, "I sat daily teaching in the temple, and you laid no hold on me," (26:55). In addition, the passage from Isaiah that appears in the opened book (61:1–10) is one of the Prophetic readings for Holy Saturday.[29]

The Purging of the Temple is not, so far as I have determined, mentioned in the texts prescribed for Lent, but it is nonetheless relevant to the season. John's version of the episode (2:12–22), read on the Friday after Easter, has Christ saying, "Destroy this temple, and in three days I will raise it up;" and John goes on to explain that this statement was a prophecy of the Resurrection. Hence the reading in which this event is related takes us back to Holy Week, and indeed to its culminating event.

---

[24] E.g., Τὸν ἰώμενον τὰ πάθη πρὸς πάθος ἑτοιμάζουσι (Συνέκδημος [note 15 above], 1049, 1056).

[25] This detail can be seen in Buschhausen, *Marienkirche* (note 1 above), pl. XXX, ill. 122. The reading for the fourth Sunday of Lent: Colwell and Riddle, *Prolegomena* (note 15 above), 117; Συνέκδημος (note 15 above), 860–61. The other healings of demoniacs or people possessed of an unclean spirit are mentioned in Lk. 4:33–36; Mt. 8:28–34, Mk. 5:1–20, Lk. 8:26–39 (Gadarene demoniac[s]); Mt. 9:32–34; Mt. 12:22–24, Mk. 3:20–30, Lk. 11:14–16; Mt. 17:14–21, Lk. 9:37–43 (lunatic child, same event as in Mk. 9:17–31); but none of these readings is prescribed for Lent.

[26] The Raising of the Widow's Son (Lk. 7:11–17) is read in September, on the third Sunday of the New Year (Colwell and Riddle, *Prolegomena* [note 15 above], 103–104; Συνέκδημος [note 15 above], 463 [where the Sunday is counted as the twentieth after Pentecost]). Healings of blind men are mentioned in nine Gospel texts, comprising five different events (Mt. 9:27–31; Mt. 12:22–24, Mk. 3:20–30, Lk. 11:14–16; Mt. 20:29–34, Mk. 10:46–52, Lk. 18:35–43; Mk. 8:22–26; Lk. 9:1–12), and the blind are mentioned also in two general references to Christ's healings (Mt. 11:5, Mt. 15:29–31). None of these readings occurs in Lent.

[27] These three descriptions of the parable are read on Monday of the ninth week after Easter, Friday of the thirteenth week of the new year, and Wednesday of the fifth week of the new year, respectively (Colwell and Riddle, *Prolegomena* [note 15 above], 96, 111, 105). A similar parable, involving more than one child, is told in Mt. 19:13–15, Mk. 10:13–16, and Lk. 18:15–17. The idea of acceptance into heaven is brought out in, among other texts, the Gospels for the third and fifth Sundays of Lent, Mk. 8:34–9:1 and 10:32–45, respectively: *ibid.*, 117, 118.

[28] As mentioned above, this scene reflects Luke's account of the incident (4:16–22), and this is read on the fifth day of the first week of the new year: Colwell and Riddle, *Prolegomena* (note 15 above), 102.

[29] Høeg and Zuntz, *Lectiones* (note 9 above), 469–71.

The Hospitality of Abraham is not mentioned, to my knowledge, in the Lenten texts, and we may assume that it was included as a prefiguration of the Last Supper. We may prefer to adduce the same reason for the inclusion of the Miracle at Cana, given the brevity of the allusion to it in the canon of Good Friday.[30]

In light of the above, even if the unidentifiable paintings, as well as any that may have appeared on the remaining surfaces of the side walls and on the north wall,[31] could be shown to have no relation to the texts read or chanted during Lent, we should have to allow that subjects upon which attention is focused during Lent dominate the layout. To be sure, some of them are more obviously associated with the season than others, but few, if any, of the references would have been lost on someone familiar with the Lenten liturgies.

The arrangement of the paintings reveals a clustering on or near the south wall of the events that occurred in conjunction with the Last Supper or that involve food and are therefore typologically related to the Last Supper, as the Buschhausens have emphasized.[32] The Hospitality of Abraham, the Washing of the Feet, Christ Instructing the Apostles, the Communion of St. Mary of Egypt, Elijah Fed by the Raven, the Annointing of Christ's Feet, and the Miracle at Cana fit this description (although the last would be situated even closer to the south wall were it placed where the Synagogue scene appears).

The arrangement of the remaining identifiable subjects in the top register of the side walls (*A1, A4, A5, C4, C5*) does not follow the order in which they are related in the Gospels or the order in which the readings occur in the Lectionary. These scenes may represent a more or less arbitrary selection and distribution of subjects from a fuller Ministry cycle. The possibility that such models existed in Palaeologan Constantinople is raised by what we know of the now vanished trapeza program at the monastery of the Chora, of about 1320. This is described by its donor, Theodore Metochites, as having paintings of Christ's "mysteries and miracles," ($\mu\nu\sigma\tau\acute{\eta}\rho\iota\alpha$ $\theta\nu\acute{\omega}\mu\alpha\tau\acute{\alpha}$ $\tau\epsilon$).[33] The precise meaning of the term "mysteries" in this context is not clear, but the reference to miracles makes it almost certain that the Chora refectory had a Ministry cycle.

A comparison of the program at Apollonia with existing programs will serve to isolate its most historically significant characteristics. Few refectories preserve paintings older than, or of roughly the same date as those of Apollonia. I am aware of three in Georgia, at Udabno (early eleventh century), Bertubani (early thirteenth century), and Kolaguiri (second half of the thirteenth century); one in Cappadocia, at Çarıklı Kilise (ca. 1050); two on

---

[30] The Hospitality narrative (Gen. 18:1–10) is read in March for the Annunciation to the Theotokos (*Monumenta Musicae Byzantinae*, I: *Prophetologium*, pt. 2: *Lectiones anni immobilis*, ed. G. Engberg [Copenhagen, 1980–81], 99–100), and the Cana narrative (Jn. 2:1–11), on Monday of the second week after Easter (Colwell and Riddle, *Prolegomena* [note 15 above], 86; Dmitrievsky, *Pamiatniki* [note 15 above], 568; cf. Mateos, *Typicon* [note 20 above], 102, 110).

[31] If the Athonite programs are any indication (the Great Lavra, Dionysiou, Xenophontos, Pantokratoros), the north wall may have contained a Last Judgment, another subject consistent with the emphasis on Lent (see above, n. 27).

[32] Buschhausen, *Marienkirche* (note 1 above), 230–31. The Annointing of Christ's Feet, as the Buschhausens remark, also establishes a correspondence with the Washing of the Feet.

[33] P. Underwood, *The Kariye Djami*, I: *Historical Introduction and Description of the Mosaics and Frescoes* (New York, 1966), 188–89.

Cyprus, the Apsinthiotissa Monastery (possibly twelfth century) and the Hermitage of St. Neophytos (the older of the two layers, ca. 1200); one on Patmos, the monastery of St. John the Theologian (twelfth and thirteenth centuries); and one on Mount Athos, the monastery of Hilandar (paintings above the present ceiling, ca. 1315–20). At Vatopedi, also on Athos, a fragment of a painting allegedly from the old refectory program there, depicting the Meeting of Sts. Peter and Paul, has been dated to the end of the twelfth century.[34]

Because the paintings are sparse everywhere but at Patmos, it is impossible to reconstruct a "canon" of subjects for the period before or contemporary with Apollonia. As shown below, several of the subjects at Apollonia have precedents in six of the eight earlier or contemporary programs.

Subjects Shared With Earlier or Contemporary Programs

	Udabno	Bertubani	Kolaguiri	Çarıklı Kilise	Patmos	Hilandar
Christ and Archangels						X
Hospitality/Abraham	X	X	X		?	X
Miracle at Cana		X	X			
Last Supper	X	X	X	X	?	?
Washing/Feet					X	
Prayer in Garden					X	
Myrrh-Bearers					X	
Stylites	X					
Standing ascetics in bottom zone					X	

Two recurring images are those of the Last Supper and the Hospitality of Abraham. The former we shall discuss in due course. The Hospitality appears in the three Georgian refectories, always near the Last Supper; and in the case of Kolaguiri it is also adjacent to the apse. At Hilandar, where it is flanked by Abraham Welcoming the Angels and the Sacrifice of Isaac, it is directly over the apse, as in the case of Apollonia.[35] At Patmos the

---

[34] Udabno, Bertubani, and Kolaguiri: A. Vol'skaia, *Rospisi srednevekovykh trapeznykh Gruzii* (Tbilisi, 1974). Çarıklı Kilise (only a Last Supper): N. Thierry, "Une iconographie inédite de la Cène dans un réfectoire rupestre de Cappadoce," *REB* 33 (1975), 177–85. Apsinthiotissa (Absinthiotissa): fragments in the apse, possibly of the twelfth century, discovered by A. Papageorghiou in 1963 (reported in personal correspondence with the author); see also A. Papageorghiou, "Ἡ Μονὴ Ἀψινθιωτίσσης," *RDAC* 1963, 82–83. St. Neophytos: C. Mango and E. J. W. Hawkins, "The Hermitage of St. Neophytos and Its Wall Paintings," *DOP* 20 (1966), esp. 186–90, 202–204. Patmos: A. Orlandos, Ἡ ἀρχιτεκτονικὴ καὶ αἱ βυζαντιναὶ τοιχογραφίαι τῆς μονῆς τοῦ Θεολόγου Πάτμου (Athens, 1970), 93–103, 175–272; and E. Kollias, *Patmos* (Athens, 1986), 10–11, 24–35. Hilandar: V. Djurić, "Peinture de Chilandar" (note 5 above), 41–53. Vatopedi: D. Mouriki, "Stylistic Trends in Monumental Painting of Greece during the Eleventh and Twelfth Centuries," *DOP* 34–35 (1980–81), 110 for references.

[35] Hilandar: V. Djurić, "Peinture de Chilandar" (note 5 above), fig. A. Directly over the apse, at the apex of the triangular surface, are Christ and two archangels, and below them the three scenes with Abraham. The paintings which have replaced the rest of this older program, and which one sees today in the trapeza, below

presence of Abraham Welcoming the Angels to the left of the window over the apse (its position also at Hilandar) suggests that the Hospitality may have been painted to the right of the window (Fig. 14). Hence in these four monuments—Patmos, Kolaguiri, Apollonia, and Hilandar—which, for lack of precise indications, we can only say were painted within a century or so of each other, scenes with Abraham were placed over or near the main apse. This much, at least, of their programs seems to have constituted a repeatable formula.

If the programs cited thus far do not coincide on many points, there are grounds nevertheless for thinking that few, if any, of them were independently conceived. That there was a tradition of refectory decoration either already formed or in the process of formation, of which these early programs are but partial reflections, is suggested by the fact that some of the subjects listed above were employed centuries later in the post-Byzantine trapeza programs of Mount Athos. These are the Hospitality of Abraham, the Miracle at Cana, the Last Supper, the portraits of stylites, and the standing ascetics in the bottom zone.[36] Apollonia adds to this list at least seven subjects not found in the other early refectories: the Communion of St. Mary of Egypt, the Prophet Elijah Fed by the Raven, the Three Youths, and four Gospel events—the Raising of the Widow's Son, the Healing of the Possessed Man, the Purging of the Temple, and Christ Teaching in the Synagogue.[37] It also offers an early example of hierarchs in the bottom zone of the apse, who furthermore are dressed not in liturgical vestments but in cowled habits, as in the Athonite refectory programs of the sixteenth century.[38]

Two of the early refectories—Bertubani and Kolaguiri—each have three of the subjects found at Apollonia, and Patmos has four; but Bertubani and Kolaguiri have too few paintings to allow further instructive comparisons with Apollonia. It is otherwise at Patmos: the four subjects that the Patmian program shares with Apollonia—the Washing of the Feet, the Prayer in the Garden, the Myrrh-Bearers, and the standing ascetics—represent only a small fraction of the paintings that are visible.[39]

We turn, therefore, to a comparison of Patmos and Apollonia. It must be acknowledged at the outset that the relative chronology of the two programs is incompletely established.

---

the present ceiling, date from 1622 and 1780: see Z. Kajmaković, *Georgije Mitrofanović* (Sarajevo, 1977), 189–267.

[36] Here and in the following notes I shall confine my Athonite examples to the programs predating the mid-nineteenth century. These lists do not pretend to be exhaustive. Hospitality: Hilandar, Dionysiou, Docheiariou, Esphigmenou, Pantokratoros, Vatopedi. Cana: Great Lavra, Pantokratoros, Philotheou. Last Supper: all but Docheiariou. Stylites: Philotheou, Vatopedi. Ascetics in the bottom zone: all of the programs.

[37] Communion: Hilandar, Docheiariou, Great Lavra, Pantokratoros. Elijah: Great Lavra. Three Youths: Dionysiou, Docheiariou, Esphigmenou (as part of the Menologion cycle). Demoniac: Dionysiou, Pantokratoros. Widow's Son: Dionysiou. Purging: Dionysiou. Synagogue: Esphigmenou. If at Apollonia the last-named subject is in fact Christ among the Doctors, this too has its Athonite examples, at Philotheou and Pantokratoros.

[38] The striped edge of the cape that we noticed on one of the figures in the south apse appears for example on the hierarchs of the apsidal wall in the refectory of Stavronikita: see M. Chatzidakis, Ὁ Κρητικὸς ζωγράφος Θεοφάνης· Ἡ τελευταία φάση τῆς τέχνης του στὶς τοιχογραφίες τῆς Ἱερᾶς Μονῆς Σταυρονικήτα (Mount Athos, 1986), figs. 206–208.

[39] Orlandos, Τοιχογραφίαι τῆς μονῆς τοῦ Θεολόγου (note 34 above), 174 and ills. 72, 75, 76.

About the earliest layer at Patmos (which according to Orlandos is comprised of the paintings *1–6, B* and *D* in Fig. 14) there is no doubt: all estimates place it in the late twelfth or
early thirteenth century, well before the earliest suggested date for the program at Apollonia.[40] The same is true of the remaining paintings located to the north of the central bay
(*A–L* in Fig. 14): the dates proffered for these range from the late twelfth to the first half of
the thirteenth century.[41] The uncertainty arises with regard to the paintings in the southern
part of the trapeza beginning with the central bay, which make up the third stylistically ho-
mogeneous set. Orlandos assigns these to the second half of the thirteenth century, and
Kollias to the third quarter of the century.[42] Djurić, it will be remembered, dates the
program at Apollonia to about 1275. Accordingly we must allow for the possibility that the
latest paintings at Patmos are contemporaneous with or even a bit later than those at
Apollonia.

The paintings revealed at Patmos may account for less than half of the original program, since large areas of the walls are still covered with plaster.[43] Nevertheless we count
about twenty-seven narrative scenes (two of them duplicates of the Appearance by the Sea of
Tiberias and the Multiplication of the Loaves). A majority of the paintings depict events or
themes commemorated during Lent. Such are the twelve Passion scenes but also the Ecumenical Councils, a subject commemorated by the reading of the Synodicon on the first
Sunday of Lent; while the Death of the Sinner and the Death of the Righteous Man call to
mind the idea of judgment and entry into heaven.

One of the principles of selection at Patmos, therefore, resembles the one employed at
Apollonia. But an important difference lies in the presence at Patmos of at least two Great
Feast images—a Crucifixion and an Anastasis—and of a Communion of the Apostles, the
liturgical analogue to the Last Supper (which may have been the subject of the painting that
has disappeared from the apse). Significant in itself, this sampling, however small, of the
most solemn subjects of a church program also raises an important, if perhaps unanswer-
able, question about the dome, an addition to the original structure and a highly unusual
feature for a trapeza.[44] One wonders whether it may not have been provided with the celestial images generally assigned to the dome of a church—Pantokrator, angels, prophets.

It is unlikely that the Communion of the Apostles or any Great Feasts—even those of
Lent (Raising of Lazarus, Entry into Jerusalem, Crucifixion)—were represented at Apollonia, for one would expect, given their importance, to find such paintings on or near the

---

[40] Orlandos: early thirteenth century (*ibid.*, 267–68). Mouriki: ca. 1180 ("Stylistic Trends" [note 34 above],
116–17). E. Kollias (who assigns to this layer only the paintings *1–6* in Fig. 13): end of the twelfth century
(*Patmos* [note 34 above], 24).

[41] Orlandos: first half of the thirteenth century (Τοιχογραφίαι τῆς μονῆς τοῦ Θεολόγου [note 34 above],
268–70). Kollias: late twelfth century (*Patmos* [note 34 above], 25). M. Chatzidakis ("Μεσοβυζαντινὴ τέχνη
[1071–1204]," in ῾Ιστορία τοῦ ἑλληνικοῦ ἔθνους, vol. 9 [Athens, 1979], 408) suggested tentatively a date of
ca. 1200 for the "second layer," by which he presumably meant all but the earliest paintings.

[42] Orlandos, Τοιχογραφίαι τῆς μονῆς τοῦ Θεολόγου (note 34 above), 268–70. Kollias, *Patmos* (note 34
above), 26. Contrary to Orlandos, Kollias includes in this group the paintings *b* and *d* in our Fig. 14.

[43] See above, n. 39.

[44] Orlandos, Τοιχογραφίαι τῆς μονῆς τοῦ Θεολόγου (note 34 above), 96–100; and 257–58, where the addition of the dome is dated to the twelfth century.

main apsidal wall. At Patmos they do not appear there, it is true. But the disposition at Patmos seems a bit haphazard and therefore possibly unrepresentative: the Ecumenical Councils are placed above the more important Anastasis and Myrrh-Bearers, and, oddly, *both* parts of the Communion of the Apostles appear on the same half of the vault, even though presumably the other half also was painted.[45]

If the Great Feasts and the Communion of the Apostles were in fact omitted at Apollonia, the program can be interpreted, in contrast to that of Patmos, as providing an early instance of a tendency that is amply documented in later refectories. This is the tendency to avoid or minimize duplication of the most solemn subjects of the central space of the church, the naos, thereby avoiding competition with it. Provincial Apollonia could not have initiated the trend, but it bears witness to the fact that this purposeful restriction of a refectory program's thematic scope was known and gaining acceptance, if it was not already common, in the Palaeologan period. The practice was to lead to the trapeza programs of the Holy Mountain, which have long been described as accommodating the "overflow" of subjects from the katholikon, and as otherwise complementing, rather than repeating, the church programs.[46] In the Athonite refectories no Communion of the Apostles ever appears, and, until the eighteenth century, images of the Great Feasts are limited to that of the Annunciation. The figures of Gabriel and the Theotokos are usually assigned to the spandrels of the main apsidal arch, raising the possibility that the very choice of the subject was prompted by the availability of a surface similar to the one that it occupies in a church.[47]

It is tempting to see in two first-hand descriptions of the now destroyed trapeza of the Peribleptos Monastery in Constantinople evidence of a transition, in one and the same building, from the—so to speak—more competitive to the less competitive type of refectory program. This monastery was an eleventh-century foundation.[48] It seems that sometime after Clavijo's visit to the Peribleptos in 1403 but before the visit of De Montconys in 1648, an ambitious mosaic cycle of Christ's life, from the Annunciation to the Crucifixion, seen in the refectory by Clavijo, may have been replaced by the paintings that De Montconys saw and described as depicting "the life of the Virgin."[49] Possibly this was a misidentified

[45] Orlandos thinks that at Patmos the placing of scenes having to do with food close to the north end of the refectory, where the abbot's table stood, explains why the Christological scenes are moved out of their proper biblical sequence (Τοιχογραφίαι τῆς μονῆς τοῦ Θεολόγου [note 34 above], 187). But this explanation would not seem to account for the apparent anomalies that I have just mentioned.

[46] H. Brockhaus, *Die Kunst in den Athos-Klöstern*, 2nd ed. (Leipzig, 1924), 84; Buschhausen, *Marienkirche* (note 1 above), 231. Remarks to the same effect in Chatzidakis, Θεοφάνης (note 38 above), 60–61.

[47] Philotheou, Dionysiou, Docheiariou, Pantokratoros, Hilandar. An Annunciation is painted also on the spandrels of an apsidal arch at Udabno: see Vol'skaia, *Rospisi* (note 34 above), pl. 12.

[48] R. Janin, *La géographie ecclésiastique de l'empire byzantin*, I. *Le siège de Constantinople et le patriarcat oecuménique, iii, Les églises et les monastères*, 2nd ed. (Paris, 1969), 218–22, for its foundation and subsequent history.

[49] Clavijo, *Embassy to Tamerlane, 1403–1406*, trans. G. Le Strange (London, 1928), 67–68; passage on refectory reproduced in C. Mango, *The Art of the Byzantine Empire, 312–1453* (Englewood Cliffs, N.J., 1972), 218; original text in *Embajada a Tamorlán*, ed. F. López Estrada (Madrid, 1943), 40. For De Montconys' account, see J. Ebersolt, *Constantinople byzantine et les voyageurs du Levant* (Paris, 1918), 133–34. Regarding the year in which the monastery was transferred to Armenian control, see H. Berbérian, "Le monastère byzantin de Péribleptos dit Soulou Manastir, Siège du patriarcat arménien de Constantinople," *REArm* n.s. 5 (1968), 145–49.

Acathist Hymn, a popular subject in Palaeologan churches (and in Athonite refectories), but one not likely to be familiar to a Western observer.[50] In any case, assuming that both travelers were describing the same interior, it would appear (although the evidence is admittedly inconclusive) that a less important cycle was substituted for a more important one.

Eastern refectories, no less than churches, were beneficiaries of the expansion of the monumental repertory in the Comnenian and Palaeologan periods. With rare possible exceptions, the images in refectories give no evidence of having been invented for refectories. They are images that have been transferred, in effect, from the church to another space, functionally and visually distinct and subordinate. Together with those in the church, many of which they consequently duplicate, they form a single system of interrelated images, the interpretation of which presupposes more than the mere identification of textual sources. The problem of their meaning, in other words, is not a narrowly iconographic one.

The partial duplication of the church's subjects by the refectory has to be seen against the variations in their locations. The placing of a Last Supper in the apse, the focal point of the interior, which is its usual—but not exclusive—location in a refectory,[51] announces both the function of the trapeza in an obvious way *and* its lower station relative to the church, the latter as a result of the fact that in both Byzantine and post-Byzantine churches the Last Supper customarily figures as merely one in the series of Passion scenes.[52] Because the actual Last Supper encompassed the institution of the Eucharist, however, and because various other Scriptural events known to have been considered types of the Last Supper are often depicted in refectories, some scholars have identified the Eucharist as being typically the central theme of refectory programs.[53] The one exception, to my knowledge, is M. Chatzidakis, who, in describing the refectory at Stavronikita, on Mount Athos (which has a magnificent Last Supper by Theophanes the Cretan), states in passing that the program there is not Eucharistic; and he appears to imply the same of refectory programs in general.[54]

The seeming disagreement is partly semantic. By describing an image as "Eucharistic," we may mean that it depicts or symbolizes the liturgical Eucharist—its institution and ritual performance; or we may mean that it leads us to contemplate any or all of the ideas and events that are recapitulated in the liturgical Eucharist, including the prophecies of Christ's Incarnation, the Incarnation itself, the Ministry, Crucifixion, and Resurrection. Since these are implicit in any image with a Christian content, however, it is desirable to try to ascertain

---

[50] The Acathist is represented in the refectories of the Great Lavra, Stavronikita, Philotheou, Xenophontos, Hilandar, Docheiariou, and Esphigmenou, as well as in the late-nineteenth-century program at St. Panteleimon (Rossikon).

[51] Exceptions in the Byzantine period are at Udabno and Bertubani (Vol'skaia, *Rospisi* [note 34 above], pls. 2 and 30), and in the post-Byzantine period, at Xenophontos and Vatopedi (unpublished).

[52] An exception appears in the church of Ubisi in Georgia, where a Last Supper is painted directly below the conch of the main apse and between the two halves of a Communion of the Apostles: Sh. Amiranashvili, *Georgian Painter Damiane* (Tbilisi, 1974), ill. 5. (The name "Damiane" should be read as "Gerasime": see J. Lafontaine-Dosogne, in A. Alpago-Novello et al., *Art and Architecture in Medieval Georgia* [Louvain-la-Neuve, 1980], 100 n. 55.)

[53] Vol'skaia, *Rospisi* (note 34 above), esp. 38–39; Djurić, "Peinture de Chilandar" (note 5 above), 45ff.

[54] Chatzidakis, Θεοφάνης (note 38 above), 60–61.

the range of intended meanings, unless we are prepared to admit no essential distinction in meaning between images of different subjects. More is at stake than the correct use of terms. The following remarks are offered as one means of conceptualizing the matter.

We can safely say that in certain settings images of the Last Supper and of subjects prefiguring it, such as Elijah Fed by the Raven or the Hospitality of Abraham, to name two seen at Apollonia, are "Eucharistic," in the sense that they are intended to accompany and to provide a visual biblical context for the Eucharistic liturgy.[55] But we become prisoners of our iconographic erudition if we conclude that such images were fated to carry this meaning regardless of the setting to which they were transferred.

In a church the Last, or "Mystical," Supper is thought of as being made present in the Eucharistic liturgy.[56] Therefore it is perfectly legitimate to assign to the *image* of the Last Supper in a church, at least hypothetically, whatever meanings are attached to the *event* of the Last Supper, including the institution of the Eucharist. But the situation changes when the image does not appear in the setting in which the event is thought to be made present—such as in a refectory. Here the liturgical Eucharist is *not* performed, however elaborate may be the ritual surrounding the monastic meal.[57] In such a setting, where the image can function only as a historical reference, pointing to something that "happens" elsewhere, as distinct from a sign of something actualized on the premises, the image is open to redefinition or reinterpretation—unlike, say, a Rembrandt that is transferred from one room in a museum to another.

Numerous things were done and said at the Last Supper, apart from those comprising the institution of the Eucharist, as we are reminded by the biblical, liturgical, and patristic texts having to do with Holy Thursday. The prediction of Judas' betrayal, the idea of redemption through suffering, assurances of a Last Judgment, hope of reunion in the Kingdom of Heaven, are all important subjects of meditation on that day.[58] It is not enough in our case to enumerate these subjects; it is also necessary to determine upon which of them the accent is placed in a refectory. Or, to alter the metaphor: we must decide which of the thematic "notes" that are sounded by a Last Supper is in harmony with a refectory program's dominant "chord." Given the emphasis on Lenten subjects that one finds at Apollonia, but also (if there were space here to demonstrate it) in most of the trapeza programs of

---

[55] One assumes that this is what J. Ştefănescu meant in speaking of the "signification eucharistique" of paintings of the Prophet Elijah Fed by the Raven that are placed in or near the church sanctuary (*L'Illustration des Liturgies dans l'art de Byzance et de l'Orient* [Brussels, 1936], 151).

[56] A. Schmemann, *Introduction to Liturgical Theology*, trans. A. Moorhouse (1966; repr. London and Bangor, Maine, 1970), esp. chap. 1.

[57] The ritual character of the monastic meal is well sketched in F. Dölger, E. Weigand, and A. Deindl, *Mönchsland Athos* (Munich, 1943), 128, 234, 236, 250. Concerning the most important trapeza ceremony, see J. Yiannias, "The Elevation of the Panaghia," *DOP* 26 (1972), 225–36.

[58] Συνέκδημος (note 15 above), 1037–68, passim. In this connection it is also instructive to read St. John Chrysostom's homily on Mt. 26:26–28 (P. Schaff, ed., *A Select Library of the Nicene and Post-Nicene Fathers of the Christian Church*, vol. 10 [New York, 1888], 491–97). Loerke draws a useful distinction between the Last Supper as a subject and the Last Supper as a setting, in pointing out that the meal scene on page five of the Rossano Gospels illustrates the prediction of Judas' betrayal: see G. Cavallo, J. Gribomont, W. Loerke, *Codex Purpureus Rossanensis* (Rome and Graz, 1987), 131.

the Athonite monasteries,[59] we may tentatively conclude that the accent falls on Christ's preparation for his own suffering and death, presented as the model for the monks' *kenosis* and control of the passions—so appropriate to a space in which the primal passion, gluttony, is supposed to be restrained.[60] The image of the Last Supper comes to the refectory from the church with its liturgical associations largely preempted by the Communion of the Apostles. One cannot assume that it gains these associations in a refectory, which does not serve as a setting for the Eucharistic celebration.

Whatever the merits of that argument, we can say that at least four important factors governing the choice of subjects in Eastern refectories are exemplified at Apollonia. One is a preference for texts—liturgical or hagiographical—that are appropriate to the season of abstinence and to the ideas closely related to it—"passion-control" and self-sacrifice. Another is what may be called visual habit, the association of certain images with certain surfaces, such as the full-length figures of standing saints with a wall's bottom zone.[61] A third is iconographic habit, as when subjects like the Hospitality of Abraham or the Wedding at Cana trail after the Last Supper, even though their meaning in a refectory may reside primarily in their being hallowed Scriptural meals, rather than in any intended evocation of the liturgical performance of the Eucharist. And a fourth factor is the desire to avoid the most solemn festal and celestial images, for the purpose of leaving the church unrivaled and undiminished as the space consecrated to the Eucharistic actualization of the history of salvation.

[59] See my essay, "The Refectory Paintings of Mount Athos: An Interpretation," to be published in John J. Yiannias, ed., *The Byzantine Tradition after the Fall of Constantinople* (Charlottesville and London, University Press of Virginia, 1991).

[60] The patristic literature on the nature and consequences of gluttony is extensive. I mention only that Gregory Palamas describes abstention from the fruit of the Tree in Eden as the first fast: see Migne, PG 151:81C.

[61] Examples in other refectories include the association of the Annunciation with the spandrels of the main apsidal arch (mentioned above); of the Theotokos and Christ Child with the conch of the main apse (a position for which they contend with the Last Supper); and of the Mandylion with the space over the crown of the main apsidal arch. See my forthcoming essay, "The Refectory Paintings of Mount Athos" (note 59 above).

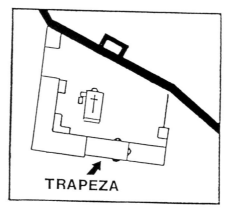

1. Apollonia, Monastery. Schematic plan (adapted from Buschhausen by the author)

APPROX.
◀ N

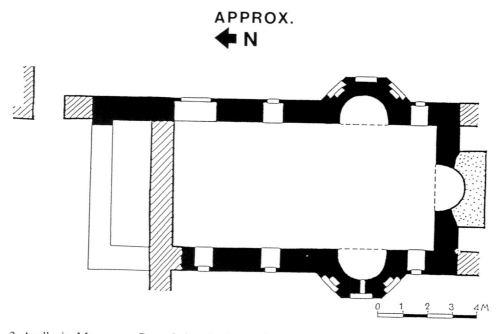

2. Apollonia, Monastery. Ground plan of refectory (Meksi, with addition by the author)

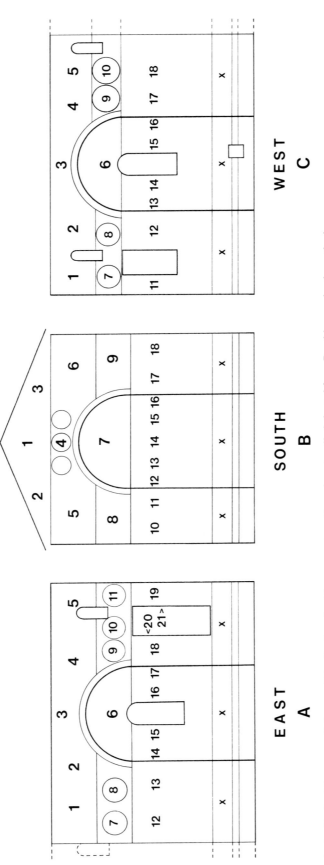

EAST

A

SOUTH

B

WEST

C

3. Apollonia, Monastery. Refectory. Distribution of subjects on east, south, and west walls (adapted from Buschhausen by the author)

East wall (**A**):

1. Christ Raising the Widow's Son. **2.** ? **3.** ? **4.** Christ Healing the Possessed Man. **5.** Christ among the Doctors *or* Christ Teaching in the Synagogue at Nazareth. **6.** Myrrh-Bearers at the Tomb (?) **7** and **8.** Saints. **9–11.** Three Youths. **12–18.** Standing saints. **19.** St. Symeon Stylite. **20 and 21.** Saints. **x.** Painted imitation marble panels

South wall (**B**):

1. Hospitality of Abraham. **2.** ? **3.** ? **4.** Christ Emmanuel and Archangels. **5.** Washing of the Feet. **6.** Christ Instructing the Apostles. **7.** Last Supper. **8.** Communion of St. Mary of Egypt. **9.** Prophet Elijah Fed by the Raven. **10–16.** Standing saints. **17.** St. Gregory the Theologian. **18.** St. John of Damascus. **x.** Painted imitation marble panels

West wall (**C**):

1. Annointing of Christ's Feet. **2.** Miracle at Cana. **3.** ? **4.** Healing of a Blind Man *or* Blessing of the Child. **5.** Purging of the Temple. **6.** Prayer in the Garden. **7** and **8.** Male saints. **9.** Abraham (?) **10.** A patriarch (?) **11.** St. Symeon the Younger (Stylite). **12.** Standing saint. **13** and **14.** Undraped standing saints. **15–18.** Standing saints. **x.** Painted imitation marble panels

4. Apollonia, Monastery. Refectory, south wall, general view (photo: Bildarchiv Foto Marburg)

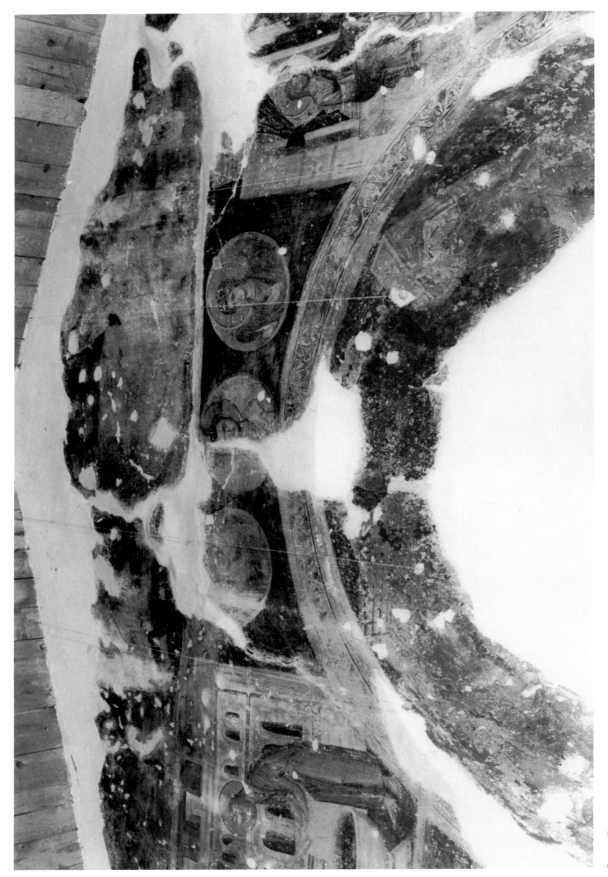

5. Apollonia, Monastery. Refectory, south apse, detail: west half and adjacent surface (photo: Conway Library, Courtauld Institute of Art)

7. Apollonia, Monastery. Refectory, east half of south wall, Communion of St. Mary of Egypt; two saints (photo: Conway Library, Courtauld Institute of Art)

6. Apollonia, Monastery. Refectory, west half of south apse, Last Supper, detail: figure with scroll (Isaiah) (photo: Conway Library, Courtauld Institute of Art)

8. Apollonia, Monastery. Refectory, west wall, detail: Christ Teaching in the Synagogue (photo: Conway Library, Courtauld Institute of Art)

9. Apollonia, Monastery. Refectory, west wall, Christ Teaching in the Synagogue. detail (photo: Conway Library, Courtauld Institute of Art)

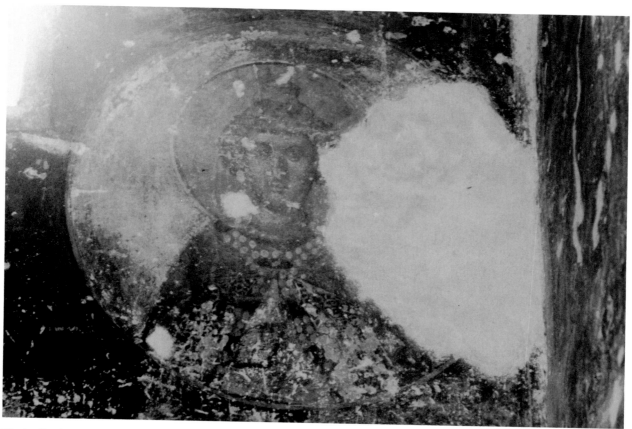

10. Apollonia, Monastery. Refectory, east wall, detail: one of the Three Youths (Fig. 3, **A11**) (photo: Conway Library, Courtauld Institute of Art)

11. Apollonia, Monastery. Refectory, west wall, detail: south portion and apse (photo: Conway Library, Courtauld Institute of Art)

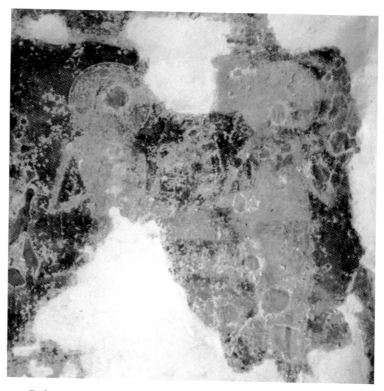

12. Apollonia, Monastery. Refectory, west apse, detail: two ascetics (photo: Conway Library, Courtauld Institute of Art)

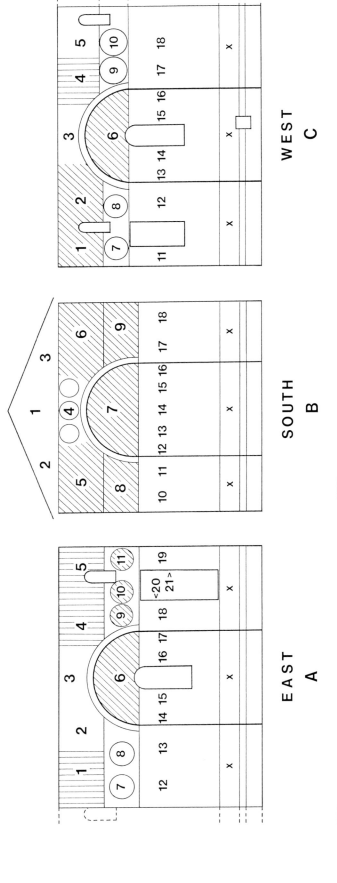

EAST
A

SOUTH
B

WEST
C

◨ (hatched) Subjects narrated or mentioned explicitly in Lenten texts   ▦ Subjects alluded to in Lenten texts

13. Apollonia, Monastery. Refectory, east, south, and west walls; distribution of subjects based on Lenten texts

East wall (**A**):
1. Christ Raising the Widow's Son. **2**. ? **3**. ? **4**. Christ Healing the Possessed Man. **5**. Christ among the Doctors *or* Christ Teaching in the Synagogue at Nazareth. **6**. Myrrh-Bearers at the Tomb (?) **7** and **8**. Saints. **9–11**. Three Youths. **12–18**. Standing saints. **19**. St. Symeon Stylite. **20 and 21**. Saints. **x**. Painted imitation marble panels

South wall (**B**):
1. Hospitality of Abraham. **2**. ? **3**. ? **4**. Christ Emmanuel and Archangels. **5**. Washing of the Feet. **6**. Christ Instructing the Apostles. **7**. Last Supper. **8**. Communion of St. Mary of Egypt. **9**. Prophet Elijah Fed by the Raven. **10–16**. Standing saints. **17**. St. Gregory the Theologian. **18**. St. John of Damascus. **x**. Painted imitation marble panels

West wall (**C**):
1. Annointing of Christ's Feet. **2**. Miracle at Cana. **3**. ? **4**. Healing of a Blind Man *or* Blessing of the Child. **5**. Purging of the Temple. **6**. Prayer in the Garden. **7** and **8**. Male saints. **9**. Abraham (?) **10**. A patriarch (?) **11**. St. Symeon the Younger (Stylite). **12**. Standing saint. **13 and 14**. Undraped standing saints. **15–18**. Standing saints. **x**. Painted imitation marble panels

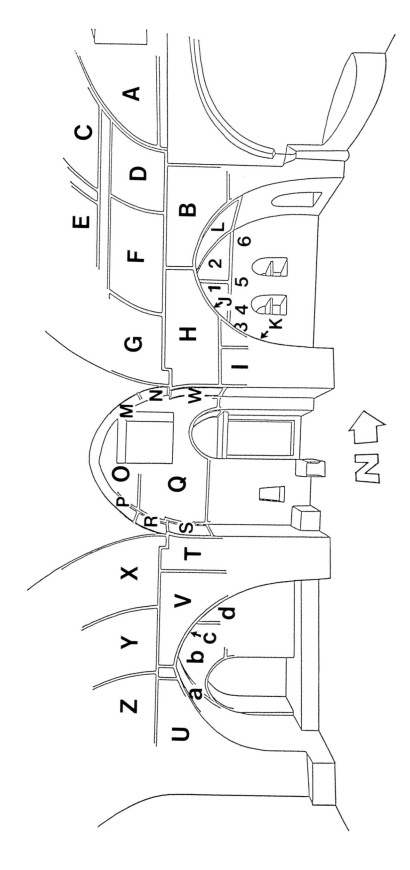

14. Patmos, Monastery of St. John the Theologian. Refectory, arrangement of paintings (adapted from Kollias by the author)

1. Appearance of Christ to the Disciples by the Sea of Tiberias. 2. Multiplication of the Loaves. 3. St. Euthymios. 4. St. Chariton. 5. St. Hilarion. 6. Unidentified saint. A. Abraham welcoming the Angels. B. Multiplication of the Loaves. C. Communion of the Apostles (Bread). D. Communion of the Apostles (Wine). E. Washing of the Feet. F. Prayer in the Garden.

G. Betrayal by Judas. H. Appearance of Christ to the Disciples by the Sea of Tiberias. I. St. Gregory of Akragas. J. St. Cyprian. K. St. Amphilochios. L. St. Dionysios the Areopagite. M. Christ before Annas and Caiaphas. N. Peter's Denial. O. Christ Led to the Cross. P. Preparation of the Cross. Q. Crucifixion. R. Distribution of Christ's Garments.

S. Descent from the Cross. T. Lamentation. U. Descent into Hell (Anastasis). V. Myrrh-Bearers at the Sepulchre. W. Mission of the Apostles. X. Second Ecumenical Council. Y. Fourth Ecumenical Council. Z. Sixth Ecumenical Council. a. Death of the Sinner (?). b. Death of the Righteous Man. c. Unidentified visionary scene. d. Monk and inscription.

Diversity in Fresco Painting of the Mid-Fourteenth Century: The Case of Lesnovo

SMILJKA GABELIĆ

THE CHURCH of the Archangel Michael of the monastery at Lesnovo is situated in the northeast section of the Yugoslav republic of Macedonia. Its well-preserved frescoes display numerous and distinct artistic trends, and for that reason they are suitable for demonstrating various currents in the contemporary wall painting of that region.

During the second quarter of the fourteenth century, the lands around Lesnovo, including the village itself, belonged to a powerful nobleman, Jovan Oliver. This high-ranking official at the court of the Serbian king, later emperor (tsar) Dušan, commissioned the rebuilding and painting of this church. Its older part, the naos, was built in 1341 and painted by 1346 or 1347; the narthex was added, most probably, in 1347 and was painted in 1349.[1]

A relatively large number of artists painted the Lesnovo church. The frescoes of the naos were done by four or five artists; the decoration was divided into horizontal zones, and the painters began working, it would be logical to assume, in the dome.[2]

Among the painters of the naos, only the one who painted the two lower zones left his signature. It is written in Greek on the figure of St. George on the north wall next to the donor's composition, but is unfortunately damaged. It reads: χ(ε)ίρ ζωγράφοῦ . . . ("By the hand of the painter . . . ").[3] Speculation that he inscribed his name on the figure of his personal protector, St. George, and that his name would therefore be George, is not provable. We prefer to call him the anonymous chief master, since his frescoes occupy prominent places in the naos and the conch of the apse. More precisely, he worked in the semidome of the apse (Virgin with Archangels), on the walls of the prothesis and diaconicon (isolated

---

[1] For the dating of the church in the Lesnovo monastery see Smiljka Gabelić, "Novi podatak o sevastokra-torskoj tituli Jovana Olivera i vreme slikanja lesnovskog naosa," *Zograf* 11 (1980), 54–62 (esp. 61–62, with bibliography). The fresco decoration of the naos was completed when Jovan Oliver, the founder, had become Sebastocrator (in 1346 or 1347): he was portrayed with the attributes of a Sebastocrator (blue robe and single-headed eagles), while in the dado below the figure of his personal protector and patron of the church, the Archangel Michael, are monograms in medallions; one of these includes the beginning letters of the title Seba-stocrator. The narthex was painted in 1349, as the inscription above the east door indicates. Jovan Oliver was portrayed in the narthex as Despot, in a red robe decorated with double-headed eagles within roundels (*ibid.*, 54–60, figs. 1, 2, 8, 10 and 11).

[2] Kosta Balabanov, "Novootkrieni iminja na zografi od 1341 godina vo crkvata na Lesnovskiot manastir," *Razgledi* IV/4 (1963), 400–407, and Vojislav J. Djurić, *Vizantijske freske u Jugoslaviji* (Belgrade, 1974), 64, distinguished four painters' hands in the naos.

[3] Cf. Gabriel Millet, *L'ancient art serbe. Les églises* (Paris, 1919), 31, fig. 16. Until recently, it was incorrectly believed that there were another three painters' signatures in the naos of Lesnovo, which are in fact monograms of the Sebastocrator Jovan Oliver and his wife Anna Maria: S. Gabelić, "Novi podatak" (note 1 above), 54–55, figs. 1–8.

saints), and, in the naos itself, in the two bottom zones of the walls and columns (cycle of the Archangels and row of standing figures).

Although he is easily distinguished from the other painters in Lesnovo and justifiably praised for his work, scholars have not yet found analogies or stylistic sources for his art.[4] In addition to strong coloring, which is the first impression of these frescoes, the main characteristics of the painter's style are clear expression, regular and beautiful shapes, and a pedantic manner (Figs. 1–4). The treatment of figures and drapery is geometrically strict, and the modeling is predominantly linear. The faces are noticeably pale, with narrow strips of shading. Especially striking are the large, carefully drawn eyes. The volume is not stressed and the compositions lack depth. On the whole, the precise work and ability to render detail indicate that this artist must have worked as an icon painter as well, and may have perhaps been a manuscript illuminator, too. From a technical standpoint, these frescoes are of extremely high quality, and are preserved in excellent condition. The painter worked on ideally smooth mortar. The use of gold leaf can be observed on the garments and haloes of some figures: *ktētor* Jovan Oliver, Archangel Michael, Saint Nicholas, the Virgin, and the Archangel Gabriel (Fig. 5).

A number of icons and mural decorations in Ohrid show that the chief master of the Lesnovo naos should be connected with artistic workshops in that town. We may even presume that an icon of St. Naum found in the church of the Virgin "Bolnička" in Ohrid was painted by this same artist. The icon (Fig. 6) is now kept in the Gallery of Icons, Ohrid (no. 1132).[5] The bust of St. Naum is wide, and the treatment has a geometrical purity and clarity. The creasing of the robe is achieved with broken lines, while thin unbroken lines are used in a confident and precise manner to draw the long, thin nose and the large almond-shaped eyes with arched eyebrows. The face is particularly bright; the shading and rosy highlights are barely accentuated, the locks of hair done separately. The peculiarities of the technique, as well as the handling of the half-figure, betray the manner of painting characteristic of the Lesnovo painter under discussion. Identical traits are evident in the execution of details (lower eyelids, linear highlights below and in the corners of the eyes), and indicate that this icon was produced by the principal painter of the Lesnovo naos.[6]

The same master of Lesnovo has close analogies among some other artists in Ohrid. Above all, the frescoes in the church of Old St. Clement, from the year 1378, show a strong resemblance with, e.g., the frescoes of the lower zones of the west and south walls.[7] The sim-

[4] Svetozar Radojčić, *Staro srpsko slikarstvo* (Belgrade, 1966), 145. Djurić, *Vizantijske freske* (note 2 above), 64, figs. 62–65. For reproductions see Gabriel Millet and Tania Velmans, *La peinture du Moyen âge en Yougoslavie*, IV (Paris, 1969), pls. 7:16, 8, 9, 14:30 and 17; Svetozar Radojčić, *Lesnovo* (Belgrade, 1971) figs. 1–7, 18–24.

[5] The icon of St. Naum was first published in Vojislav J. Djurić, *Icônes de Yougoslavie* (Belgrade, 1961), p. 33, cat. 27, pl. XL. He dated it to the second half of the fourteenth century. According to Kosta Balabanov, *Icons from Macedonia* (Belgrade-Skopje, 1969), p. xx, fig. 48 and *idem*, *Icons from Macedonia* (Zagreb, 1987), p. 100, cat. 29, figs. 60 and 61, the icon was brought from the church of St. Nicholas "Bolnički" in Ohrid.

[6] Based on this analogy we can assume that the icon belongs either to the middle or to the second half of the fourteenth century.

[7] See Djurić, *Icônes* (note 5 above), 33; Balabanov, *Icons* (note 5 above), p. xx; Djurić, *Vizantijske freske* (note 2 above), 89–90; Cvetan Grozdanov, *Ohridsko zidno slikarstvo XIV veka* (Belgrade, 1980), 153, fig. 154;

ilarities include the setting of the figures, the shapes of their heads and the rendering of their pale, delicate faces. On the other hand, strong colors and white highlights are missing and the figures have smaller dimensions. These frescoes were probably done by a pupil of the chief Lesnovo master. Other, less similar analogies from Ohrid are the icon of St. Nicholas from the church of the Virgin Peribleptos, dated to the second half of the fourteenth century (Fig. 7), frescoes of 1364/65 in the chapel of St. Gregory in the church of the Virgin Peribleptos (Fig. 8), and wall painting in the church of St. Nicholas "Bolnički" from ca. 1330–40.[8] We propose still another parallel: the icon of St. Stephen Protomartyr from the Menil Collection in Houston, Texas (Fig. 9).[9] The delicacy of the portrait, the facial features (large eyes, sharp nose ridge), and the strong, bright colors recall the style of the main artist of the Lesnovo naos (Fig. 10). The characteristics that show these two works to be strikingly similar suggest a period around the middle of the fourteenth century or slightly earlier. At the same time, they reveal that the provenance of the icon could not be far from Ohrid and northern Greece.

The style of the Lesnovo master was not too popular in the fresco decoration of contemporary churches. His predilection for beautiful, pale faces and the wide setting of his rather monumental figures are features that link his frescoes with monumental painting of the late thirteenth or the beginning of the fourteenth century (Protaton and Olympiotissa in Greece, and Peribleptos in Ohrid are the best analogies).[10] Conservative in comparison with

idem, *Portreitite na svetitelite od Makedonija od IX–XVIII vek* (Skopje, 1983), 108–109. Balabanov and Grozdanov consider that the painter of the icon of St. Naum and the painter from Old St. Clement are the same person.

[8] Djurić, *Icônes* (note 5 above), 33, cat. 22, pls. XXXII–XXXIII; *idem*, *Vizantijske freske* (note 2 above), 67–68 (St. Nicholas "Bolnički"), 73–74, fig. 79 (Virgin Peribleptos); Grozdanov, *Ohridsko zidno slikarstvo* (note 7 above), 37–45, figs. 4–9 (St. Nicholas "Bolnički"), 137–44, figs. 110–114 (St. Gregory chapel).

[9] On this icon: Jacqueline Lafontaine-Dosogne, *Splendeur de Byzance*, exh. cat. (Brussels, 1982), 40; Bertrand Davezac, *Spirituality in the Christian East. Greek, Slavic, and Russian Icons from the Menil Collection* (Houston, 1988), 13–15; Ellen C. Schwartz, "The St. Stephen Icon," *Fourteenth Annual Byzantine Studies Conference, Abstracts of Papers* (Houston, 1988), 34. Davezac dates this icon to ca. 1300 and relates it to Constantinople. Schwartz dates it to the first quarter of the fourteenth century and believes that the painter was from Thessaloniki.

[10] On the Protaton at Karyes, Mount Athos, see Gabriel Millet, *Monuments de l'Athos*, I (Paris, 1927), pls. 5–56; Andréas Xyngopoulos, *Thessalonique et la peinture macédonienne* (Athens, 1955), 29–34; *idem*, *Manuel Panselinos* (Athens, 1956), 9–28, pls. 1–11; Petar Miljković-Pepek, *Deloto na zografite Mihailo i Eutihij* (Skopje, 1967), 203–212, pls. L–LXXX (especially LII, LIII, LXXII–LXXX); Doula Mouriki, "Stylistic Trends in Monumental Painting of Greece at the beginning of the Fourteenth Century," in *L'Art byzantin au début du XIVe siècle. Symposium de Gračanica 1973* (Belgrade, 1978), 64–66, fig. 14; Branislav Todić, "Protaton et le peinture serbe des premières décennies du XIVe siècle," in *L'Art de Thessalonique et des pays balkaniques et les courants spirituels au XIVe siècle. Recueil des rapports du IVe colloque serbo-grec, Belgrade 1985* (Belgrade, 1987), 21–31. On the painting of the katholikon of the Olympiotissa at Elasson: M. G. Soteriou, "Ἡ πρώϊμος παλαιολόγειος ἀναγένησις εἰς τὰς χώρας καὶ τὰς νήσους τῆς Ἑλλάδος κατὰ τὸν 13ον αἰῶνα," Δελτ.Χριστ.Ἀρχ.Ἑτ. ser. 4, vol. 4 (1964–65), 271–73, figs. 63, 64; Mouriki, "Stylistic Trends," 69–70, fig. 27. (D. Mouriki stresses the stylistic differences between the various parts of the fresco painting in this church.) On the Virgin Peribleptos in Ohrid: Gabriel Millet and Anatole Frolow, *La peinture du Moyen âge en Yougoslavie*, III (Paris, 1962), x, xii–xiii, xv, pls. 1–18; Horst Hallensleben, *Die Malerschule des Königs Milutin* (Giessen, 1963), 51–54, 128–33; Miljković-Pepek, *Deloto na zografite*, 43–51, pls. I–XLIX (especially pls. I, II, XXIII, XXII, XXXIX, XXXVI); Djurić, *Vizantijske freske* (note 2 above), 17–19.

contemporary tastes in wall painting, this painter's style is centered geographically, we believe, in Ohrid.

Quite a different path was taken by another painter of the naos of Lesnovo, who worked on the upper portions of the walls and the pendentives as well as on the bottom zone of the drum, painting most of the busts of the Forty Martyrs of Sebaste, the Evangelists, and the Great Feasts cycle, with the exception of the Dormition (Figs. 11, 12).[11] The dramatic manner that he used was highly popular in contemporary wall- and icon-painting. By using deep colors, vivid movement of the figures and, especially, strong contrasts of light and dark, he achieved an expressive style. Without any intention of creating dignified or beautiful forms, he created figures marked by raw power. Animation and expressiveness are the most emblematic results of this artist's manner. It is likely that he should be connected with one of at least six painters that decorated the narthex in the church of the Pantokrator at the monastery of Dečani (1346/47), specifically the artist who illustrated the lower registers of the Calendar cycle.[12] These frescoes also possess strong expressive character: forms and figures are robust, colors are vivid, and modeling is achieved by using contrasts of dark and light (Fig. 13). The expressionistic painter from Lesnovo, scholars agree, continued to work in some other churches in Macedonia. He took part in the decoration of the church dedicated to St. Demetrios in Markov Manastir (1376/7), famous for the dynamic character of its wall paintings.[13] Among the artists who worked there, his hand is recognized in the bottom zone of the sanctuary and in the middle zones of the naos and narthex (Akathistos to the Virgin; part of the St. Nicholas cycle). There he developed fully a style that may be called anti-classical. This trend was sometimes accompanied by a decline in quality: the figures have squat proportions and the compositions often lack a deeper spatial background. Sometimes, however, the result was extraordinarily impressive, such as in the figures depicted in the lower zone of the apse, which are characterized by an abstract treatment (Fig. 14). The same artist also painted the church of St. Nicholas in the village of Čelopek near Tetovo in northwest Macedonia. The wall painting of this church has only recently been discovered and is not yet fully published, and as far as we know, there is no historical information on this church. The frescoes, depicting the Life and Suffering of Christ, are preserved only in the central zone of the naos, and should be dated in the late eighties of the fourteenth cen-

---

[11] For the frescoes painted by this artist, Balabanov, "Novootkrieni iminja na zografi," (note 2 above), 400ff.; Djurić, *Vizantijske freske* (note 2 above), 64; Smiljka Gabelić, "Jedna lokalna slikarska radionica iz sredine XIV veka," in *Dečani i vizantijska umetnost sredinom XIV veka, Symposium Belgrade 1985* (Belgrade, 1989), 370–72, 374–75, figs. 7–13.

[12] The connection between these two painters has been analyzed by Gabelić, "Jedna lokalna slikarska radionica" (note 11 above), 368–69, 374–75, figs. 1–6. See also the reproductions in Vladimir R. Petković and Djurdje Bošković, *Dečani*, II (Belgrade, 1941), pls. LXXVI, LXXVII:1, LXXXVIII:1, LXXIX, CIII:2, CVI–CXI, CXII–CXXXI:1, CXXII–CXXVIII:1, CXXXIX–CXXXXI:1, CCXVII. On Dečani: Radojčić, *Staro srpsko slikarstvo* (note 4 above), 131–40; Djurić, *Vizantijske freske* (note 2 above), 56–58. For the chronology of the fresco decoration: Gojko Subotić, "Prilog hronologiji dečanskog zidnog slikarstva," *Zbornik radova Vizantološkog instituta* 20 (1981), 111–36.

[13] Radojčić, *Staro srpsko slikarstvo* (note 4 above), 157; Vojislav J. Djurić, "Markov manastir—Ohrid," *Zbornik za likovne umetnosti* 8 (1972), 140; *idem*, *Vizantijske freske* (note 2 above), 157; Gabelić "Jedna lokalna slikarska radionica" (note 11 above), 372–73, figs. 14–18. For the dating: Cvetan Grozdanov and Gojko Subotić, "Crkva Svetog Djordja u Rečici kod Ohrida," *Zograf* 12 (1981), 73–74, fig. 17.

tury.[14] The painter whom we follow from Lesnovo and Markov Manastir, perhaps from Dečani too, in Čelopek fell into provincialism by using a simplified color palette and by drawing disproportionate figures. Thus, the artist began with an expressive but still sufficiently balanced style at Lesnovo, and perhaps at Dečani. Afterwards, his manner changed into an extremely intense, anti-classical style in Markov Manastir and Čelopek.

Such a trend, as already mentioned, appears widely diffused around the middle of the fourteenth century and represents one of the two main stylistic movements in the wall painting of Serbia and Macedonia.[15] One sees it, for example, in the monastery of the Transfiguration in Zrze, where the frescoes were commissioned in 1368/69.[16] The painter of the lower zone at Zrze, another representative of the expressionistic trend, achieved these effects through the manipulation of light and shadow and vigorous, expressive modeling of the facial features. The same can be said for the style of the wall painting in the badly damaged church of St. Athanasios near Lešak, from around 1350,[17] the church of the Apostles in Pećka patrijaršija from approximately the same period (frescoes on the arch on the west side of the naos),[18] St. Nicholas "Šiševski" dated ca. 1380, Lipljan from ca. 1376, and finally, a layer of frescoes from the fourth decade of the fourteenth century on the south wall in the narthex at Pećka patrijaršija (Virgin Galaktotrophousa with angels),[19] belonging to the "expressionistic" trend, all of which resemble the work of the Lesnovo artist.

The roots of such a trend may be found among monuments of the workshop of the so-called King Milutin's artists, a workshop that was directed by the famous painters Michael and Eutychios, who, it is believed, came from Thessaloniki.[20] This workshop decorated several churches founded by the Serbian king Milutin and was active until the end of the second decade of the fourteenth century. It worked at the churches of the Virgin Peribleptos in Ohrid, of the Virgin "Ljeviška" in Prizren, of St. George in Staro Nagoričino, and of St.

[14] Gabelić, "Jedna lokalna slikarska radionica" (note 11 above), 373–74, fig. 19. Cf. the preliminary report on this church: Petar Miljković-Pepek, "Pregled na crkovnite spomenici vo tetovska oblast od XI do XIX vek," *Spomenici za srednovekovata i ponovata istorija na Makedonija*, III (Skopje, 1980), 465–66.

[15] The other current could be described as more harmonious and, more particularly, subdued in coloring (see the church of the Virgin and of St. Demetrios in Pećka patrijaršija, Ljuboten, Konče and Pološko, for example). On the stylistic characteristics of the wall paintings of the middle and the second half of the fourteenth century in Serbia: Djurić, *Vizantijske freske* (note 2 above), 60 and passim; Gordana Babić-Djordjević, "Razgranavanje umetničke delatnosti i pojave stilske raznorodnosti," in *Istorija srpskog naroda*, I (Belgrade, 1981), 641–63; *eadem* and Vojislav J. Djurić, "Polet umetnosti," in *Istorija srpskog naroda*, II (Belgrade, 1982), 144–91.

[16] Djurić, *Vizantijske freske* (note 2 above), 85; Zorica Ivković, "Živopis iz XIV veka u manastiru Zrze," *Zograf* 11 (1980), 80–81, figs. 8–13.

[17] Djurić, *Vizantijske freske* (note 2 above), 65; Petar Miljković-Pepek, "Crkvata Sv. Atanasij Aleksandrijski kraj manastirot Lešok," *Spomenici za srednovekovata i ponovata istorija na Makedonija*, III (Skopje, 1980), 497–502.

[18] Djurić, *Vizantijske freske* (note 2 above), 59; Branislav Todić, "Patrijarh Joanikije-ktitor fresaka u crkvi sv. Apostola u Peći," *Zbornik za likovne umetnosti* 16 (1980), 102, figs. 1–11; Gabelić, "Jedna lokalna slikarska radionica" (note 11 above), 369, figs. 20, 21.

[19] Djurić, *Vizantijske freske* (note 2 above), 83, fig. 90 (Lipljan); 83, figs. 91 and 92 (St. Nicholas Šiševski); 59 (Pećka patrijaršija, narthex).

[20] On the so-called "painting school" of King Milutin: Svetozar Radojčić, *Majstori starog srpskog slikarstva* (Belgrade, 1955), 20–28; Horst Hallensleben, "Zu den Malerinschriften der 'Milutin-Schule'," *BZ* 53/1 (1960), 112–17; *idem*, *Die Malerschule des Königs Milutin* (Giessen, 1963); Miljković-Pepek, *Deloto na*

Nikita at Čučer; it also presumably participated in the decoration of the Holy Apostles church in Pećka patrijaršija, the King's Church in Studenica, and Gračanica (Figs. 15, 16). Staro Nagoričino (1316–18), for example, is the monument where the representative, narrative style of Milutin's painting workshop reached its full development. The mural painting of this church possesses high aesthetic quality and the classical manner of Palaeologan style is dominant. At the King's Church (ca. 1320) and St. Nikita (1314), the compositions are full and detailed and include numerous subsidiary figures. These possess expressiveness and typological traits that would eventually prevail in painting around the middle of the century.[21]

In the hands of the most expressive master from Lesnovo (master of the Great Feasts cycle, Evangelists, and Forty Martyrs), the prominent Palaeologan style turned to anticlassicism; the facial features and "drama" were inherited but they were intensified both in typology and in modeling. This trend, as we have seen, was accompanied by a gradual decline of this painter's quality.

The other painters of the naos of the church at Lesnovo left frescoes of a low artistic quality. The artist responsible for the Pantokrator, the Heavenly Liturgy and prophets in the dome and drum, the figures of saints in the upper portions of the columns, the Christ-patriarch in the apse and, most likely, the officiating prelates and some busts of saints in the altar area, is the worst in the Lesnovo artistic hierarchy.[22] His frescoes appear to follow monumental models but the results show poor expression, raw color palette, and very often complete ugliness of form. The figures have anatomic deviations, e.g., huge hands, deformed heads, lop-ears, and twisted postures (Figs. 17, 18). The drapery is flat and covered with very large, simple decorative motifs. Schematically separated segments of muscles and wrinkles which are far too strong are used for depicting the faces of old persons such as St. Athanasios (Fig. 19). In their shear ugliness, the church fathers in the apse of Lesnovo resemble frescoes in some small monuments in Ohrid, although direct links are difficult to draw.[23] We later find faces which are similar to a certain degree, with very deep parallel lines, in the church of St. Nicholas "Šiševski."[24] Despite all the defects in the work of this painter at Lesnovo, he managed on occasion to achieve results of fairly high quality, as seen in the head of the Archangel Gabriel of the Annunciation (Fig. 20).

---

zografite (note 10 above); Djurić, Vizantijske freske (note 2 above), 18–19, 47–54; Gordana Babić, in Istorija srpskog naroda, I (Belgrade, 1981), 488–493; eadem, Kraljeva crkva u Studenici (Belgrade, 1987), 215, 218 and passim; Branislav Todić, Gračanica, slikarstvo (Belgrade-Priština, 1988), 232–34.

[21] For the literature on Staro Nagoričino, King's Church, and Gračanica see note 20 above. For illustrations of the frescoes, see Miljković-Pepek, Deloto na zografite (note 10 above), pls. LXXII–CII (King's Church), CIII–CXV (Nikita), CXVI–CLXXVIII (Staro Nagoričino). For the new dating of St. Nikita: Petar Miljković-Pepek, "Crkvata Sv. Nikita vo skopska Crna Gora kako istorijsko-umetnički spomenik," in Spomenici na Makedonija, I (Skopje, 1975), 381–83.

[22] Cf. Balabanov, "Novootkrieni iminja na zografi," (note 2 above), 406; Djurić, Vizantijske freske (note 2 above), 64. For reproductions see Millet and Velmans, Peinture du Moyen âge (note 4 above), IV, pls. 6:13, 11:24.

[23] Compare, for example, frescoes in the church of Mali Sveti Vrači (ca. 1340): Grozdanov, Ohridsko zidno slikarstvo (note 7 above), 48–54, figs. 22–26.

[24] Djurić, Vizantijske freske (note 2 above), figs. 91, 92.

It is not always easy to separate the painter of the dome from the one who worked beneath him on the Passion and the Christological cycles. Certain details are identical, for instance the small prolongation below the ears. Nevertheless, we can safely attribute to him some of the busts of the Forty Martyrs on the south side, most of the scenes of the Passion cycle and the complete cycle of the Miracles and Parables of Christ, as well as the Communion of the Apostles in the bema.[25] The style of this painter is characterized specifically by an intense, warm-colored palette and the physiognomical types of his figures (Figs. 21–23). Among these features we may point out the round, reddish cheeks and the faces with their naive expressions. The figures are elongated, lacking in weight, and seem uncertain in their movement: they often appear to be drifting above the ground. The compositions tend to be either monotonous, with constantly repeated groups of the same type of figure (e.g., Miracles) or, on the contrary, disperse, rather comic, and too garish (e.g., the Cleansing of the Temple, the Mocking of Christ). We cannot find close parallels for these frescoes, but some general similarities can be observed with frescoes of at least one of the three artists who worked in the church of the Virgin in Pećka patrijaršija (before 1377).[26]

The narthex of Lesnovo, smaller than the naos, was decorated by only one painter. It was previously believed that his name was Michael because of the inscription МНХАНА inscribed on the sword of the Archangel Michael whose figure is painted next to the entrance into the naos. Most probably the inscription actually refers to the bearer of the sword, i.e., Michael the Archangel, patron of the church, and very hypothetically, to the painter as well. The same name, in abbreviated form, was also inscribed on the sword of the Archangel Michael presented in the donor's composition in the naos.[27]

The style of this artist shows the influence of Palaeologan painting from the beginning of the fourteenth century.[28] The forms and proportions are elaborate and the figures have a plastic quality, although the architectural motifs have lost a good deal of their heaviness. The frescoes appear subdued, calm, and are characterized by a palette of cool colors. Intense red and blue tones predominate in the naos, while the main colors in the narthex are green and light ochre. Apart from the soft and plastic modelling, the artist's heritage from the

---

[25] Cf. Balabanov, "Novootkrieni iminja na zografi," (note 2 above), 405–406; Djurić, *Vizantijske freske* (note 2 above), 64. Good reproductions may be found in Millet and Velmans, *Peinture du Moyen âge* (note 4 above), IV, pls. 6:14, 7:15, 10:21, 12:25–26, 13:27, 14:31, 15:32–33, 16:34; Radojčić, *Lesnovo* (note 4 above), ills. 8–17.

[26] Cf. Milan Ivanović, *Bogorodičina crkva u Peći* (Belgrade, 1972) ills. 10, 15.

[27] On those inscriptions: Millet, *L'ancient art serbe* (note 3 above), 26, fig. 16; Radojčić, *Majstori starog srpskog slikarstva* (note 20 above), 35; Babić, in *Istorija srpskog naroda*, I (note 20 above), 655; and Vojislav J. Djurić, "Ime Merkurije iz Psače," *Zbornik za likovne umetnosti* 7 (1971), 231–35, who points out the medieval custom of placing on garments and armor the names of their wearers, suggesting that these types of inscriptions in frescoes are not necessarily the painters' signatures.

[28] For the style of painting in the narthex of Lesnovo cf. Radojčić, *Staro srpsko slikarstvo* (note 4 above), 146–48; *idem*, "Der Klassizismus und ihm Entgegengesetzte Tendenzen in der Malerei des 14. Jahrhunderts bei den Orthodoxen Balkanslaven und den Rumänen," in *Actes du XIVe Congrès International d'Études Byzantines, Bucharest 1971*, I (Bucharest, 1974), 198; Djurić, *Vizantijske freske* (note 2 above), 65, fig. 64. See illustrations in: Millet and Velmans, *Peinture du Moyen âge* (note 4 above), IV, pls. 18–28; Radojčić, *Lesnovo* (note 4 above), pls. 25–48. It should be mentioned that some major repairs of a more recent date are in evidence in the upper portions of the walls on the east side of the narthex. Alterations to the frescoes can be recognized in the compositions above the door that leads into the naos (the underside of the arch), on the lower

Palaeologan style can be seen in his ability to fit compositions into the available wall space. On the whole, the painting of the Lesnovo narthex is of high quality; the heads of St. Savel (Fig. 27) and St. John the Baptist (Fig. 24) provide good examples of the painter's skill. The busts of Sts. Menas Kalikelados, Hermogenios, and Eustathios (Figs. 25, 26) reveal unusual renderings of the ears and the use of grouped parallel white lines on faces and hands not found elsewhere in the narthex, but these need not be considered the work of another painter. The plasticity of the drapery is achieved through a sophisticated distribution of light, while the faces are soft and voluminous. In contrast to the so-called expressionistic painter of the naos, whose stylistic approach, though also rooted in the Palaeologan tradition is overstressed and overdramatized, the artist of the narthex, sharing the same stylistic roots, took an interest in refined types and manner. In the narthex of Lesnovo the frescoes attained a high degree of refinement, although their treatment lacks emotional and spiritual qualities. As Svetozar Radojčić has already observed, they relate with astonishing fidelity to the text spelled out on the scroll next to St. John Chrysostom on the southeast pendentive. This text addresses directly to the painters, and advises them to imitate nature, but to mix and refine it with wisdom.[29]

There are few monuments which are analogous to the Lesnovo narthex. It bears similarities to the wall painting at the Treskavac Monastery, specifically with the layer from around 1340.[30] The busts of the figures of Sts. Savel (?) and Ananias (?) (Figs. 28, 29) demonstrate this analogy best. In a similar way, this painter fostered an academic, classical style by emphasizing plastic modelling.

The investigation of the style of the painters of Lesnovo contributes, we believe, to our knowledge of the phenomenon of local painters' workshops in the Byzantine art of the Balkans. Artists certainly gathered at Lesnovo a few years after the erection of its naos in 1341 and worked until 1346 or 1347, when they finished the fresco ensemble. Subsequently this group departed and another painter came to decorate the narthex. The painters of Lesnovo are true representatives of their period. Their work corresponds to M. Chatzidakis' assessment of the style of painting between 1330 and 1360. That period, he wrote, is "une époque de stagnation, sinon de regression, qui ne fait que conserver et transmettre les formules reçues."[31] The art of this period has not been widely investigated. The number of adequately published monuments is still relatively small. Perhaps the most interesting features of the wall painting of this period are the absence of direct influence from Thessaloniki and Constantinople, and, above all, the range of stylistic diversity. Striking differences, as we see in Lesnovo, could occur even within the same monument.

---

portions of the east pair of pendentives, and on the frescoes that cover the east side of the vault on the south side. These alterations can be observed even in reproductions. Cf. N. L. Okunev, "Lesnovo. L'art byzantin chez les Slaves," in *Les Balkans*, vol. 1 part 2 (Paris, 1930), 222–59, pls. XXXIV, XXXVI; and Radojčić, *Lesnovo* (note 4 above), pls. 30, 36 (all of the signs of the zodiac on the east side are repainted).

[29] Svetozar Radojčić, "Die Entstehung der Malerei der paläologischen Renaissance," *JÖBG* 7 (1959), 116, fig. 2.

[30] On this layer of frescoes in Treskavac and its dating: Djurić, *Vizantijske freske* (note 2 above), 56.

[31] Manolis Chatzidakis, "Classicisme et tendances populaires au XIVᵉ siècle. Les recherches sur l'évolution du style," in *Actes du XIVᵉ Congrès International des Études Byzantines, Bucharest 1971*, I (Bucharest, 1974), 172.

1. Lesnovo, Church of the Archangel Michael. St. Nicholas (photo: author)

2. Lesnovo, Church of the Archangel Michael. St. Symeon Nemanja (photo: author)

3. Lesnovo, Church of the Archangel Michael. St. Euthymios (?) (photo: author)

4. Lesnovo, Church of the Archangel Michael. St. Sava of Serbia (photo: author)

5. Lesnovo, Church of the Archangel Michael. Archangel Gabriel (photo: author)

6. Ohrid, icon of St. Naum (photo: V. J. Djurić, Institut za istoriju umetnosti, Belgrade)

8. Ohrid, Virgin Peribleptos. Chapel of St. Gregory the Theologian (photo: author)

7. Ohrid, icon of St. Nicholas (photo: V. J. Djurić, Institut za istoriju umetnosti, Belgrade)

9. Icon of St. Stephen Protomartyr. The Menil Collection, Houston (photo: courtesy of the Menil Collection)

10. Lesnovo, Church of the Archangel Michael. St. Euplos (photo: author)

11. Lesnovo, Church of the Archangel Michael.
Evangelist Mark (photo: author)

12. Lesnovo, Church of the Archangel Michael.
Evangelist John (photo: author)

13. Dečani. Calendar scene (photo: Republički zavod za zaštitu spomenika kulture, Belgrade)

15. Gračanica. Christ Preaching (photo: V. Savić, Institut za istoriju umetnosti, Belgrade)

14. Markov Manastir. St. Athanasios of Alexandria (photo: G. Subotić, Institut za istoriju umetnosti, Belgrade)

17. Lesnovo, Church of the Archangel Michael. Prophet Habakkuk (photo: author)

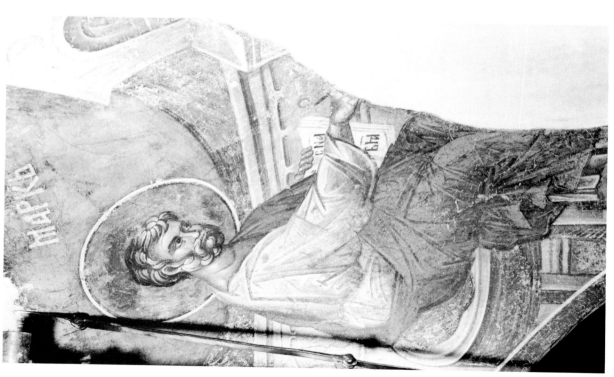

16. Gračanica. Evangelist Mark (photo: V. Savić, Institut za istoriju umetnosti, Belgrade)

18. Lesnovo, Church of the Archangel Michael. Unknown bishop (photo: author)

19. Lesnovo, Church of the Archangel Michael. St. Athanasios of Alexandria (photo: author)

20. Lesnovo, Church of the Archangel Michael. Archangel Gabriel of the Annunciation (photo: author)

21. Lesnovo, Church of the Archangel Michael. Communion of the Apostles (photo: National Museum, Belgrade)

22. Lesnovo, Church of the Archangel Michael. Cleansing of the Temple (detail) (photo: National Museum, Belgrade)

23. Lesnovo, Church of the Archangel Michael. One of the Forty Martyrs of Sebaste (photo: author)

24. Lesnovo, Church of the Archangel Michael. John the Baptist Preaching (photo: author)

25. Lesnovo, Church of the Archangel Michael. Sts. Menas Kalikelados and Hermogenios (photo: author)

26. Lesnovo, Church of the Archangel Michael. Sts. Eustatios and Theopiste (photo: author)

27. Lesnovo, Church of the Archangel Michael. St. Savel (photo: author)

28. Treskavac. St. Savel (?) (photo: V. J. Djurić, Institut za istoriju umetnosti, Belgrade)

29. Treskavac. St. Ananias (?) (photo: V. J. Djurić, Institut za istoriju umetnosti, Belgrade)

The Wall Paintings of the Pantanassa at Mistra: Models of a Painters' Workshop in the Fifteenth Century

DOULA MOURIKI

THE WALL PAINTINGS of the katholikon of the Pantanassa Monastery at Mistra (hereafter Pantanassa) cannot be considered an isolated work of the pictorial arts of Byzantium during the last decades of its existence.[1] The creation of this monument in the capital of the Despotate of Morea makes it a most significant witness to the latest artistic developments in Constantinople during this period. It also asserts the specific role played by Mistra in the last phase of the cultural phenomenon that has often been termed the Palaeologan Renaissance.[2]

The Pantanassa was built and decorated ca. 1430 through the patronage of the second most important political figure in the Despotate, who held an office equivalent to that of prime minister. The imposing size and lavish decoration, both on the exterior and the interior of the church, already bespeak the pretensions of its donor. But, above all, the commanding position of the monastery in the center of the hill occupied by the town of Mistra (Fig. 1) makes this monument the most impressive of all Mistra churches and illustrates the semi-feudal character of Late Byzantine society.

Following an established Constantinopolitan tradition regarding patronage of the highest order, the name and title of the *ktētor* of the Pantanassa are preserved in several locations in the church. The identity of the patron, Ioannis Frangopoulos, and his offices, *protostrator* and *katholikos mesazon*, appear in the form of six painted monograms on the west facade of the church. Four further monograms with his name and title are carved on the sides of the impost of the capital of the westernmost column of the south colonnade. In addition, a painted dedicatory inscription in metric verses surrounds the medallion of the Virgin Blachernitissa with the Child in the summit of the cupola of the west gallery. It includes the patron's name and title and reveals that the church was offered as a modest token of his gratitude for the many graces he had received from the Virgin and with the hope for his

---

[1] A monographic study on the Pantanassa paintings is in preparation. A number of the frescoes is illustrated in G. Millet, *Monuments byzantins de Mistra* (Paris, 1910) pls. 137–150. A brief commentary on the frescoes is included in M. Chatzidakis, Μυστράς, 2nd ed. (Athens, 1956), 90–91. See also the English edition: M. Chatzidakis, *Mystras* (Athens, 1985), 95–96, 98 (with color illustrations). See also S. Dufrenne, *Les programmes iconographiques des églises byzantines de Mistra* (Paris, 1970), 9–13 and passim. Brief references to these frescoes have consistently appeared in handbooks on Byzantine art and in more specialized studies thus acknowledging the importance of this monument for the history of Late Byzantine painting.

[2] The key monograph for the history of Mistra is D. Zakythinos, *Le despotat grec de Morée*, I (Paris, 1932), II (Athens, 1953) (revised edition: London, 1975).

future salvation.[3] The most important inscription for dating purposes and for further information on the monastery was on the slab of the altar table. This inscription, now lost, was
recorded in 1730 by the French traveler Michel Fourmont. It reveals that the monastery
was dedicated to the Virgin Pantanassa, defines it as an imperial and patriarchal foundation, and gives September, 1428 as the consecration date.[4]

The wall paintings of the Pantanassa confirm the not easily proven observation that
behind the creation of a Byzantine decoration there is an older monument, an ambitious
model, which the subsequent patron wants to emulate. In the case of the Pantanassa, the
models were actually two: the Hodegetria or Aphendiko (painted ca. 1320)[5] and the Peribleptos (painted ca. 1370),[6] the most famous churches built at Mistra until that time. The
relationship of the Pantanassa with the Hodegetria is a direct one, since here the special
architectural form of the earlier church, the so-called "Mistra type", a combination of a
basilica on the ground floor, and a cross-in-square church with five subsidiary domes, on the
upper floor, has been copied.[7] The adoption of this plan explains the close adherence of the
iconographic program of the Pantanassa to that of the earlier monument, as can be deduced
from the decoration of the upper floor and the domes; it should be noted that, in all probabil-
ity, the decoration of the ground floor was never completed.[8] Moreover, the decoration of the
Hodegetria, in addition to the iconographic program, inspired many stylistic features in the
masters who completed the frescoes of the later monument. As far as the Peribleptos is
concerned, its Dodekaorton scenes, in particular, lent compositional devices and numerous
iconographic features to the corresponding cycle of the Pantanassa. The same applies to the
figure style. The manner in which the painters of the Pantanassa used the models provided
by the frescoes of the Hodegetria and the Peribleptos lends interesting insights into Byzantine painting of the first half of the fifteenth century.

An attempt will be made in this paper to provide a sketch of the physiognomy of the
wall paintings of the Pantanassa, and to point out some significant elements of affinity or
dissimilarity of this decoration with the frescoes of the Hodegetria, of ca. 1320,[9] and those of

---

[3] For the monograms and the metric dedicatory inscription, see G. Millet, "Inscriptions byzantines de
Mistra," *BCH* 23 (1899), 134–37, nos. XXXI–XXIII; *idem*, "Inscriptions inédites de Mistra," *BCH* 30
(1906), 462.

[4] G. Millet, "Inscriptions byzantines de Mistra," *BCH* 23 (1899), 137–38, no. XXXIV.

[5] For the wall paintings of the Aphendiko, see Millet, *Mistra* (note 1 above), pls. 92, 93:1, 93:3, 93:4,
95–100, 104. Chatzidakis, *Mystras* (note 1 above), 59–62, 64, 66–67 (with color illustrations). Dufrenne,
Programmes (note 1 above), 8–13 and passim.

[6] For the wall paintings of the Peribleptos, see Millet, *Mistra* (note 1 above), pls. 108–131. Chatzidakis,
Mystras (note 1 above), 77, 80–84, 86–89 (with color illustrations). Dufrenne, *Programmes* (note 1 above),
13–18 and passim.

[7] Cf. H. Hallensleben, "Untersuchungen zur Genesis und Typologie des 'Mystratypus'," *MarbJb* 8
(1969) 105–18.

[8] Aside from the well-known fifteenth-century funerary portrait of an aristocrat at the arcosolium of the
south wall of the narthex, no traces of paintings from the Late Byzantine period have been detected at the level
of the ground floor during the recent work of cleaning and restoration of the frescoes. Since the extant sections
of two layers of paintings in this area are datable to the post-Byzantine period, it may be suggested that the
original decoration of the church was not completed.

[9] The date for the decoration of the sanctuary, the naos, and the narthex, as well as the northwest and the

the Peribleptos, of ca. 1370.[10] The focus will be on stylistic forms, compositional principles, which reveal the approach to both pictorial and real space, as well as on iconographic details insofar as these condition the function of the images in the church. The differences in the iconographic programs of these monuments and their theological implications are beyond the scope of this paper.

The wall paintings of the Pantanassa illustrate several trends, and can be safely attributed to more than one artist. In its most classical and subdued expression, the figure style reverts to the early fourteenth-century Constantinopolitan trend that is represented by the mosaics and frescoes of the katholikon of the Chora. There is no need, however, to imply a direct relationship between the two monuments, although the master painters of the Pantanassa had most probably seen this decoration in Constantinople. Previously, the artists who completed the wall paintings of the Peribleptos had gone back to excellent Constantinopolitan models of the early fourteenth century, which also illustrate the trend of the mosaics and frescoes of the Chora. It was through the Peribleptos frescoes that at least one of the Pantanassa painters experimented with the sophisticated features of early fourteenth-century Palaeologan style. A comparative study of portraits and scenic compositions in both monuments leads to the conclusion that, within the restrictions imposed by copying an important model, the artists of the Pantanassa introduced their own interpretation in accordance with the spirit of the age. This new spirit was expressed through a more complex vocabulary of forms, which as a consequence had a large number of ambiguities in the reading of the contents and, in the final analysis, the desacralization of religious art.

Whereas one group of paintings of the Pantanassa and the Peribleptos share similar facial types and modelling devices in accordance with the norms established by early fourteenth-century monuments, such as the katholikon of the Chora, the faces in the Pantanassa are more fleshy and earthbound, and the use of color for enhancing volume is more arbitrary. A clear departure from classical norms is apparent in many groups of figures in the fifteenth-century monument. For instance, one of the angels supporting the glory of Christ in the Ascension (Fig. 2), with a fleshy face and prosaic profile, reddish hair, and long fingers, is much less classical than an angel in the Ascension in the Peribleptos (Fig. 3). The idealistic approach to this category of figures in the fourteenth-century decoration has given way to a sensuous rendering of their counterparts in the later monument. The stylistic character of the Pantanassa figures is largely due to the use of light and color treated in a way that enhances their dynamic, though rhetorical and decorative aspect. This is also evident in the modelling of the flesh-tones and in the rendering of hair and beards.

A telling example of the rendering of the body in the Pantanassa is provided by a depiction of one of the Seventy Apostles in the south gallery (Fig. 4), which seems to be a close

---

southwest chapels has usually been determined by the earliest and the latest dates, i.e., 1312/1313 and 1322, provided by the painted chrysobulls in the southwest chapel.

[10] The chronology of the Peribleptos frescoes has generally been placed within the rule of the despot Manuel Kantakouzenos (1348–1380). Close stylistic affinity with the illustrated manuscript with the *Theological Works* of John Kantakouzenos (Paris, Bibliothèque Nationale, gr. 1242) in particular has provided arguments for a dating in the seventies of the fourteenth century. Cf. H. Buchthal, "Toward a History of Palaeologan Illumination," in *The Place of Book Illumination in Byzantine Art* (Princeton, 1975), 172, 175.

copy of the prophet Habakkuk in the cupola of the Peribleptos (Fig. 5). However, the theatrical pose and the over-emphasized volume of the body, the bare neck and part of the chest and, above all, the fact that now the life-size figure is at eye level with the viewer who stands in the gallery, create an impression of stark realism. A comparison of these two figures illustrates, moreover, the special manner of rendering the drapery in the Pantanassa. A dense web of lines, looking as if they had been incised with a knife, conveys a stiff appearance which contradicts the seemingly soft texture of the material. This manneristic approach to the garments draws attention away from the faces and directs it instead to the arabesque of the fold lines, which function autonomously. Compared to the Pantanassa figures, those in the Peribleptos seem to adhere closely to the classical principles which underline much of fourteenth-century Constantinopolitan painting. Such comparisons yield interesting insights into the special approach of the painters of the Pantanassa towards their models. In this case, as in all other instances, the artists of the later monument did not blindly copy the principal iconographic features of identical subjects in the earlier monuments of Mistra. Instead, they adapted, in an eclectic way, iconographic features and stylistic devices from various groups of figures in the earlier decorations of Mistra, thus showing their independence vis-a-vis their models.

An unclassical solution in the compositions of the Pantanassa is exemplified by the Pentecost (Figs. 7 and 8), which also derives from the same depiction in the Peribleptos (Fig. 9). Whereas in the earlier monument the scene occupies half of the north barrel vaulted arm of the cross, in the Pantanassa the composition has been split into two parts and accommodated on the north and south walls of the bema. Each of these sections is further divided into two compartments dictated by the arched opening in the middle of each wall. As a consequence of such manipulations of architectural surfaces, an important iconographic component of the scene, the personification of Kosmos, has been omitted. Looking at the compositional devices used in the rendering of this scene in the Pantanassa, we perceive a new approach in the handling of space, both pictorial and real. With devices like this one the transcendental character of Byzantine painting has disappeared, and action has been transposed into an illusionistic world.

The Pantanassa painters introduced into the church's decoration new principles of composition and numerous anecdotal elements. In both cases the pictorial tradition represented by the earlier monuments at Mistra was taken into consideration. The results, however, indicate complexities which can be viewed only against the cultural climate of the period. One of the obvious consequences is that the hieratic quality of the models has vanished.

A study of the Nativity scene in the Pantanassa (Fig. 10) and in the Peribleptos (Fig. 11) is revealing for the new directions to which the paintings of the later monument point. The composition in the Peribleptos shows an emphasis on the central axis by the placement of the Virgin and the cradle of the Child in the middle and by the disposition of the secondary episodes in balanced units on either side. Anecdotal elements are used judiciously. The fresco preserves its function as an iconic image by the remoteness of the Virgin and the Child. This is not the case with the scene in the Pantanassa, for which the composition of the Peribleptos doubtless served as a model. By the omission of certain elements, such as the third hill to the right, and by the transfer of isolated figures and groups, such as the Virgin, Joseph and the shepherds, and the Bathing of the Child, the Nativity in the Pantanassa has lost the perfect balance this scene possesses in the earlier monument. Numerous elements of anecdotal realism have invaded the scene, conveying an immediacy, which is lacking in the corresponding scene in the Peribleptos. The changes that the model underwent show not only the exploratory character of the work of the Pantanassa painters, but also their complex visual equipment, i.e., their acquaintance with a far greater number of models than those provided by the previous decorations at Mistra. For instance, three shepherds holding or playing musical instruments are depicted here, whereas in the Peribleptos there is only one. In the Pantanassa the shepherd playing his horn for the pleasure of a goat who stands on its hind legs (Fig. 12) is the counterpart of the youth who also plays his horn near his flock of sheep in the Peribleptos scene (Fig. 13). However, the serene atmosphere in the earlier painting has given way to an atmosphere charged with interaction and humor: Joseph, in an impossibly twisted posture, is charmed by the horn-blowing of a young shepherd garbed in a picturesque outfit (Fig. 14). The shepherd is preceded by his sheep, who turns backward in the direction of the lagging sheep at the left of the scene. Nearby, a youthful shepherd has ceased his music and offers picked flowers to his lambs who leap excitedly at this vegetal delicacy (Fig. 15).

The juxtaposition of the representations of the Entry into Jerusalem in the two monuments (Figs. 16 and 17), hardly leaves any doubt as to the fact that again the earlier representation has served as a model in this case as well. Such rare features as the two groups of Israelites coming out of the two gates of Jerusalem appear in both scenes; the male figure with the striped cloak is common to both depictions, as well as the woman displaying her child as a palladium. In both instances the cityscape has taken a complex appearance, with numerous rooftops and people witnessing the entry of Christ from the ramparts and the various openings in the walls. We may also point out an unusual feature shared by both compositions: two trees in the background, both with children; one child, in particular, is hanging in an acrobatic pose from a branch (Fig. 18). Common to both depictions are also the numerous episodes with children playing in the foreground. On the other hand, several major differences are noted in the compositional principles applied in each case, and also in many iconographic details. Whereas in the Peribleptos, Christ occupies the center of the composition, in the Pantanassa Christ's figure has been shifted to the left. In the former monument the genre themes in the foreground are grouped in a frieze (probably derived from manuscript illuminations, as suggested by the miniature in the Berolinensis gr. quarto 66)[11] which breaks the unity of the composition. By contrast, these themes have become an integral part of the composition in the Pantanassa. Here, the pictorial elements are disposed in three planes, of which the front and the back planes show an emphasis on the alternation of architecture and landscape; in the middle zone, on the other hand, there is a dense frieze of numerous figures. Compared to the scene in the Peribleptos, this new handling of the

---

[11] See G. Millet, *Recherches sur l'iconographie de l'Evangile aux XIVe, XVe et XVIe siècles* (Paris, 1916; reprinted 1960), fig. 244. The manuscript is presently in the University Library of Tübingen.

composition resulted in the illusion of a vaster expanse of space. The scene could be read either as the illustration of a tale or as a rendering of everyday life, which comes closer to the viewer through anecdotal elements and other realistic details.

Regarding the relation of figures to the architecture and landscape elements in the scenic representations in all three monuments considerable differences can be noted. In the Pantanassa this relationship is balanced. Even when crowded groups are included, and despite an apparent *horror vacui*, there is always a sense of space and atmosphere. Both architecture and landscape create an illusion of materials and depth, while at the same time forms are closer to nature. Thus, the buildings tend to be more realistic in appearance through their imposing scale vis-a-vis the human figures, their relatively sober morphology, and the use of color on the outside which gives the impression of large plastered surfaces recalling contemporary secular architecture of Mistra. In the Annunciation, and more so in the Presentation in the Temple, the various planes of color on the exterior surfaces of the buildings also recall real and painted architecture in Italy, as seen in Siena. It is remarkable that the conventional red draperies, extensively used in both earlier monuments at Mistra, are altogether absent. As for the rendering of the landscape, although it often possesses an atmosphere of a dream world through its color scheme and majestic expanse, it tends to be closer to nature in its judicious use of the stepped planes employed by the landscape in Late Byzantine painting. The handling of color and light contributes to the creation of a sense of space and atmosphere. In the Peribleptos the compositions tend to be crowded, although emphasis has been placed on the spatial context according to the requirements of the narrative. The figural elements are not organically integrated with the architecture, which plays the role of strictly background scenery. Its unrealistic character is enhanced by the combination of various disparate elements with an ambiguous function. The use of stairs and canopies with no obvious purpose is compensated only by an emphasis on the central axis which preserves the hierarchical organization of the compositions. The materials used imitate marble and have neutral tonalities. A feeling of compression is accentuated by the airless atmosphere in the scenic representations. In the Aphendiko the handling of figures and space is in keeping with the metropolitan trend of the early fourteenth century as illustrated in the mosaics and frescoes of the monastery of the Chora. Following a tendency to exploit intricate relations between figures and architecture, as in late antique painting, there is an interaction of figures and architecture. However, the disproportionate difference in scale between these two components contributes to the creation of an architectural fantasy permeated with a lyrical atmosphere. More than in any other monument at Mistra, these paintings convey a sfumato effect.

The tendency to present quotations from classical art under the guise of genre, apparent in practically all Mistra decorations, is even more intensified in the Pantanassa frescoes. In the Entry into Jerusalem this tendency is illustrated by including two variants of the "Spinario" theme, as opposed to only one in the Peribleptos. The most complex variant in the Pantanassa involves three children, the actual suffering child leaning against a tree, while the two other children attempt to extract the thorn from his foot. The simpler variant shows the single "Spinario" motif. In the Peribleptos, on the other hand, we see the two-figure variant.[12] This indicates that, as in so many other instances, the Pantanassa painters did not copy literally individual iconographic details from the decorations at Mistra that served as their models. Instead, they adopted types of iconographic details provided by the earlier local decorations, but also chose different variants which they copied from model books.

Other depictions of children in the Entry into Jerusalem in the Pantanassa, though with no clearly identified antique sources, also betray an antique derivation, due to their genuine *joie de vivre*. This is the case with the small mischievous children who taunt and play with each other in the foreground, and likewise with the child who plays with the water from the fountain. In the process of the desacralization of religious painting, the abundance of classical features, their rendering, and the way they have been used, acquire special significance. From these examples we can see clearly that, compared to the decoration of the Peribleptos, with its more traditional iconography, the wall paintings of the Pantanassa reveal a strong taste for anecdotal features and other eccentricities which distract the viewer from the principal theme of the compositions. If such a tendency is a component of Late Byzantine painting as a whole, its results have not been preserved as fully in any other monument as in the Pantanassa.

The refined, antiquarian tastes apparent in the decorations of the earlier monuments of Mistra are even more evident in the Pantanassa frescoes, as illustrated by a large number of grisaille ornaments reproducing human and animal masks, and non-representational decorative features such as floral motifs, shells, etc. Despite the fact that, as in their local models, these elements are usually integrated into the architectural backgrounds and furniture,[13] it is the overwhelming presence of these motifs and their placement in relation to the human figure that assign a special significance to them. Moreover, the ambiguity in the interpretation of antiquarian motifs such as masks, partly due to a new dynamism that invigorates them, sometimes distances these details from their antiquarian heritage and makes them energetic components in a playful fantasy world. This is well illustrated by the use of the mask motif in the pendentives of the cupola of the west gallery (e.g., Fig. 20). The medallions with portraits of four holy persons are surrounded by human and animal masks with substantial vegetal elements issuing from their mouths. The impressive scale of these masks, as well as their direct relation to portraits of holy figures represent a clear departure from the conventions of antiquarian grisaille elements in Byzantine painting. Despite the obliteration of the inscriptions with the names of these figures, under normal circumstances we should be able to identify at least the class to which these portraits belong. However, this is not the case here since the hands of the figures are not shown and thus no attributes are included. The identification of these figures as prophets,[14] based on the fact that prophets are depicted in the drum of this cupola, which includes at its summit the medallion of the

---

[12] For this theme in the Peribleptos and the Pantanassa, see D. Mouriki, "The Theme of the 'Spinario' in Byzantine Art," Δελτ.Χριστ.Ἀρχ.Ἑτ. ser. 4, vol. 6 (1970–1972) 58–59, pls. 22:b and 23:a. *Eadem*, "Palaeologan Mistra and the West," *Byzantium and Europe. Delphi 1986* (Athens, 1987), 242–43, fig. 28.

[13] For these features, see D. Mouriki, "The Mask Motif in the Wall Paintings of Mistra," Δελτ.Χριστ. Ἀρχ.Ἑτ. ser. 4, vol. 10 (1980–1981), 307–38.

[14] Millet, *Mistra* (note 1 above), pls. 146:1, 146:2 and 148:3. This identification is accepted by Chatzidakis, Μυστράς (note 1 above), pl. 27b, and by Dufrenne, *Programmes* (note 1 above), pl. 26 (drawing).

Virgin and Child, is not altogether convincing. A second alternative could be that we have here the four evangelists, whose facial features roughly correspond to those of the four anonymous portraits in the Pantanassa.[15] The latter hypothesis is reinforced by related Western depictions of evangelist portraits associated with rinceaux and masks.

A direct relationship of the grisaille elements to the content of the frescoes of the Pantanassa is perhaps best illustrated in the scene of the Presentation in the Temple. Here, a rather large grisaille figurine of an armed soldier holding a lance is depicted on the ambo of Symeon (Fig. 19). This representation may be a reference to the well-known prophecy of Symeon in connection with the Passion of Christ as recorded in Luke 2:35. If this interpretation is correct, we are faced with an innovative use of grisaille elements as carriers of symbolical implications.

A symbolical interpretation may also be applied to some stock motifs of the antique repertoire as illustrated by the scene of the Annunciation (Figs. 22 and 23). The theme of the fountain, rare in the Byzantine iconography of this scene,[16] has received an Early Christian appearance by the addition of two partridges drinking from the life-giving water. In this way, the well becomes the Fountain of Life (*Zoodochos Pigi*), an allegory of the Virgin which is encountered in various homiletic and hymnographic texts.[17] For such an interpretation monumental painting at Mistra may have once more provided a visual source, as suggested by the rendering of the Annunciation in the church of Ai-Yiannakis.[18]

The treatment of ornament in the wall paintings of the Pantanassa is particularly revealing for the differences which separate this monument from its fourteenth-century models at Mistra. Some of the antique-like motifs in the ornament of the frescoes of the Hodegetria and the Peribleptos have been sacrificed in order to allow for the use of an ornamental vocabulary of a different character. A survey of the ornament in both fourteenth-century decorations shows a profound indebtedness to a "fantastical" repertoire of motifs with an antique derivation.[19] A favorite motif in both monuments consists of variants of the "peopled" or "unpeopled" scroll, used as separating elements of scenes, or as fillers of secondary architectural surfaces; in both cases the floral or vegetal band frequently issues from a vase imitating a kantharos. The foliate scroll has been taken over into the group of ornamental themes in the Pantanassa, but, rendered differently, it points again to the freedom with which the Pantanassa painters approached the earlier models provided by the monuments of Mistra.[20] A telling example of this approach is provided by the foliate motif with partridges and other birds, which surrounds the medallion portrait of a saint on the

[15] Mouriki, "The Mask Motif" (note 13 above), 312–13.

[16] For some examples of the fountain motif in the context of the Annunciation, see D. Mouriki, "The Wall Paintings of the Church of the Panagia at Moutoullas, Cyprus," in *Byzanz und der Westen. Studien zur Kunst des Europäischen Mittelalters*, ed. I. Hutter (Vienna, 1984), 180–81.

[17] Cf. K. Weitzmann, "Eine spätkomnenische Verkündigungsikone des Sinai und die zweite byzantinische Welle des 12. Jahrhunderts," in *Festschrift für Herbert von Einem zum 16. Februar 1965* (Berlin, 1965), 302.

[18] See Millet, *Mistra* (note 1 above), pl. I. Cf. Millet, *Recherches* (note 11 above).

[19] Cf. C. Lepage, "L'ornementation végétale fantastique et le pseudo-réalisme dans la peinture byzantine," *CahArch* 19 (1969), 191–211.

[20] Cf. Mouriki, "Palaeologan Mistra and the West" (note 12 above), 242, fig. 27.

spandrel of the double-arched opening on the east side of the west gallery of the Pantanassa (Fig. 21). As in the case of the masks in the pendentives of the west gallery cupola, here, too, substantial decorative elements are placed in close proximity to the portraits of the holy persons, thus generating a different attitude on the part of the viewer. On the other hand, we no longer find striking examples of antique ornaments of the "fantastical" type, such as garlands issuing from cusps and decorated with ribbons or wires of precious metals with imitations of semi-precious stones, as seen respectively in the Aphendiko and in the Peribleptos.[21] In the Pantanassa, the floral ornament on the whole has lost its antique flavor by the special emphasis placed on the symmetrical spreading-out of the leaves in the manner of an arabesque. This is particularly the case with the integrated green leafy pattern with red fruit seen on the east side of the north arched opening in the easternmost section of the south gallery (Fig. 24). The floral ornament in the Pantanassa covers broad surfaces and, moreover, has acquired a pseudo-realistic quality clearly removed from the antique repertoire. This type of ornament enhances the decorative character of the paintings. An important place is assigned to the geometric motifs and the multiple variants of the ribbon motif as elements that accentuate architectural units. Worthy of note is the extensive use of the geisipodes with their illusionistic rendering, appropriately placed in many instances for outlining the bases of saucer domes and drums of cupolas. By the type and function of this group of ornamental motifs the Pantanassa frescoes conform to a novel approach in early fifteenth-century Byzantine painting.[22] In fact, some of the transformations that ornament has undergone in the last Palaeologan decoration of Mistra may have been inspired by Islamic art.[23]

The function of ornament in the Pantanassa, when compared to the two previous monuments at Mistra, is indicative of the different aims which it served in each case. In the Pantanassa, ornament was used in an imaginative and innovative way, devoid to a great extent of its frame-like function. When it is employed, it forms a substantial complement of certain representations or even fills large secondary areas as their sole decoration. However, in some cases, the ornament is altogether missing where one would expect it to be used as a framing element. The difference in the approach to ornament in the Pantanassa, as opposed to that in the Aphendiko and the Peribleptos, can be seen clearly in the Feast scenes in the barrel-vaulted arms of the cross. In the Hodegetria the dividing elements of these scenes are foliate strips, whereas in the Peribleptos we find plain red-brown bands. On the other hand, the painters of the Pantanassa dismissed any type of separating devices for the Feast scenes. Such an approach resulted in innovative iconographic solutions which go beyond the Byzantine tradition. For instance, a continuous beam of light connects the scenes of the Annunciation and the Nativity in the south barrel vault and denotes, in the former, the

[21] Cf. Mouriki, "Palaeologan Mistra and the West" (note 12 above), figs. 23 and 25.

[22] See C. Lepage, "Remarques sur l'ornementation peinte à l'intérieur des églises de la Morava," in *L'école de la Morava et son temps. Symposium de Resava 1968* (Belgrade, 1972), 229–37.

[23] For Islamic sources of Palaeologan ornament see R. S. Nelson, "Palaeologan Illuminated Ornament and the Arabesque," *WJKg* 41 (1988), 7–22. The Islamic sources of Palaeologan ornament, with special emphasis on examples from the wall paintings of Mistra, have been dealt with in a seminar report by Maura C. Donohue at the Department of Art and Archaeology of Princeton University in April 1989.

presence of the Holy Spirit and, in the latter, the appearance of the Star of Bethlehem. Such devices emphasize the continuity of the painted walls and at the same time enhance the decorative, tapestry-like, function of the paintings. By the omission of dividing elements the images have lost to a great extent their iconic function.

As in the case of ornament, an ample use of illusionistic devices is a conspicuous characteristic of the wall paintings of the Pantanassa. For instance, a simulated marble plaque in opus sectile on the dado of the west face of the easternmost pier of the south gallery (Fig. 25) was placed at right angles to a real parapet slab, now lost, thus creating a confusion as to the nature of the painted element, when seen from a distance.

The fact that the frescoes of the Hodegetria have not been preserved in their entirety, as in the case of the Peribleptos, prevents a detailed comparison with the frescoes of the Pantanassa. One can be confident, however, that the inspiration from the early fourteenth-century monument mainly concerns the shaping of the iconographic program[24] and the stylistic approach to certain sections of the paintings, rather than the iconography of individual scenes and figures. A revealing comparison which confirms this observation concerns the depictions of the Seventy Apostles in both monuments. A different approach to iconography has resulted in differences in the rendering of these figures in the two monuments, as shown by the juxtaposition of one apostle from the Pantanassa (Fig. 4) and a pair of portraits of the same group in the Aphendiko (Fig. 6). Thus, the omophorion, which is usually combined with the antique garb in the depictions of this group in the Hodegetria (e.g., Fig. 6), is often omitted in the same figures in the Pantanassa, or it becomes inconspicuous through the use of various devices. On the other hand, the freer style in the rendering of the paintings in the Pantanassa, in contrast to the more linear approach observed in those of the Peribleptos, may be explained through the influence of the decoration of the Hodegetria. A comparison of the Nativity of the Pantanassa and the Baptism in the Hodegetria shows a similar aesthetic appearance, marked by a preference for light tones in the landscape elements. In the Aphendiko the colors, modified by light, create the impression of a soft luminous atmosphere which envelops the figures. Thus they contribute to the unified appearance of individual compositions and of whole painted surfaces on the walls. This effect has been transmitted to some extent to the fifteenth-century decoration, but the similar result has a much more decorative character, mainly due to the absence of strong tonal contrasts and to the blurring of colors in general. In the Peribleptos, on the other hand, color is used clearly as a complement to line for the purpose of defining form. As opposed to the two earlier monuments, the painters of the Pantanassa have exploited several times the effect of cast shadows as, for instance, in the sarcophagi of the Righteous in the Anastasis. In this monument it is color that is used to evoke space and light.

As is the case with other monuments of the Late Byzantine period,[25] it is possible to trace vague Western elements in the Pantanassa frescoes, which indicate that its artists were looking towards new sources of inspiration during this period. Western works could explain such rare iconographic features in the Pantanassa paintings as the depiction of a window on

[24] See especially Dufrenne, *Programmes* (note 1 above), 9–13.

[25] For this subject see T. Velmans, "Infiltrations occidentales dans la peinture murale byzantine au XIVe et au debut du XVe siècle," in *École de la Morava* (note 22 above), 37–48.

a building behind the Evangelist Luke in the southwest pendentive of the main cupola. The artist painted the window in such a way as to give the impression that natural light penetrates into the room (Fig. 26).[26] A further iconographic detail of Western derivation is the flowerpot on the parapet placed between Gabriel and the Virgin in the Annunciation (Fig. 22). This rare motif does not appear in Byzantine depictions of this scene before the fourteenth century, and in the case of the Pantanassa the iconographic source might have been the corresponding scene in the Peribleptos. However, this motif certainly has a longer tradition in Western painting.[27] In the Pantanassa, the conspicuous representation of a wall in the foreground of the Annunciation, in combination with the fountain motif, gives the impression of a walled court, a kind of *hortus conclusus*, a reference to the Song of Songs (IV:12), which again has symbolic connotations related to the Western tradition.[28] The inclusion of two trees with children in them in the Entry into Jerusalem can also be attributed to Western infiltrations.[29] Unlike other contemporary or even earlier decorations which are characterized by strong Western influence in the attire, this is not the case with the Pantanassa frescoes. The rare relevant examples may include the striped cloak of a male figure in the Entry into Jerusalem; another literal quotation from the corresponding scene in the Peribleptos.[30] The most obvious individual iconographic feature of Western origin is doubtless the masks with foliate elements issuing from their mouths in a dynamic way,

[26] The fascination with openings in architecture is a constant feature of Tuscan painting of the fourteenth and the fifteenth centuries. Devices like the one observed in the depiction of the evangelist in the Pantanassa are very common in the context of this pictorial material. For instance, in the Last Supper and the Washing of the Feet in the frescoes of the Scrovegni Chapel in Padua, half- or entirely open windows let the blue of the sky be seen through: G. Previtali, *Giotto e la sua bottega* (Milan, 1967), pls. LII and LIII. Moreover, in the fresco depicting the death of St. Martin, painted by Simone Martini in the Lower Church of Saint Francis in Assisi, the sky is shown through the arcade of a loggia: E. Carli, *La pittura senese del trecento* (Venice, 1981), fig. 115. In a resurrection miracle of St. Silvester in the frescoes of the Cappella Bardi in Santa Croce in Florence by Maso di Banco, the sky is shown behind arched openings: *La pittura in Italia. Il duecento e il trecento*, ed. E. Castelnuovo (Milan, 1986), fig. 464.

[27] For this feature in the Pantanassa see Mouriki "Palaeologan Mistra and the West" (note 12 above), 238, fig. 15. In Western depictions of the Annunciation we usually find the motif in the form of a vase with lilies. Among the earliest examples are Cavallini's Annunciation mosaic in Santa Maria in Trastevere, Rome: G. Matthiae, *Pietro Cavallini* (Rome, 1972), fig. X. However, a Western example that is very close to the Pantanassa fresco is the depiction of the Annunciation in the central panel of the triptych in the Louvre which is attributed to Carlo Braccesco. Here a golden vase holding a plant with red flowers is placed on a parapet near the Virgin: *La pittura a Genova e in Liguria dagli inizi al cinquecento*, ed. E. Poleggi (Genova, 1987), figs. 99–100. For the flowerpot in the Annunciation and its Western sources cf. Millet, *Recherches* (note 11 above), 91.

[28] In a few depictions of the Annunciation from the Middle and Late Byzantine periods the idea of the *hortus conclusus* is visualized through the inclusion of a tiny garden on a terrace of the architectural background behind the Virgin. One such example is included in the Late Comnenian Annunciation icon at Sinai. K. Weitzmann, "Eine spätkomnenische Verkündigungsikone," (note 17 above), color illustration on p. 305.

[29] This feature characterizes the rendering of this scene in the panel by Guido da Siena in the Pinacoteca Nazionale, Siena, on the reverse side of the Maesta by Duccio, in the Opera del Duomo, Siena, and in the fresco of Giotto in the Arena Chapel in Padua. For the first two examples, see Carli, *Pittura senese* (note 26 above), figs. 15 and 56, 57. For Giotto's Annunciation see C. Gnudi, *Giotto* (Milan, 1958), fig. 99. It may be noted that two trees with children appear eventually in Armenian and Georgian painting.

[30] Striped garments are often included in Western painting, as, for instance, in the portrait of a donor depicted on a Crucifix in the Galleria dell'Accademia, Florence. Maria G. Ciardi Dupré dal Poggetto, *Il maestro del codice di San Giorgio e il Cardinale Jacopo Stefaneschi* (Florence, 1981), fig. 229.

which cover the pendentives of the cupola in the western gallery.[31] Unlike grisaille motifs in Byzantine painting, which play a subordinate role and possess an ornamental function, the scale of the masks and their relationship to the human figures here convey a Western character. On the whole, Western iconographic features in the frescoes of the Pantanassa are very rare and of secondary importance, an observation all the more interesting since the Western impact on the architectural decoration of this monument is much more obvious.

Unlike the iconography, the Western connections of the Pantanassa frescoes may be detected more forcefully in compositional principles as well as in the use of color. Some of the new devices in the organization of scenes and in the adaptation of painting to the architecture share affinities with fourteenth- and fifteenth-century developments in Italy. In fact, the systematic disregard of the central axis and symmetry as a means for enhancing hierarchy, the interplay of the various levels of action, the use of light pastel tonalities in uniform surfaces in certain scenes, the importance assigned to architecture and landscape with a care for accurate detail, and, above all, the insistence on subsidiary narrative episodes could all be attributed to a creative assimilation of genuine Western works of art. Tuscan painting of the fourteenth and fifteenth centuries provides some of the most characteristic examples of this approach. The gift of an illustrator which characterizes one of the masters engaged in the completion of this decoration can be related to the basic character of Sienese painting of this period. The Entry into Jerusalem, as in its renderings in Sienese pictorial examples, lends itself to the display of this talent. As in the case of Late Byzantine painting in general, stylistic affinities of the Pantanassa frescoes with Western art, in whatever degree they may appear, can be better illustrated through comparisons with Sienese painting of the same period.

A vaguely Western character, responsible for the distinct mood of at least one group of scenes in the Pantanassa, is provided by their color. The Presentation of Christ in the Temple is one of the scenes that possess this quality. It is enough to compare this scene with, for instance, the Incredulity of Thomas in the Peribleptos in order to understand their difference. The pastel colors used in several scenes of the Pantanassa, such as in the Presentation of Christ, give the impression that the buildings have painted walls recalling those in Sienese painting of the fourteenth and fifteenth centuries. In addition, an interest in spatial illusionism, which constitutes one of the prevalent characteristics of the paintings of the Pantanassa, can also be explained in terms of the Western experience. Color plays an important role in this aspect and often produces effects of aerial perspective. In contrast to the basic uses of color in Byzantine painting, namely, to provide rhythmical effects by the use of vivid contrasts in tone, the Pantanassa colors function in an equivalent way, but despite their great variety, are blended and of nearly uniform tonality, producing the effect of a tapestry. It is interesting to note that the typical red of Palaeologan painting was not used in the Pantanassa.[32] It must be stressed that connections with Western painting appear in only

---

[31] Cf. Mouriki, "The Mask Motif," (note 13 above), 312–13.

[32] For some observations on color used in the Pantanassa see U. Max Ruth, *Die Farbgebung in der byzantinischen Wandmalerei der spätpaläologischen Epoche (1341–1453)*. Doctoral Dissertation. Rheinische Friedrich-Wilhelms-Universitat, Bonn 1977, 496–511.

one group of paintings in this church. However, even in this group, all familiar features of Western painting have been abstracted so as to become faint recollections of their sources of inspiration. These Late Palaeologan paintings are so deeply anchored in the earlier Byzantine tradition that slavish copying of Western models seems to be precluded from the outset.

The decoration of the Pantanassa at Mistra, perhaps the most important work of monumental painting to have been preserved from the end of Byzantium, reveals complexities which cannot be explained only through the availability of models at Mistra itself. Compared to the fourteenth-century paintings produced in this town or those of equal standards created elsewhere during the same period that have survived,[33] the Pantanassa frescoes show a novel, distinct physiognomy which easily contradicts an old-fashioned but still prevalent view that Byzantine painting died around 1320.[34] In this monument of around 1430 an idiom has developed which reveals a new vigor and self-assertion that makes the mosaics and frescoes of the Chora look mannered in their over-refined elegance.

The major shortcoming in an attempt to place the Pantanassa frescoes within the history of Late Byzantine painting is the lack of comparative material preserved in Constantinople from the second half of the fourteenth and the first half of the fifteenth centuries. On the other hand, historic coincidence made Mistra the representative center of metropolitan art during this period, and one which has come to us in a relatively good state of preservation. Moreover, some important decorations preserved in Thessaloniki, in the territory of Byzantium's cultural neighbors, and in Venetian-occupied Crete can also help us gain interesting insights into artistic developments in Constantinople during this period. On the evidence provided by a substantial number of samples, it is possible to sustain that Constantinopolitan painting of the first half of the fifteenth illustrates two trends, whose common denominator is a varying indebtedness to Western art. The two trends are differentiated by the ways they received Western features.

One of these trends is illustrated by the painting of the so-called Morava school of North Serbia from the end of the fourteenth and the beginning of the fifteenth centuries.[35] The figures in these frescoes are detached from the viewer, and enclosed in a separate, frozen world. They convey no sense of passion which would invite the viewer to interact with them. The focus on luxury in garments and weaponry emphasizes the aulic, profane aspirations of the patrons. This approach is paired with the use of costly painting materials, such as gold leaf and lapis lazuli. The pictorial devices, which negate the piety of holy

[33] The first half of the fifteenth century was very prolific in the creation of Byzantine painting, as can be deduced from an impressive number of monuments which are still, for the most part, unpublished.

[34] The most important contribution for an assessment of the creativity of this period is S. Radojčić, "La pittura bizantina del 1400 al 1453," *RSBN* n.s. 15 (1968), 41–60; reprinted in Serbocroatian in *École de la Morava* (note 22 above), 1–12.

[35] For various aspects of the paintings of this school, see the volume of the Acts of the Symposium dedicated to it in 1968 (note 22 above). For the definition of the special characteristics of this school, both in iconography and style, see, V. J. Djurić, "La peinture murale de l'école de la Morava," in *La peinture de l'école de la Morava. Galerie des fresques de Belgrade* (Belgrade, 1968), 30–60. *Idem*, "La peinture murale de Resava. Ses origines et sa place dans la peinture byzantine," in *École de la Morava* (note 22 above), 277–91.

[36] Cf. Velmans, "Infiltrations occidentales," (note 25 above), 47.

persons, link the School of Morava to the International Gothic.[36] This particular trend had a considerable diffusion, as is shown by the Trinity image painted by Rublev. Russian mysticism hardly conceals the fin-de-siècle quality presented by this composition.

A second trend is exemplified by certain decorations created in Venetian-occupied Crete, which never came under Palaeologan rule.[37] These decorations reveal close and continuous contacts with Constantinople, but also show an increasing awareness of the Italian artistic experience.[38] Unlike the decoration of the Pantanassa, Cretan paintings often display substantial iconographic borrowings from the West, such as the portraits of St. Francis, or even certain architectural details taken from real garden architecture in the Italian style. Some of the Cretan paintings from this period show, though on a different scale, a research parallel to that undertaken by the painters of the Pantanassa.

The study of iconographic schemes and details in the paintings of the Pantanassa, as well as in those which exemplify the two trends described above, reveals the circulation of common models as illustrated, for instance, by the acrobatic pose of a child in the Entry into Jerusalem, which can be detected in the Peribleptos and the Pantanassa (Fig. 18) at Mistra, at Ravanica, and at Sklaverohori on Crete.[39] The frescoes of the Pantanassa represent a unicum among extant Late Byzantine decorations. In fact, these paintings can be considered as representing a synthesis of the two trends described above. The leading members of the workshop which was engaged in this decoration came in all likelihood from Constantinople. This conclusion is based on the extremely high quality of this decoration, its up-to-date features, and the complexity of visual sources beyond those available at Mistra, which can only be explained through the availability of a variety of models, still extant in the imperial city. This conclusion is reinforced by the abased quality of the extant monumental painting at Mistra datable between the Peribleptos and the Pantanassa, which implies that new masters had to be brought from outside. However, the special character of the Pantanassa wall paintings is partly due to the creative assimilation of the two fourteenth-century pictorial models at Mistra. Thus, the complexities of this decoration should be viewed against the unique political and cultural climate of Mistra. The ties of this town with the court of Constantinople had become more intensified under the late Palaeologi. The presence of the most progressive thinker of Europe of this period, George Gemisthos Pletho, and his followers enhanced the prestige of Mistra, which became a brilliant center of Byzantine culture.

[37] The wall paintings that are interesting as comparative material for the study of the decoration of the Pantanassa include those of the Virgin at Sklaverohori, St. Antonios at Vrontisi and St. Phanourios at Valsamonero, as well as a group of paintings executed by the family of Phokas in the churches of St. George at Embaros (1436/1437), Sts. Constantine and Helen at Avdou (1445), and St. George at Apano Symi (ca. 1453). For some observations on these paintings see M. Chatzidakis, "Τοιχογραφίες στὴν Κρήτη," Κρ. Χρον. 6 (1952), 59–91. M. Borboudakis, in K. Gallas, K. Wessel, and M. Borboudakis, *Byzantinisches Kreta* (Munich, 1983), passim. Th. Gouma-Peterson, "Manuel and John Phokas and Artistic Personality in Late Byzantine Painting," *Gesta* 22 (1983), 159–70.

[38] For Western iconographic elements in Cretan wall paintings of the Late Byzantine period, see M. Vassilakis-Mavrakakis, "Western Influences on the Fourteenth Century Art of Crete," *JÖB* 32/5 = *XVI. Internationaler Byzantinistenkongress, Vienna 1981, Akten* II/5 (Vienna, 1982), 301–11.

[39] For this detail cf. J. Albani, "Die Wandmalereien der Kirche Hagios Athanasios zu Leondari," *JÖB* 39 (1989), 271.

On the other hand, the special circumstances of the genesis of the Despotate of Mistra in the Frankish Peloponnese, and the constant contacts of the despots with the West through trade and marital alliances, intensified the osmosis from Western culture. The presence of Cleope Malatesta, the western-born wife of Theodore II, might account for a new wave of Western infiltrations in the art of Mistra.[40]

The semi-imperial aspirations of the donor of the Pantanassa frescoes, as shown by the grandiose scale of the monument and its commanding position on the site, explain not only the assumed metropolitan provenance of the master painters of the Pantanassa but also the eagerness to emulate previous distinguished local donors by borrowing artistic forms and even the architectural type from their foundations. The adherence to the earlier Mistra tradition would not only establish this town in the Peloponnese as a brilliant center of culture, but would also reinforce the claims of the donor occupying the highest offices in the civil hierarchy of the Despotate. The amalgam of the old and the new, a common procedure in medieval decorations, finds a concrete justification in the case of the Pantanassa.

The dream world of the Pantanassa demonstrates a lack of anxiety concerning the imminent collapse of the Byzantine world, which can be seen to correspond to Pletho's ideology that promoted a return to the Olympian deities. This return to the past in his philosophy and the return to antiquarian motifs in the frescoes of the Pantanassa reveal a type of escapism at this time, where the myths of the invincible Doreans might have proven more reassuring than contemporary political and military vicissitudes. The question may be raised whether the Pantanassa frescoes represent the direction which Byzantine painting was taking towards something new and different which was cut off when Constantinople fell and further contacts with Western ideas were ended. I believe that these frescoes already represent an end in the evolution of Byzantine painting, since they no longer function as images carrying with them the eternal truths of Orthodoxy.

---

[40] For the official engagements taken by the despot Theodore II for his western-born wife's free exercise of the Catholic rite and her adherence to Western customs, see V. Laurent, "Un argyrobulle inédit du Despote de Morée Theodore Paléologue en faveur de Mastino de Cattanei, gentilhomme toscan," *REB* 21 (1963), 213–14.

1. Mistra, Pantanassa. Exterior view (photo: Makis Skiadaressis)

2. Mistra, Pantanassa. Angel supporting the glory of Christ in the Ascension (photo: Makis Skiadaressis)

3. Mistra, Peribleptos. Angel supporting the glory of Christ in the Ascension (photo: Makis Skiadaressis)

4. Mistra, Pantanassa. One of the Seventy
Apostles (photo: Makis Skiadaressis)

5. Mistra, Peribleptos. The Prophet Habakkuk (photo: Makis
Skiadaressis)

6. Mistra, Hodegetria. St. Mark, bishop of Apollonias, and St. Caesar, bishop of Dyrrachium (photo: Makis Skiadaressis)

8. Mistra, Pantanassa. Pentecost, detail (photo: Makis Skiadaressis)

7. Mistra, Pantanassa. Pentecost, detail (photo: Makis Skiadaressis)

9. Mistra, Peribleptos. Pentecost (photo: Makis Skiadaressis)

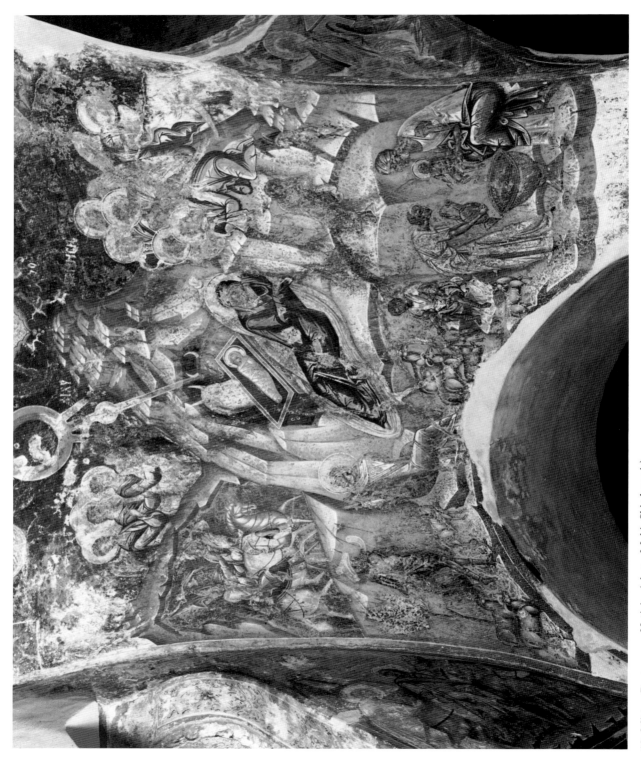

10. Mistra, Pantanassa. Nativity (photo: Makis Skiadaressis)

11. Mistra, Peribleptos. Nativity (photo: Makis Skiadaressis)

13. Mistra, Peribleptos. Nativity, detail (photo: Makis Skiadaressis)

12. Mistra, Pantanassa. Nativity, detail (photo: Makis Skiadaressis)

15. Mistra, Pantanassa. Nativity, detail (photo: Makis Skiadaressis)

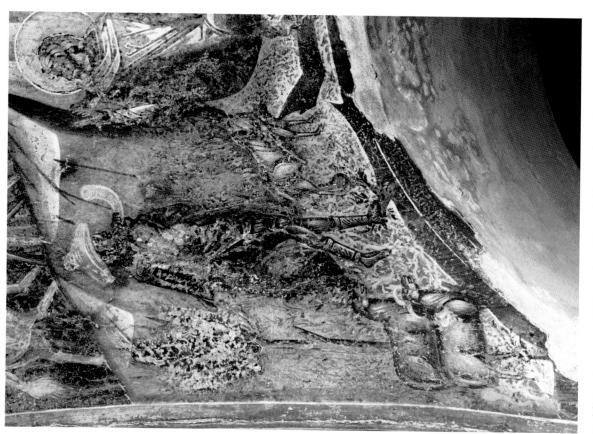

14. Mistra, Pantanassa. Nativity, detail (photo: Makis Skiadaressis)

16. Mistra, Pantanassa. Entry into Jerusalem (photo: Makis Skiadaressis)

17. Mistra, Peribleptos. Entry into Jerusalem (photo: Makis Skiadaressis)

18. Mistra, Pantanassa. Entry into Jerusalem, detail (photo: Makis Skiadaressis)

19. Mistra, Pantanassa. Presentation of Christ, detail (photo: Makis Skiadaressis)

20. Mistra, Pantanassa. Saint's medallion with masks (photo: Makis Skiadaressis)

21. Mistra, Pantanassa. Saint's medallion with peopled rinceau (photo: Makis Skiadaressis)

22. Mistra, Pantanassa. Annunciation (photo: Makis Skiadaressis)

23. Mistra, Pantanassa. Annunciation, detail (photo: Makis Skiadaressis)

24. Mistra, Pantanassa. Floral arabesque
(photo: Makis Skiadaressis)

25. Mistra, Pantanassa. Simulated marble panel (photo:
Makis Skiadaressis)

26. Mistra, Pantanassa. Evangelist Luke, detail of architecture (photo: Makis Skiadaressis)

Late Byzantine *Loca Sancta?* Some Questions Regarding the Form and Function of Epitaphioi*

SLOBODAN ĆURČIĆ

To the Memory of Laskarina Bouras

EPITAPHIOI represent the quintessential creation of the Late Byzantine art of embroidery. A substantial number of Late Byzantine epitaphioi survive, and they belong to several distinct groups according to their form and, most likely, their function. Only two epitaphioi—the one in the Art Museum of Princeton University (Fig. 1), and the other at the Museum of the Serbian Orthodox Church in Belgrade (Fig. 2)—constitute one of these distinctive groups by virtue of their idiosyncratic form and iconography.[1] It has been postulated that their origins may be traceable to a common workshop of fourteenth-century Constantinople.[2] Both epitaphioi have undergone subsequent repairs, the Princeton epitaphios having suffered considerably on account of these interventions.[3] From both stylistic and technical viewpoints, it is apparent that only certain sections of the Princeton piece have escaped subsequent reworking. Thus, in its present form the Princeton epitaphios can be considered only an iconographically accurate replica of the original.

The Princeton epitaphios evokes the memory of one Michael, the son of Kyprianos, as may be gleaned from the inscription which runs along its bottom edge.[4] Precisely the same

---

* This article constitutes a substantially revised version of the paper delivered at the colloquium "The Twilight of Byzantium," on May 9, 1989. In rewriting my paper I have benefited from the comments and suggestions of my colleagues Professors Anna Kartsonis, Henry Maguire, and Doula Mouriki, to whom I am most grateful. I would also like to thank Professor Robert Thomson, who kindly helped me locate certain literature on the Cathedral of Mtskheta.

[1] S. Ćurčić, "Epitaphios," in *Byzantium at Princeton*, S. Ćurčić and A. St. Clair, eds. (Princeton, 1986), 135–38, is the first, preliminary account of the Princeton epitaphios. A more thorough publication of the piece is planned. For the Belgrade epitaphios see M. Jovanović-Marković, "Dve srednjovekovne plaštanice. Zapažanja o tehnici izrade," *Zograf* 17 (1986), esp. 58–64, who, though dealing largely with technical issues, cites the older literature.

[2] Ćurčić, "Epitaphios" (note 1 above), 138. Jovanović-Marković, "Dve srednjovekovne plaštanice" (note 1 above), 71, considers the Belgrade epitaphios to be a Constantinopolitan work, but (p. 64) suggests that the Princeton epitaphios was made in a "provincial workshop" because of the crudeness of its execution. This conclusion is erroneous and is based on observations made from photographs which could not reveal the extent of re-workings easily observed on the original piece.

[3] Ćurčić, "Epitaphios" (note 1 above), 135, where I indicated that the piece was the result of a remounting. Subsequent examination suggests that *at least two* major remountings must have occurred. Further work on various technical aspects of the Princeton epitaphios are in order.

[4] In its remounted version the somewhat jumbled inscription reads: ΜΙΧΑΗΛΤΟΥΚΥΠΡΙΑΝΟΥΨΥ-

formula was used on the Belgrade epitaphios, though the language there is Old Church Slavonic instead of Greek.[5] The Belgrade epitaphios commemorates Serbian King Uroš II Milutin (1282–1321), and is thought to have been the gift of his widow to Milutin's mausoleum church at Banjska Monastery.[6] The same, or very similar formulae for the commemorative inscription appear on a number of related epitaphioi of this period.[7] This paper will attempt to demonstrate that the epitaphioi bearing such inscriptions were actually made for churches which contained tombs of important individuals whose names are invoked in such inscriptions.

According to the most basic definition, an epitaphios is "a veil embroidered with the scene of Christ's burial. It is carried in procession on Good Friday and Good Saturday, and remains on the altar during the Eastertide."[8] Considerable scholarly literature is in basic agreement that in this form epitaphioi appear first toward the end of the thirteenth century, that is, at the beginning of the Palaeologan era.[9] Scholars also seem to concur regarding the general function of epitaphioi, finding them predominantly liturgical in nature.[10] Stylistic and technical issues pertaining to epitaphioi have only recently begun to receive the kind of scrutiny they deserve.[11] The iconography of most epitaphioi suggests links with the Lamentation, a biblical event, distinct from their symbolic, liturgical role. Relying on earlier assumptions that the type of epitaphios in question evolved from the liturgical cloth known as the *aer*, Pauline Johnstone has argued that by the end of the fourteenth century the liturgical type of epitaphios was superceded by the so-called "Good Friday" epitaphios which was used in processions and was specifically related to the Lamentation.[12] She has also postulated that in the course of time epitaphioi had become too large and too cumbersome for

---

XHNTOYΔΛOYCOYMNHCΘHTIKETHN. Unscrambled it should read: [+]MNHCΘHTI $\overline{\text{KE}}$ THN ΨYXHN TOY Δ[OY]ΛOY COY MIXAHΛ TOY KYΠPIANOY ("Remember, O Lord, the soul of Thy servant Michael, the son of Kyprianos").

[5] +ПОМѦНН Ь[ОЖ]Е ДОУШѦРАЬА СВОЕГО МНЛОУТНА ОУРЕШН ("Remember, O Lord, the soul of Thy servant Milutin Ureši").

[6] S. Mandić, "Svilen pokrov za dar manastiru," *Drevnik. Zapisi konzervatora* (Belgrade, 1975), 72.

[7] Suffice it to mention the following examples: the epitaphios of Matthew and Anne from Bachkovo, now in Sofia; the epitaphios of Archbishop John of Skopje, now at Hilandar Monastery; and the epitaphios of one Antonios of Heraclea, now at Studenica Monastery; see G. Millet, *Broderies religieuses de style byzantin* (Paris, 1947), 90, 95, and 99, respectively.

[8] *The Concise Oxford Dictionary of the Christian Church*, E. A. Livingstone, ed. (Oxford, London, New York, 1977), 176, under alternative spelling "epitaphion."

[9] In addition to the major general work by G. Millet already cited (note 7 above, esp. 86–109), we should also mention L. Mirković, *Crkveni umetnički vez* (Belgrade, 1940), esp. 13–27; and P. Johnstone, *The Byzantine Tradition in Church Embroidery* (London, 1967), esp. 25–40 and 117–28.

[10] The most important recent studies on the liturgical aspects of epitaphioi are D. I. Pallas, *Die Passion und Bestattung Christi in Byzanz. Der Ritus, das Bild*, Miscellanea Byzantina Monacensia, 2 (Munich, 1965); R. F. Taft, *The Great Entrance = OCA* 200 (Rome, 1978), esp. 216–19; and H. Belting, "The Image and Its Function in Liturgy: The Man of Sorrows in Byzantium," *DOP* 34–35 (1980–81), 1–16; and more recently *idem, The Image and Its Public in the Middle Ages. Form and Function of Early Paintings of the Passion* (New Rochelle, N.Y., 1989), esp. chap. 5.

[11] L. Bouras, "The Epitaphios of Thessaloniki, Byzantine Museum of Athens No. 685," in *L'art de Thessalonique et des pays balkaniques et les courants spirituels au XIVe siècle* (Belgrade, 1987), 211–31; and also Jovanović-Marković, "Dve srednjovekovne plaštanice" (note 1 above), 57–72.

[12] Johnstone, *Byzantine Church Embroidery* (note 9 above), 26.

covering the eucharistic elements on the altar table, and that consequently they were probably hung on the walls of the sanctuary.[13]

Although Johnstone, unlike most other authors, has raised some important practical questions, her explanations have not gone far enough. Her postulation that an epitaphios may have been hung in the sanctuary does not pursue the question far enough, asking where in a given sanctuary it could have been hung. It is well known that the walls of most sanctuaries were covered with frescoes, some of which would have had to be covered up by such an arrangement. Furthermore, even if one were to accept as plausible that the size of epitaphioi did not matter much in their being used for covering the eucharistic elements, one could not ignore the fact that most Late Byzantine altar tables were square and that their sides seldom exceeded one meter in length. This would mean that most epitaphioi would have been draped awkwardly over the side edges of any altar table.

Ignoring the conventional *ex-silentio* argument that epitaphioi must have been stashed away somewhere during the entire year, to be brought out only for the Easter services, I would like to suggest that they had a more visible role throughout the year and were displayed in some fashion within churches. One possibility is that an epitaphios may have been displayed directly on the tomb of the deceased individual in whose memory the inscription on the epitaphios was spelled out. This idea was first put forth by Svetislav Mandić writing about the Belgrade epitaphios.[14] While we have no contemporary texts alluding to such an arrangement, neither do we have any texts referring to an alternative one.

Casting our net wider in search for potential clues, we find that the general custom of covering tombs of prominent individuals with precious or embroidered cloth has a very long history. Ammianus Marcellinus, for example, refers to a purple pall (*velamen purpureum*) as having covered the sarcophagus of the Emperor Diocletian in his mausoleum at Split.[15] Nichetas Choniates refers to a "splendid cover interwoven with gold" over the sarcophagus of Constantine the Great in the church of the Holy Apostles in Constantinople.[16] Ruy Gonzalez de Clavijo describes the tomb of an empress in the church of St. George of Mangana in Constantinople, as having been made of jasper and "covered with a pall of silk."[17] Clavijo visited Constantinople in 1403, which suggests that the custom of covering imperial tombs with precious fabrics in the Byzantine capital endured for over a millenium. Because none of these fabrics survive, we do not know what decorative motifs, if any, may have embellished them. It should be noted that the custom of covering important tombs with cloth is still practiced in churches of the Orthodox world, as it is in the world of Islam.[18]

[13] *Ibid.*

[14] Mandić, "Svilen pokrov" (note 6 above), 71.

[15] Ammianus Marcellinus XVI.8.4: " . . . he had stolen a purple robe (*velamen purpureum*) from Diocletian's tomb . . . " (trans. J. C. Rolfe, The Loeb Classical Library, I [Cambridge, Mass. and London, 1935], 235).

[16] *O City of Byzantium, Annals of Niketas Choniates*, transl. by H. J. Magoulias (Detroit, 1984), 263.

[17] C. Mango, *The Art of the Byzantine Empire, 312–1453, Sources and Documents* (Englewood Cliffs, N.J., 1972), 220.

[18] For some embroidered nineteenth- and twentieth-century examples see M. Šakota, *Studenička riznica* (Belgrade, 1988), 194–95. We should also note that plain red fabric covers are still used on the royal tombs at Sopoćani, Gradac, and Dečani, and on the archibishops' and patriarchal tombs at Peć. Cloth tomb covers,

Relatively few Byzantine covers for saints' tombs or reliquaries have survived, or are known from written sources.[19] The practice of embroidering images of saints on tomb covers is recorded in Byzantium as early as the twelfth century.[20] It is of some consequence to observe that this apparently coincided in time with the appearance of the epitaphios type showing the stretched-out body of Christ.[21] André Grabar has argued that the two phenomena were related, and that this eventually (in the fourteenth century and later) gave rise to the appearance of gisant sculptures on Byzantine and Russian saints' tombs.[22] In his interpretation of this development Grabar stopped short of suggesting that epitaphioi were ever used as covers for saints' tombs; this notion remains in the realm of speculation.[23] Possible iconographic links with western monumental tombs should not be overlooked, though this is a subject for a separate investigation.[24]

The second possibile manner in which epitaphioi may have been displayed involves the consideration of a special type of arched or domed baldachin, which would have signified the "tomb of Christ". Such pieces of furniture, albeit relatively modern in origin, do exist in

---

predominantly of green color, are also commonly employed in the world of Islam; see D. G. Shepherd, "A Pall from the tomb of Ali ibn Muhammad," *The Bulletin of the Cleveland Museum of Art*, 49, no. 4 (1962), 72–79; esp. 72 and 77; also F. Ollendorff, "Two Mamluk Tomb-Chambers in Western Jerusalem," *IEJ* 33, no. 4 (1982), esp. 246, and note 9. I am grateful to Maura Donohue for the last two references.

[19] As, for example, the cover for the relics of Serbian Prince Lazar, dated 1402, now in the Museum of the Serbian Orthodox Church in Belgrade, or the pall of St. Sergius of Radonezh, made in the 1420s, in the Trinity-Sergius Monastery at Zagorsk. For the former see Mirković, *Crkveni umetnički vez* (note 9 above), 30–31, and pl. XIII–1; for the latter see M. A. Ilyin, *Zagorsk. Trinity-Sergius Monastery* (Moscow, 1967), 48–50, and figs. 32 and 33. The former cover consists of an embroidered text of a poem in Old Church Slavonic; the latter depicts a full-length frontal image of St. Sergius. A number of comparable later Russian tomb covers exist: for example, the 1574 tomb cover of a Metropolitan Peter in the Novodevichevii Manastir, Moscow; the 1648–69 tomb cover of a Metropolitan Peter in the Imperial Collection, Moscow; and the 1713 tomb cover of a Metropolitan Alexei in the N. L. Trakhanitovaia Collection, Moscow; cf. N. A. Maiasova and I. I. Vishnevskaia, *Russkoe khudozhestvennoe shitie XIV–nachala XVIII veka* (Moscow, 1989), no. 11 (p. 73), no. 27 (p. 77), and no. 33 (p. 79), respectively. An example of textual evidence for fabric reliquary covers is found in the Life of King Milutin, written by Serbian Archbishop Danilo II. Describing the gifts prepared by Queen Simonida (Simonis) for her husband's tomb, the author includes the following comment: " . . . i takodje platna skupocena i zlatna, imajući na sebi divnu lepotu izgleda, kojim će pokriti raku ovoga hristoljubivoga . . . " (" . . . and furthermore, precious and golden fabrics embellished with splendid and beautiful decorations, with which she would cover the tomb of this Christ-loving man . . . "); Danilo Drugi, *Životi kraljeva i arhiepiskopa srpskih. Službe*, G. MacDaniel and D. Petrović, eds. (Belgrade, 1988), 149.

[20] The earliest evidence is believed to be the description of the transfer of a piece of fabric with an embroidered image of St. Demetrius from Thessaloniki to Constantinople, carried out at the orders of Emperor Manuel Komnenos; cf. A. Grabar, "Le thème du 'gisant' dans l'art byzantin," *CahArch* 29 (1980–81), 144.

[21] The earliest evidence for the existence of an epitaphios with an embroidered image of the dead Christ was deduced from a representation of such a piece on a twelfth-century Byzantine enamel, now in the Hermitage in Leningrad; cf. Belting, "The Man of Sorrows" (note 10 above), 13, and fig. 19.

[22] A. Grabar, "Le thème du 'gisant'" (note 20 above), 143–56, esp. 149.

[23] See note 7, above.

[24] Grabar, "Le thème du 'gisant'" (note 20 above), 149ff. The degree of western input in the development of later Byzantine funerary practices is broached by S. Ćurčić, "Medieval Royal Tombs in the Balkans: An Aspect of the 'East or West' Question," *The Greek Orthodox Theological Review* 29, no. 2 (Summer, 1984), 175–94, and esp. 180–81 regarding the 'gisant' question.

the Orthodox world; witness the example from Gračanica Monastery (Fig. 3). Unfortunately, no authentic medieval installations of this kind have survived. Thus, our path of investigation will take us in a slightly different, though parallel direction.

We will start by examining the role of the baldachin as a shrine marker in the Byzantine world. The four-columned baldachin, taken over from Roman art, was used widely in Byzantium. As the marker of a "sacred spot", it rose over thrones, altars, reliquaries, etc., as illustrated by this ciborium shrine from ca. 500, now in the Treasury of San Marco in Venice (Fig. 4).[25] I will consider briefly the Byzantine uses of baldachins within the strictly funerary context. To my knowledge, no Byzantine tomb baldachins survive intact. Fragments of two such structures are preserved at the Byzantine Museum in Athens.[26] A hypothetical reconstruction of a "pseudo-baldachin", based on the surviving fragments, has been proposed for the tomb of the Serbian Archbishop Sava II at Peć.[27] Equally important is the much later (1628) Russian example—the tomb of the Tsarevich Dimitry, in the Cathedral of the Archangel Michael in Moscow.[28] The mentioned examples illustrate the sparse nature of the surviving physical evidence. At the same time, this underscores the pressing need for the continuation of careful recording and analyses of archaeological remains in hopes of retrieving more information about various types of Byzantine church furniture, including monumental tombs. At the present, our understanding of such tombs must depend on other sources.

Byzantine manuscript illuminations preserve the largest number of relevant examples illustrating funerary uses of baldachins. For example, an illumination of fol. 311v of the eleventh-century manuscript, known as Codex Taphou 14, from the Patriarchal Library in Jerusalem, illustrates the Seven Wonders of the Ancient World (Fig. 5).[29] One of these, the Mausoleum at Halikarnassos, is depicted using a fictitious convention, but one which would have been readily understood as a monumental tomb by contemporaries. It shows the famous tomb as a four-columned domical baldachin rising above the reposing effigy of King Mausolos. Comparable conventions appear in the scene of the Burial of St. John the Baptist in the eleventh-century Gospels (Bibliotheque nationale, Paris Gr. 74, fol. 76), and in the Prothesis of St. Athanasios in the twelfth-century Homilies of Gregory Nazianzenus (Bibliotheque nationale, Paris Gr. 543, fol. 260v).[30] The oldest and the most compelling of the related illuminations is the one depicting the tomb of Christ in the so-called Khludov Psalter (Historical Museum, Moscow, cod. 129, fol. 9v) (Fig. 6).[31] Here we see the body of Christ in the tomb below a four-columned domical baldachin.

[25] D. Gaborit-Chopin, "Marble Ciborium with Greek Inscription," in *The Treasury of San Marco, Venice,* D. Buckton, ed. (Milan, 1984), 96–97. For a more general discussion see K. Wessel, "Ciborium," *RBK,* I (Stuttgart, 1966), 1055–65.

[26] A. Grabar, *Sculptures byzantines du Moyen Age,* II (Paris, 1976), 124–25, nos. 126 and 127.

[27] D. Popović, "Nadgrobni spomenik arhiepiskopa Save II iz crkve sv. Apostola u Pećkoj Patrijaršiji," *Zbornik za likovne umetnosti* 21 (1985), 71–88.

[28] H. Faensen and V. Ivanov, *Early Russian Architecture* (London, 1972), 42, and pl. 194.

[29] K. Weitzmann, *Greek Mythology in Byzantine Art* (Princeton, 1951), 35–37, and fig. 35.

[30] C. Walter, "Death in Byzantine Iconography," *Eastern Churches Review* 8 (1976), 125 and 126; figs. 10 and 11.

[31] M. V. Shchepkina, *Miniatiury Khludovskoi psaltyri* (Moscow, 1977), fol. 9v.

Chronologically and functionally more relevant for our discussion are two fourteenth-century frescoes—from the prothesis of Markov Manastir (painted ca. 1376–7), and from the narthex of Dečani (painted probably ca. 1350) (Figs. 7 and 8).[32] The general liturgical implications of both scenes are obvious. The relevance of the former—within the prothesis niche—requires no further explanation.[33] The second scene, which shows the tomb of Christ as an altar, with the two principal authors of the Eastern Orthodox liturgy—St. Basil the Great and St. John Chrysostomos—officiating, deserves closer scrutiny. The fresco is situated on the east wall of the northeastern corner bay of the spacious narthex. Along the northern wall of the same bay is a sarcophagus-tomb and next to it three additional floor tombs. Two of these have identifiable inscriptions, while the third has been disturbed and is now covered by various disparate slab fragments.[34] The bay is adjacent to and accessible through the north narthex portal with its own distinctive funerary iconography—a carved foliated cross in the tympanum (Fig. 9).[35] An additional floor tomb without an inscription is located in the northwestern corner of the narthex. All of these elements taken together suggest that the north aisle of the Dečani narthex functioned essentially as a funerary chapel, a pendant to the southern aisle and portal with their distinctive baptismal function and iconography (Fig. 10).[36] The funerary function of the narthex is corroborated by the general typikon of the Serbian Church, introduced in 1319 by the Archbishop Nikodim.[37] Such a juxtaposition of the funerary (north) and baptismal (south) functions recalls a

[32] For Markov Manastir following the most recent cleaning of frescoes see C. Grozdanov, "Iz ikonografije Markovog manastira," *Zograf* 11 (1980), 83–93, esp. 83–87. For Dečani see V. R. Petković and Dj. Bošković, *Manastir Dečani* (Belgrade, 1941), vol. 2, pls. XCV:1 and XCVI. Other related examples are discussed by D. Iliopoulou-Rogan, "Sur une fresque de la période des Paléologues," *Byzantion* 41 (1971), 109–21. I am grateful to Lois Drewer for bringing this article to my attention.

[33] In addition to Grozdanov, "Iz ikonografije Markovog manastira," (note 32 above), see also R. Hamman-MacLean, *Grundlegung zu einer Geschichte der mittelalterlichen Monumentalmalerei in Serbien und Makedonien*, Die Monumentalmalerei in Serbien und Makedonien, Band 4 (Giessen, 1976), 154–55.

[34] The identity of the sarcophagus-tomb and the adjacent floor tombs is discussed in detail by D. Popović, "Srednjovekovni nadgrobni spomenici u Dečanima," *Dečani i vizantijska umetnost sredinom XIV veka*, V. J. Djurić, ed. (Belgrade, 1989), esp. 232–35.

[35] For the sculpture of this portal see J. Maglovski, "Dečanska skulptura—program i smisao," *Dečani i vizantijska umetnost sredinom XIV veka*, V. J. Djurić, ed. (Belgrade, 1989), esp. 203–204, who also analyzes in depth the meaning of the corresponding south portal (199–203). A more concise interpretation of the sculptural decoration of these portals along with a functional interpretation of their relationship to the narthex is given by I. Nikolajević, "Portali u Dečanima," *ibid.* 185–91.

[36] Regarding the changing functions of narthexes in Serbian and Byzantine church architecture of this period see S. Ćurčić, "The Twin-Domed Narthex in Paleologan Architecture," *ZVI* 13 (1971), 333–44. On the baptismal font and its iconographic setting see S. Ćurčić, "The Original Baptismal Font of Gračanica and Its Iconographic Setting," *Zbornik Narodnog muzeja* 9–10 (1979), 313–23, esp. 317–20; also Z. Gavrilović, "Divine Wisdom as Part of Byzantine Imperial Ideology," *Zograf* 11 (1980), 44–52; *eadem*, "Kingship and Baptism in the Iconography of Dečani and Lesnovo," *Dečani i vizantijska umetnost sredinom XIV veka*, V. J. Djurić, ed. (Belgrade, 1989), 297–304.

[37] V. Petković, "Žiča," *Starinar* n.s. 1 (1906), 183. The original manuscript of Nikodim's typikon was burned in the German air raid which destroyed the National Library of Belgrade on April 6, 1941. A photocopy of the manuscript made before its demise is preserved in the Library of the Serbian Academy of Sciences and Arts in Belgrade, no. 473. The relevant information is on fol. 137v. A critical edition of this typikon has

much earlier arrangement of a pair of chapels linked to the narthex of the katholikon at Hosios Loukas Monastery.[38]

Scrutinizing the Dečani fresco more closely, we discover that, in addition to its obvious liturgical connotations, it also represents the burial and the tomb of Christ. This is suggested by the manner in which Christ's body is depicted: it is comparable to conventional Lamentation scenes and therefore evokes the historical event of Christ's Deposition.[39] At the same time, the rendition of Christ's body, covered only by a loin cloth and laid out on a red cloth, is clearly related to epitaphioi in general. This "non-historical" formulation is fully confirmed by the presence of four arcs in the four corners of the flat part of the cloth on which Christ's body reposes. Such arcs appear on a number of epitaphioi and normally enclose representations of the four apocalyptic beasts.[40] The edges of the red cloth hang over the rectangular edges of the bier on which Christ's body is resting. Below the decorative fringes of the cloth we see a flat surface articulated by a frieze of discs containing characteristic Byzantine ornamental motifs. This decoration may be related to some contemporary Byzantine sarcophagi.[41] The relationship of this seemingly solid block to the ground is somewhat ambiguous. It is shown not quite touching the surface of the ground, while not being significantly elevated above it either. Elevation of a stone slab upon a columnar support, of course, would have made an unmistakable allusion to the altar table. That formula was indeed employed on some epitaphioi, such as the fine 1538–39 example from Zerbitsa Monastery in Lakonia (Fig. 13).[42] The Dečani rendition, therefore, appears to place deliberate emphasis on the ambiguity between the altar and the tomb of Christ, while minimizing the associations with the Lamentation. The conflation of liturgical with historical and topographical iconography in the Dečani fresco bespeaks its multiple meanings, and possibly its multiple functions. Hence it may bring us closer to a fuller understanding of the meaning, functions, and the manner of display of epitaphioi in general.

A particular association of the Dečani fresco, and of epitaphioi in general, which has not received thorough scrutiny is that with the "tomb of Christ". While the symbolic aspect of this concept has been recognized, the functional and topographical ones have not. I propose that epitaphioi were displayed in a manner which would have reinforced their associations with the tomb of Christ. Furthermore, bearing in mind that juxtapositions of liturgical and topographical functions were not uncommon in Byzantine art from the earliest times

not yet been published. For the history of the typikon and the role of Archbishop Nikodim see L. Mirković, "Ein Typikon des serbischen Erzbischofs Nikodemos: vom Einfluss Konstantinopels auf den Gottesdienst der serbischen Kirche," *Atti dello VIII Congresso internazionale di studi bizantini*, 2 (Rome, 1953), 429–33.

[38] Th. Chatzidakis, "Particularités iconographiques du décor peint des chapelles occidentales de Saint-Luc en Phocide," *CahArch* 22 (1972), 89–113.

[39] H. Maguire, *Art and Eloquence in Byzantium* (Princeton, 1981), 101–108.

[40] Johnstone, *Byzantine Church Embroidery* (note 9 above), 36–37.

[41] Th. Pazaras, Ἀνάγλυφες σαρκοφάγοι καὶ ἐπιτάφιες πλάκες τῆς μέσης καὶ ὕστερης βυζαντινῆς περιόδου στὴν Ἑλλάδα (Thessaloniki, 1984), pls. 58 and 74.

[42] M. Acheimastou-Potamianou, et al., eds., *Byzantine and Post-Byzantine Art* (Athens, 1985), 218, no. 247.

on, I would suggest that such displays, were in fact, veritable "*loca sancta*".[43] Although no specific epitaphios installations can be pointed to, we may consider several other types of shrines in Middle and Late Byzantine churches. In a very general sense, these may be regarded as medieval versions of earlier martyria.

One of the oldest and best known of these is the shrine of Hosios Loukas within the katholikon of the monastery bearing his name (Fig. 11).[44] Installed shortly after the completion of the katholikon in the first quarter of the eleventh century, the cenotaph-shrine is thought to have been introduced, directly above the holy man's tomb in the crypt, with the idea of facilitating numerous visitations by pilgrims. Located in the northeastern corner of the naos and close to the north portal, the shrine took the form of a four-columned baldachin tomb, presumably topped with a pyramidal roof.[45]

Shrines of this type were once far more common than one is led to believe on the basis of meager surviving evidence. A comparable four-piered bronze shrine dedicated to the Forty Martyrs of Sebaste and containing their relics once existed in Constantinople, according to the written sources.[46] Written sources also attest the existence of canopied tombs of Sts. Spyridon and Polyeuktos in a chapel to the left (i.e., to the north) of the sanctuary of the church of the Holy Apostles in Constantinople.[47] A six-columned, canopied silver shrine of St. Demetrios once adorned the north nave arcade of the basilica of St. Demetrios in Thessaloniki, while a comparable marble shrine of unknown function, referred to as "il capitello", still stands in the north arcade of the western bay of San Marco in Venice.[48]

Canopied aedicules were employed for other, related purposes as well. A case in point is the elaborate *proskynetarion* framing a pair of icons on a iconostasis screen of the church of the Taxiarchs at Kalyvia-Kouvara in Attica.[49] It is curious, though not necessarily fortuitous, that the parapet below its two icons is actually a re-used front of a stone sarcophagus.

The most relevant example of a baldachin shrine in this context is the fifteenth-century so-called *Sveti Tskhoveli*, or "Life-Giving Pillar", under the south nave arcade of the Cathedral of Mtskheta in Georgia (Fig. 12).[50] The shrine, with its four-piered baldachin and fresco decoration illustrating scenes from the Life and Passion of Christ, was clearly inspired by the aedicula over the tomb of Christ in Jerusalem. The Cathedral of Mtskheta was the burial church of Georgian kings. The floor of its nave is covered with royal tombs clustered in the vicinity of the "Life-Giving Pillar".

---

[43] K. Weitzmann, "*Loca Sancta* and the Representational Arts of Palestine," *DOP* 28 (1974), esp. 36–41.

[44] E. Stikas, Τὸ οἰκοδομικὸν χρονικὸν τῆς Μονῆς ῾Οσίου Λουκᾶ Φωκίδος (Athens, 1970), 248–58, pls. 180–84.

[45] *Ibid.*, figs. 130–31.

[46] G. P. Majeska, *Russian Travelers to Constantinople in the Fourteenth and Fifteenth Centuries* (Washington, D.C., 1984), 230–31.

[47] *Ibid.*, 148.

[48] D. I. Pallas, "Le ciborium hexagonal de Saint-Démétrios de Thessalonique," *Zograf* 10 (1979), 44–58. Pallas also illustrates the shrine in San Marco (fig. 8).

[49] *Ibid.*, 57, fig. 11.

[50] R. Mepisashvili and V. Tsintsadze, *The Arts of Ancient Georgia* (New York, 1979), 115–16, figs. 156–57.

The Cathedral of Mtskheta preserves another piece of evidence of crucial importance in our discussion—the epitaphios of the Georgian Queen Mariam (ca. 1638–78) (Fig. 14).[51] Extensively restored in the nineteenth century, the epitaphios preserves the essentials of its iconographic program. In addition to the depiction of the dead Christ attended by two angels, the scene is also elaborated by the inclusion of the Lamentation with a multitude of participants. Such elaborations were already in evidence in earlier epitaphioi, as the fine 1538–39 epitaphios from Zerbitsa Monastery illustrates (Fig. 13).[52] The scene obviously conflates the liturgical subject of the epitaphios with a historical one—the Lamentation. The epitaphios of Queen Mariam, however, is much more complex. It includes two additional registers of related scenes—the Two Marys at the Tomb, at the bottom, and the Ascension, at the top. Finally, in the right corner of the lower scene, the artist has also included the kneeling figure of queen Mariam herself (Fig. 15). This is one of the rare examples of epitaphioi which include an actual depiction of the donor.[53]

In the case of the epitaphios of Queen Mariam, I believe, we have the final proof that epitaphioi were made for specific churches and with a specific function in mind. Prominently displayed within a church, they were intended to evoke the Holy Sepulchre itself.[54] Specifically, however, each epitaphios had an additional purpose—to commemorate a person of some distinction whose tomb was located in the same church for which the epitaphios was made. The custom of creating palpable associations with the Holy Sepulchre had a long history in Byzantium and in the West. It became particularly widespread during the eleventh and twelfth centuries, at the time of close contacts with the Holy Land.[55]

Among the many such associational creations, the most veritable ones were, of course, those which were sanctified by an authentic holy relic. It is of some significance that in the course of the twelfth century the Stone of Unction, also known as the Red Stone of Ephesus and the Burial Shroud used by Joseph of Arimathea were both brought to Constantinople.[56]

The Stone of Unction was deposited in the church of the Archangels, the middle church of the Pantokrator monastery complex, by the Emperor Manuel I Komnenos. The same

[51] G. Tschubinaschwili, *Georgische Kunst. Ihre Entwicklung vom 4.–18. Jahrhundert* (Berlin, 1930), 27, figs. 11 and 12. A detailed description of this and other epitaphioi once in the Cathedral of Sveti Tskhoveli, with the translations of the main inscriptions into Russian may be found in A. Natroev, *Mtskhet i ego sobor Sveti-Tskhoveli* (Tblisi, 1900), 427–28. I am most grateful to Professor Robert Thomson for this reference, and for providing me with the copies of the relevant pages. See also V. Beridze, et al., *The Treasures of Georgia* (London, 1983), 227, for a fine color reproduction of the epitaphios in question.

[52] See note 42 above.

[53] The other example is the epitaphios of Prince Serban Cantacuzene, dated 1681, originally given to the monastery of Tismana in Wallachia, now in the Museum of Art, Bucharest; cf. Johnstone, *Byzantine Church Embroidery* (note 9 above), 125, and fig. 111. This epitaphios is unusual also because it depicts Deposition and Lamentation scenes side-by-side. The donor, Prince Serban, his wife, and their two children are depicted in the lower right-hand corner, below the Lamentation.

[54] The original location and the manner of display of the epitaphios of Queen Mariam are not known. The possibility that it may have hung on the "Life-Giving Pillar" should be explored.

[55] R. Ousterhout, "Loca Sancta and the Architectural Response to Pilgrimage," *The Blessings of Pilgrimage*, R. Ousterhout, ed. (Urbana and Chicago, 1990), 108–24.

[56] *O City of Byzantium* (note 16 above), 125 (Stone of Unction); Belting, "The Man of Sorrows" (note 10 above), 14 (Burial Shroud).

emperor was eventually buried in its immediate vicinity.[57] Being buried *ad sanctum* had always been the ultimate wish of all Christians, but for practical reasons was accessible to only a few select individuals. Thus, the associational emulation of *"ad sanctum"* burials in various forms proliferated throughout the Christian world. Within the Byzantine sphere we find such examples as that seen in Mileševa Monastery in Serbia. Here, the tomb of King Vladislav (d. 1243) was situated below the composition depicting the king being led by the Virgin and being presented to the enthroned Christ (Fig. 16).[58] Above this depiction is the scene of the Two Marys at the Tomb. The relative positions of the king's tomb and this scene constituted a conscious juxtaposition in the same sense that we have seen on the epitaphios of the Georgian Queen. These were all, in other words, "burials *ad sanctum*" in the minds of contemporary beholders. Late Byzantine society, as has been repeatedly demonstrated by scholars, was preoccupied with notions about Death and Salvation. Rapidly losing its grip on the political and military fronts, it became exceedingly conscious of its past, both secular and religious. The decoration of Palaeologan churches amply attests to the latter phenomenon. Elaboration of the themes of Christ's Miracles and Passion, and an ever-increasing interest in martyr saints and their lives, are among the most obvious dimensions of this new trend. One could go so far in generalizing as to state that in Late Byzantine times the church building, in addition to its established symbolic role of Heavenly Jerusalem, assumed the symbolic role of Earthly Jerusalem as well.

Within such a framework it is easier to understand the functions of the monumental epitaphios, the quintessential new creation of the Late Byzantine art of embroidery. In addition to its previously known liturgical uses, the epitaphios appears to have served other purposes as well. Our current perceptions of this piece of liturgical cloth being carried in solemn processions on Good Friday and Good Saturday, as illustrated in an eighteenth-century drawing of the procession in the monastery of Hosios Loukas, by a Russian monk Vasilii Grigorovich Barskii and by a number of Byzantine and post-Byzantine frescos illustrating the Divine Liturgy, must be broadened.[59] The great cloth was surely not kept in storage for a year between solemn ceremonies celebrating the Easter week.[60] As a veritable

---

[57] On the archaeological evidence for the location of the Stone of Unction in the Pantokrator Monastery see A. H. S. Megaw, "Notes on Recent Work of the Byzantine Institute in Istanbul," *DOP* 16 (1963), 342.

[58] G. Babić, "Vladislav na ktitorskom portretu u naosu Mileševe. Značenje i datovanje slike," *Mileševa u istoriji srpskog naroda*, V. J. Djurić, ed. (Belgrade, 1987), 9–15.

[59] On the latter see J. D. Ştefanescu, "L'Illustration des Liturgies dans l'art de Byzance et de l'Orient," *AIPHOS* 1 (1932–33), esp. 71–77, who discusses and illustrates a number of Athonite and Rumanian examples.

[60] Practicalities regarding the storage of epitaphioi when not "in use" have never been considered. It would seem very unlikely that these heavy embroidered fabrics would have been rolled or folded up for prolonged periods of time. Important insights into this matter may be gleaned from an unusual epitaphios from Hvosno, dated ca. 1300, and now in the Patriarchate at Peć. The Hvosno epitaphios is unique insofar that it was painted on linen cloth. Excavated in the ruins of the monastery of the Virgin at Hvosno, the epitaphios had been folded up along with two other liturgical cloth pieces and buried inside a church bell. This was clearly an act of desperation, presumably on the eve of an impending Turkish attack. In the process of being folded the piece was badly damaged, as the paint has flaked off along the folds. This suggests unequivocally that the Hvosno epitaphios was meant to be hung, not stored by being rolled or folded up. For the Hvosno epitaphios see D. Tasić, "Hvostanska plaštanica," *Starinar* N.s. 13–14 (1962–63), 151–60.

link between this world and the Heavenly realm, the epitaphios must have been displayed prominently in the church for which it was made. As a symbolic tomb of Christ it would have provided a symbolic *locus sanctus*, a Late Byzantine version of the Holy Sepulcher, comparable in function, if not in form, to those which proliferated in the West during the twelfth and later centuries.

1. Princeton epitaphios (photo: The Art Museum, Princeton University)

2. Belgrade epitaphios (photo: D. Tasić)

4. Ciborium shrine. Venice, Treasury of San Marco

3. Epitaphios "shrine". Gračanica (photo: author)

6. Tomb of Christ. Moscow, Historical Museum, cod. 129, fol. 9v

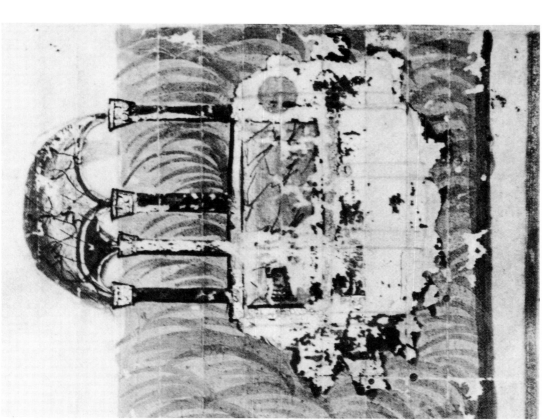

5. Mausoleum at Halikarnassos. Jerusalem, Patriarchal Library, codex Taphou 14, fol. 311v

7. Tomb of Christ. Fresco, Markov Manastir, prothesis niche (photo: G. Subotić, Institut za istoriju umetnosti, Belgrade)

8. Tomb of Christ. Fresco, Dečani, narthex (photo: Republički zavod za zaštitu spomenika kulture, Belgrade)

13. Zerbitsa epitaphios

14. Epitaphios of Queen Mariam

16. Tomb of King Vladislav. Mileševa, southwest corner of the naos (photo: Republički zavod za zaštitu spomenika kulture, Belgrade)

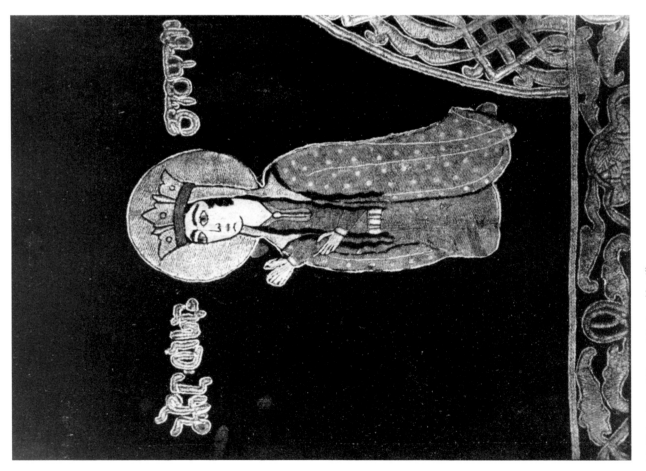

15. Epitaphios of Queen Mariam (detail)

Index

Index

DATE DUE

1 6 2004		